SECRET OF THE MUSES RETOLD

PIER PAOLO PASOLINI
UMBERTO ECO
JOSEPH TUSIANI
ITALO CALVINO
ROBERTO CALASSO

Secret of the Muses Retold

Classical Influences on Italian Authors of the Twentieth Century

John T. Kirby

THE UNIVERSITY OF CHICAGO PRESS
CHICAGO AND LONDON

John T. Kirby is Professor of Classics and chair of the Program in Comparative Literature at Purdue University.

The University of Chicago Press, Chicago 60637
The University of Chicago Press, Ltd., London
© 2000 by The University of Chicago
All rights reserved. Published 2000
Printed in the United States of America
09 08 07 06 05 04 03 02 01 00   1 2 3 4 5
ISBN: 0-226-43747-7 (cloth)
ISBN 0-226-43748-5 (paper)

Chapter 3 originally appeared, in different form, in a Festschrift for Joseph Tusiani (listed in my References list as Giordano 1994b). Chapter 4 is a significantly expanded version of an essay that originally appeared in *Quaderni d'italianistica* 12 (1991). A version of chapter 5 was presented orally as a public lecture and radio broadcast in Purdue University's "Books and Coffee" series.

"The Two Kings and the Two Labyrinths," from *Collected Fictions* by Jorge Luis Borges, translated by Andrew Hurley (London: Allen Lane The Penguin Press, 1999), pp. 263–264, copyright © 1998 by Maria Kodama; translation copyright © 1998 by Penguin Putnam Inc. Used by permission of Viking Penguin, a division of Penguin Putnam Inc. Reproduced by permission of Penguin Books Ltd.

"Diffugere Nives," from *More Poems* from *The Collected Poems of A. E. Housman,* © 1936 by Barclays Bank Ltd. © 1964 by Robert E. Symons. Reprinted by permission of Henry Holt and Co., LLC; and by the Society of Authors as the literary representative of the estate of A. E. Housman.

Library of Congress Cataloging-in-Publication Data
Kirby, John T.
    Secret of the muses retold : classical influences on Italian authors of the twentieth century / John T. Kirby.
        p. cm.
    Includes bibliographical references and index.
ISBN 0-226-43747-7 (cloth : alk. paper)—ISBN 0-226-43748-5 (pbk. : alk. paper)
    1. Italian literature—20th century—Classical influences.
2. Civilization, Classical, in literature.   I. Title.
PQ4088 .K57 2000
850.90091—dc21   00-030254

♾ The paper used in this publication meets the minimum requirements of the American National Standard for Information Sciences—Permanence of Paper for Printed Library Materials, ANSI Z39.48-1992.

FOR SUSANNAH AND DAVID

O tu che leggi, udirai nuovo ludo:
ciascun da l'altra costa li occhi volse,
quel prima, ch'a ciò fare era più crudo.
—Dante, *Inferno* 22.118–120

CONTENTS

*T*he Muses I invoke in my title are those lovely goddesses, the daughters of Zeus and Memory, who were thought by the ancient Greeks and Romans to inspire every great artist in every medium: not just the arts of language, prose as well as poetry, but also such forms as music and dance. Indeed, as we see in Homer, Hesiod, and Vergil, an artist would pray to the Muses when special inspiration was necessary. Their invocation here is really a signal to my reader, an indication that we are reaching into the distant past of the Western heritage: my subject matter in this book is nothing less than the legacy of the Greek and Roman classics as they have come down to the present day, and some of the ways in which they continue to be appreciated.

A hundred years or so ago, one would not have entitled this book *Secret of the Muses Retold,* because there was no secret to tell, at least not in our culture. *Song of the Muses Resung,* perhaps, because it is a long way back in time to ancient Greece and Rome; but most people in the West who would be reading such a book as this would already have had intimate familiarity with the texts of what we here call classical antiquity. One can no longer, for better or for worse, make such an assumption. The shift has been rather quick. "We are all Greeks," wrote Shelley in his 1822 preface to *Hellas;* "Our laws, our literature, our religion, our arts, have their roots in Greece." By 1920, T. S. Eliot could write:

> The Classics have, during the latter part of the nineteenth century and up to the present moment, lost their place as a pillar of the social and political system—such as the Established Church still is. If they are to survive, to justify themselves as literature, as an element in the European mind, as the foundation for the literature we hope to create, they are very badly in need of persons capable of expounding them. . . . We needed an eye which can see the past in its place with its definite differences from the present, and yet so lively that it shall be as present to us as the present.[1]

1. Eliot 1932:47, 50.

This, from a man who was capable of affixing to "The Waste Land" an epigraph in Greek and Latin from the *Satiricon* of Petronius. In another poem, the first of his "Choruses from 'The Rock,'" he seems to put his finger on the same problem in a different way:

> Where is the Life we have lost in living?
> Where is the wisdom we have lost in knowledge?
> Where is the knowledge we have lost in information?

To offer a more personal anecdote: I remember a day in graduate school when I walked past a stranger on campus as he was scrutinizing his campus map so as to get his bearings. I asked if I could help, and since his destination was on my way, we walked together. "What are you studying?" he asked. "Classics," I replied. To rescue him from the embarrassed ignorance that evidenced itself on his face, I quickly added, "Greek and Latin." "Oh," he said. "That's pretty esoteric, isn't it." I resisted the impulse to tell him—what was true—that when the university had opened its doors nearly two hundred years earlier, its entrance requirements had not included the ability to perform simple arithmetical functions, but *had* included a reading knowledge of ancient Greek. *Panta rhei,* said Heraclitus, Everything flows, everything changes; and the parameters and canons of education are no exception to that rule.

This is the pass to which we have come in Western culture, at least in the United States. If the situation for classics is somewhat less dire in Italy, that may be partly because Italians as a nation have more reverence for ancient things generally, and partly because they themselves still carry in their veins the blood of Julius Caesar. Whatever the cause, one does find, even among those whom one might consider avant-garde or postmodern, Italian authors of the twentieth century who do not disdain to tap into the wellspring of ancient tradition that is their classical heritage. The secret of the Muses. By these authors it is still retold, still sung anew. Sometimes the refrain is surprising, the tune modulated beyond immediate recognition, but that is simply testimony to its enduring fascination, its undying power.

According to conventional wisdom—a convention that I will call into question in a moment—the history of the classical tradition might be mapped out into five periods or ages.[2] First, of course, comes antiquity itself. From this period comes virtually all the "art"—whether verbal or

---

2. This schema is my own representation, give or take a few details, of how such periods might be parsed out. For traditional, and still very useful, expositions of the material, see, e.g., Sandys 1903–1908; Wilamowitz 1921; Pfeiffer 1968–1976.

visual—that is likely to concern the classical scholar. The Middle Ages are conventionally regarded as what we may deem Period II of the classical tradition. Here one must distinguish between work produced in the Latin West from that in the Greek (Byzantine) East. From this period in Greek come important scholia on Homer, by such scholars as Michael Psellus (eleventh century) and Eustathius (twelfth century). The same period in the West produced important writers of its own, such as Boethius (d. ca. 524), but their access to the Greek material of Period I (as we shall see in chapter 2) was severely limited, and in some cases almost nil. Typically, classicists attend to the textual remains of Period II only insofar as they find the latter useful for shedding light on various aspects of Period I materials. Those who study Period II materials lovingly for their own sake tend to be called Byzantinists (for Greek) or mediaevalists (for Latin).

The great efflorescence of Greek studies in the West heralds what we call the Renaissance. This may in conventional terms be considered as Period III because of the tremendous explosion of scholarly activity on ancient texts, both Greek and Latin, and because of the wholehearted embracing of what the people of this time perceived as classical models for culture—literary, architectural, even political. Period III also coincides with the momentous advent of a new technology that would truly revolutionize the reception and appreciation (dilettante or expert) of ancient literature from then on: the invention of the printing press. Once the manuscript—that is, the handwritten copy—was no longer the only, or even the preferable, mode of information storage and retrieval (to use a modern phrase), the dissemination of texts, both primary and secondary, could take place with unprecedented rapidity and ease.

What might count as Period IV (and here, as in Period III, we are most concerned with the classical tradition in the West) is perhaps the trickiest to demarcate. There are many differences between the eighteenth and nineteenth centuries, including developments of philosophical thought, of technological advance, and of political evolution, but there is a discernible scholarly continuity in the period from, say, Richard Bentley (1662–1742) to A. E. Housman (1859–1936). Bentley may be chosen as a *terminus a quo* because as a textual critic, though undeniably the heir of the Renaissance humanists, he raised the practice of classical scholarship to a level of virtuosity that has arguably never been exceeded. He set new standards of exactitude and industry in the editing of texts—that is, in the producing of printed editions by studying and analyzing the ancient manuscripts—and attained to a truly inspiring breadth of scholarly interest. There were plenty of other textual virtuosi in Period IV (Richard Porson, for example, Karl Lachmann, and Housman himself), and many other scholars whose greatest contribution to the study of antiquity was other than the narrowly textual (I think of such people as Wilamowitz, Gilbert Murray, and Eric Dodds). But the things that unite them as being of the same period are (a) a common foundation of basic texts, bequeathed to them from Period III, (b) an increased sophistication in the practice of editing texts, which led to the production of critical editions of unprecedented quality, and—in some ways most significantly—(c) a positivistic approach to the interpretation of those texts that evinced a common and traditional worldview. Which leads us to the matter of Period V.

It is difficult to posit a moment of ending for Period IV. In fact, someone embracing this system of periods might well make a cogent case that it has yet to end. The fact that classics in some quarters has not availed itself of, or has even vigorously repudiated, the use of current literary-theoretical approaches, has given it a reputation as the tweediest of humanistic disciplines. Some, on the other hand, eager to keep step with colleagues in other branches in the humanities, have embraced all the latest fashions of poststructuralism—sometimes in the process scoffing at what they see as a hidebound traditionalism in their colleagues.

I think that both of these positions do insufficient justice to the facts of the matter. I would rather say that they are indicative of two different epistemologies, perhaps even of two different metaphysics—indicative, in short, of two different ways of being in, and interacting with, the world around us. If I am right, this would account for some broad disparities of style in the classical scholarship being produced today, and for some radical differences of approach to the ancient world, even among those most expert in its study. It would account, in short, for the fact that, while Period V seems demonstrably to have begun, Period IV has perhaps also not yet ended.

By Period V, then, one might intend our own era—beginning, let us say, at some point in the latter half of the twentieth century—in which there has been a vast shift away from traditional modes of understanding language (and thus of reading). This had its immediate precursors in the work of such thinkers as Nietzsche and Wittgenstein, and came to prominence in the poststructuralist project. There have, predictably, been backlashes, retrenchments, and recriminations on both sides, and the whole topic is one of bitter conflict in (and sometimes even outside) the academy. And the question of the literary canon has been formulated with unparalleled urgency. I shall have more to say about all this in my Coda.

Having delineated for the convenience of my reader this more or less traditional approach, I would like now to confront some of its limitations.

Like most systems of historical demarcation, it has both strengths and weaknesses—it is tidy, and thus clear, but also arbitrary, and sometimes simplistic. In fact I would say that we run into trouble before we are even out of Period I. There are at least three problems that confront us here. First, the outer boundaries. Where does Period I come to an end? Shall we extend it as far as Ausonius? Augustine? Perhaps, then, Boethius belongs in Period I after all? The divisions seem increasingly arbitrary as one continues to stretch the parameters. Second, scholars have historically felt the need to subdivide this period further. We use terms like archaic, high classical, and Hellenistic to demarcate periods of Greek antiquity, but these do not come easily apart, and arguments can be made on either side for authors who stand on the threshold. Aristotle, for example: favored pupil of Plato, giant of ancient philosophy—surely he "deserves" to be classified as an author of the high classical period? And yet he was also the tutor of Alexander the Great, by whom we mark the beginning of the Hellenistic period.[3]

The third problem I discern here is that, *grosso modo,* Period I is typically regarded as the era whose works form a corpus of primary texts upon which "secondary" works of scholarship are written in latter days. But this is clearly an inadequate assessment, because many of the works that really cannot be later than Period I are themselves secondary works in this sense. It is not possible to stipulate a moment where literary production ends and scholarship begins.[4] There was already scholarship on ancient Greek literature in the high classical period: Plato engages in a subtle and complex form of literary criticism, for example, in his *Republic,* where Socrates is made to espouse some highly incendiary opinions about the Homeric epics and the Attic drama. Later antiquity offers self-conscious literary reflection on earlier works; Asconius, a first-century C.E. scholar, wrote commentaries on Cicero's speeches, and there were scholia on the odes of Pindar by the second century C.E. The Second Sophistic was in some respects a consciously nostalgic reiteration of certain prized rhetorical values of earlier antiquity.[5] Schiller's literary

3. I have put the word "deserves" in quotes to remind my reader that scholars also tend to think in terms of decline: Silver Latin, for example, must (in sheerly metallic terms) be worth less than Golden. This notion of cultural decline is already in evidence as early as Hesiod (*Works and Days* 106–201). and is given a specifically aesthetic slant at the beginning of Petronius' *Satiricon.* It is time for such modern scholarly conventions to come under scrutiny as well, and indeed there are signs that this is slowly beginning to happen.

4. Nor is this subtlety entirely resolved today. Without even leaving the field of classics, one can point to the complex and beautiful work of Ann Carson (1986, 1997). Is this scholarship, or art? I am tempted simply to answer, Yes.

5. Kirby 1996c.

distinctions of the Naïve and Sentimental will not suffice for us here,[6] but our inquiry indeed entails the pressing question of self-reflexivity— how much, and of what sort, the writers of antiquity engaged in when looking at their cultural forebears, their coëvals, and themselves.

No more will the attempt to demarcate Greek literature neatly from Latin help us keep things tidy here, because there is much cross-pollination artistically between Greece and Rome in this period, at both the creative and the scholarly levels. It is possible, for example, to read Vergil's *Aeneid* as a learned meditation on the *Iliad* and *Odyssey,* as Georg Knauer has amply demonstrated.[7]

These problems are recapitulated, *mutatis mutandis,* in the ensuing periods of this schema. Many mediaevalists, for example, now feel that terms like "Renaissance" and (worse) "Dark Ages" condescend to the culture under consideration before Period III, and would prefer to consider both periods together as "Middle Ages." And so on, to our own time. Certainly there are many professional academics working today who would not dissent from Cardinal Newman's idea of what a university might aspire to.[8] This points, once again, to that rivalry of metaphysics that I alluded to earlier, but also to some other factors that I think are at play here. The somewhat arbitrary division required by this five-part schema is, in important part, a matter of convenience, meant to provide some relief to the modern scholar: it is simply not practicable for the average professional academic to control all the primary and secondary bibliography of ancient *and* mediaeval literatures and arts, for example (to look no further forward in history). Such a schema, then, has a utility that is at least partly administrative. In this, it reflects the modern academic division of disciplines. There is no clear reason why Plato should be read only as literature or as philosophy, rather than as both. But to teach a university course, or to write a book, on "Greek literature" or "Greek philosophy," declares one's disciplinarity, and signals to some extent one's intended audience. In this way the workload of the university is divided into disciplines, faculties, and hours of work.

My work in this book is to some extent a work of resistance. Rather than accept these facile traditional ruptures, either of period or of discipline, I would like to suggest that these continuities emerge and re-emerge in ever-changing form, and that they affect and are affected by

6. Schiller 1981.
7. Knauer 1964.
8. Newman 1960.

the different historical circumstances with which they are engaged. Implicit in such a project, of course—and I imagine it will sound fairly explicit by the time I am done, if it does not already—is that an awareness of such continuities is worth having. I will go further and suggest that, if the concept of "humanities" or "humanistic study" is to continue to have value for us, as we stand on the threshold of a new millennium, we should take our courage in both hands and look hard at these ancient texts in order to see whether, in fact, they have something worthwhile to tell us about what it means to be human. That, after all, is what Cicero had in mind when he used the word *humanitas*.

At the outset I should indicate my awareness that a project such as this is fraught with a number of difficulties, not to say perils. First of all, I hope I will not be taken to mean that only Italian authors continue to cling to the classical tradition. Such a position would be absurd and ignorant. We see similar signs all around us, and in a variety of cultures and artistic media. Nor should my reader assume that I think the authors I have chosen are the only Italians to carry the flame. Indeed the tradition in Italy is unbroken from Dante and Petrarca on, down through authors like Machiavelli and Leopardi, and there are plenty of other twentieth-century authors (such as Anna Banti or Cesare Pavese) who might well have been included here. Nor, yet again, I hope, will my reader conclude that my project is meant as mindless flag-waving for the most traditional of Western-European cultural values. Again, this last is a question to which I shall return in my Coda.

Meanwhile, the body of this work consists of five studies, each of which may be read more or less independently of the others, but all of which, taken together, illuminate my thesis. Each of the five authors I have chosen exemplifies a different kind of textuality: Pasolini for screenplay, Eco for the novel, Tusiani for lyric poetry, Calvino for the essay, and Calasso for a *sui generis* form of writing that I have named "critical fiction." Each author produces a different kind of writing; each, too, deploys the classical tradition in a different way. Sometimes the prevailing flavor is Hellenic, sometimes Roman. One might well have shuffled the categories in a number of other ways—Calvino, for example, is perhaps principally thought of as a writer of fiction; Tusiani is an eminent scholar and translator; Pasolini made his first reputation as a poet; Calasso is a major entrepreneur in the international publishing arena; and Eco is, well, Eco—but I felt that a selection of this sort would most cogently make my point: that the secret of the Muses is still being retold in our time by Italian authors. That although many (particularly in the academy) delight in dancing on the grave of classical antiquity, there are those—even today—who move to the strains of a different dance: the melody that still wafts down, ever so softly, from Helicon.

℘

As usual, in producing this book I have many friends and colleagues to thank for their generous help. First, the institutional: Purdue University was generous in providing a semester's sabbatical leave during which I produced the prototype of the chapter on Calasso. The Istituto di Cultura Italiana in New York City graciously hosted an event at which a version of the chapter on Tusiani was presented.

Many have helped me in the completion of this project. Ann Astell, Geoffrey Huck, Richard King, Ben Lawton, Floyd Merrell, Kip Robisch, Colleen Ryan, Carol Saller, and Paul Streufert read some or all of the manuscript, and made useful and provocative comments and suggestions. Elizabeth Belfiore and Carol Poster each read it in its entirety and proffered exhaustive and learned critique, for which it is much less weak than it would otherwise be. Ruby Blondell, Stephen Martin, Kirk Ormand, Neil O'Sullivan, and Charles Segal gave information, bibliography, and encouragement.

Of the colleagues to whom I am indebted, and they are legion, none deserves my thanks more than Anthony Julian Tamburri, who believed in this project from the beginning and gave me tireless advice and encouragement. For this, as for his steadfast friendship through thick and thin, I am indeed grateful.

There are several others to whom heartfelt gratitude is due, for other reasons: to my parents, Edward and Jean Kirby, who were my first, greatest, and most humane teachers, and who many years ago began sowing the seeds for this book; to my brother, Robert Kirby, and my *sœur-en-cœur,* Janice Bragg, who had unflagging confidence in me and stood behind me as the project came to fruition; and finally (and profoundly), to Robert Wright, who with his characteristic wisdom, generosity, and acuity, helped me to explore some of the thorniest issues discussed here; his love and support, in this and other ways, have meant more to me than words could acknowledge.

Secret of the Muses Retold is dedicated to my dear children, Susannah and David, with much love, and in the hope that they may someday know this and all the other secrets they so profoundly desire to know.

CHAPTER 1

THE RIDDLE OF FATE
≫⟨

Sophocles' *Oedipus the King* and
Pier Paolo Pasolini's *Edipo re*

Quello che cerco l'ho nel cuore, come te.
—Cesare Pavese, *Dialoghi con Leucò*

*I*t takes a certain audacity to set oneself the task of not just filming, but actually rewriting, Sophocles' *Oedipus the King*,[1] but I suppose Pier Paolo Pasolini was never known primarily for his modesty. Nor is he the only one to find the allure of Oedipus irresistible. Even Sophocles himself was hardly the first author to treat this subject: we find reference to Oedipus as early as Homer's *Iliad* (23.679–680), and Aeschylus wrote an Oedipus play, indeed an Oedipus trilogy, himself.[2] In fact the Oedipus motif is one of the most widely, even universally, treated themes in world folklore and literature, as the work of Lowell Edmunds and others has documented.[3] Other modern playwrights have certainly tried their hand at reworking the Sophoclean drama, ranging from Corneille in the sev-

---

1. A word on nomenclature. The Latin title of this play is *Oedipus Rex*. The Greek title, which is not only post-Sophoclean but post-Aristotelian, is *Oidipous Turannos*, which is sometimes latinized as *Oedipus Tyrannus*. On the meaning of the word *turannos*, see Knox 1954.

2. Only one play of that trilogy—the third—survives: the *Seven against Thebes*. The first two seem to have been called *Laius* and *Oedipus*; the trilogy would thus track the family curse over three generations. The satyr play accompanying this trilogy, which has also not survived the wrack of time, was the *Sphinx*. Euripides too wrote an *Oedipus*, which survives only in fragments; the story is also treated in his (extant) *Phoenician Women*.

3. See, e.g., Edmunds and Dundes 1983, Edmunds 1985, and Johnson and Price-Williams 1996 for a staggering collection of variants on the Oedipus legend, from many different cultures. A most useful handbook on this and Greek mythology generally is that of Gantz 1993. Still authoritative on Oedipus specifically is the work of Robert 1915.

I

enteenth century, and Voltaire in the eighteenth, to Hofmannsthal, Cocteau, and Gide in the twentieth. Ruggiero Leoncavallo wrote an opera, *Edipo re,* that was produced posthumously. The playwright Ola Rotimi has adapted the legend[4] to African lore in *The Gods Are Not to Blame.* Igor Stravinsky wrote an oratorio, *Oedipus Rex,* and musical comedian Peter Schickele, writing as P. D. Q. Bach, has produced an uproarious oratorio of his own, in a southwestern setting: *Oedipus Tex.*

Among classical scholars the play does not cease to inspire the most ingenious and multifarious of interpretations—spanning from that of Philip Vellacott, who maintains that, by the evening of his first day in Thebes, Oedipus had full cognizance of the fact that he had killed his own father and married his mother, to that of Frederick Ahl, who has argued that one *cannot* prove, purely from the evidence in Sophocles, that the man Oedipus killed on the road was Laius, nor that Jocasta was his mother, and that Oedipus jumps to this conclusion in convicting himself of those crimes.[5]

The allure of Oedipus has not been felt by scholars and playwrights alone. Among political and psychological theorists as well, Oedipus has been a powerful figure to conjure with. Even readers who have not delved deeply into the writings of Sigmund Freud will have heard of his famous (notorious?) formulation of the "oedipal complex" and its implications for psychoanalysis. Indeed, it is probably fair to say that most non-classicists interact with Oedipus by way of Freud, whether to revise and extend his views for use in psychoanalysis and literary criticism (for example, Jacques Lacan) or to repudiate them for the bourgeois values they reinscribe in political theory (for example, Gilles Deleuze and Félix Guattari).[6]

Whatever the sources of our attraction to Oedipus, no one can pay any substantial attention to him without falling under his spell: his story, in some mysterious sense, we feel to be our own, and we return to him again and again. Some of us do so more memorably than others, perhaps,

---

4. On the technical distinctions elucidated by the terms "myth," "legend," and "folktale," see Edmunds 1985:3 n. 9. Most scholars, of course, speak of the "myth" of Oedipus, and we all understand what that means. Pasolini himself uses the term "myth": see, e.g., Stack 1969:122, 126–127.

5. Vellacott 1971, Ahl 1991.

6. See, e.g., Lacan 1977, Deleuze and Guattari 1983 (and Barthes 1964:6: "al di sopra di Edipo, o dietro Edipo, Freud si è sostituito ad Apollo"). As Lacan is pretty universally acknowledged even among theorists to be extremely opaque, it may be prudent for me to suggest as well the elucidations attempted in (e.g.) Evans 1996, Hogan and Pandit 1990, Lemaire 1977, MacCannell 1986, Ragland-Sullivan 1986, Ragland-Sullivan and Bracher 1991, Roudinesco 1990 and 1997, and Žižek 1992.

and none has revisited this legend more powerfully than Pasolini. Before engaging in a close examination of his screenplay, it is worth looking at the Sophoclean text and—before that—the tradition of Attic tragedy from which it emerged. We will then be able to see the ways in which Pasolini is depending on Sophocles specifically, the aspects of his work that come not from Sophocles but from other ancient sources, and the remarkable ways in which Pasolini himself has innovated upon this immemorial theme.

℮

The origins of Greek tragedy[7] are shrouded in centuries of darkness, but by the fifth century B.C.E. it had reached its apogee in the plays of Aeschylus, Sophocles, and Euripides. In a culture where we are used to perhaps daily exposure to television and cinema, we easily lose sight of the fact that preindustrial civilizations had far less to choose from in the way of entertainment; also, that the performance of these plays in classical Athens was an integral part of a *religious festival,* the Great Dionysia celebrated each spring. Moreover, the scripts of these plays are written in formal, metrical verse, using at times a vocabulary quite distinct from the daily vernacular of the Athenian populace. To have his plays performed at the Dionysia, a playwright had to enter a competition; if his plays were selected, he was "granted a chorus" by the *polis,* which is to say that his performance (and we are speaking, typically, of a *single* performance) was produced at civic expense. The playwright wrote the script, and the music for the solo and choral numbers; directed the actors and chorus; and, in the early period, acted in the performance himself. Each playwright presented a "tetralogy," composed of three tragedies (the "trilogy") and a satyr play, and a panel of judges ranked these finalists for first, second, or third prize.

The tragedies were generally on "serious" themes, as Aristotle tells us in the *Poetics* (6, 1449b), but by no means always ended "tragically" as we now use that term; very often, perhaps even typically, they were more like what we call melodrama, featuring near calamities and happy endings.[8] The satyr play was a single, short play offering comic relief from the serious issues treated in the trilogy: if the very scant relicts of this genre give any normative indication, these plays were hilarious, silly,

---

7. This mysterious issue is addressed in (among many others) Pickard-Cambridge 1927, Else 1965, Herington 1985, Winkler 1989, Zeitlin 1989.

8. A point provocatively made by John J. Winkler in his still-to-be-published manuscript *Rehearsals of Manhood,* which he kindly showed to me before his death.

slapstick, and relied heavily on earthy sexual humor. The performance of a playwright's tetralogy—three tragedies and a satyr play—occupied an entire day in the Dionysia, and typically the festival included three such days each year. Earlier in the tradition, the three plays of the trilogy could be conceived as parts one, two, and three of a single story, as we see from the *Oresteia* of Aeschylus; later on, this practice seems to have fallen into disuse. Playwrights might, however, find themselves drawn, in several tetralogies, to writing about different parts of the same myth or legend, and this was the case for Sophocles in writing what is misleadingly called the "Theban trilogy": the *Antigone, Oedipus the King,* and *Oedipus at Colonus* were each produced—in that order—in different years, each of them written as part of a different trilogy.[9]

If Sophocles could see today the gigantic impact his play has had on Western culture, he would likely be as surprised as pleased: the tetralogy in which *Oedipus the King* was originally performed did not win first prize at the Great Dionysia. Time, however, has awarded a different prize, that of literary immortality—the continual ratification that succeeding generations of transfixed readers and viewers bestow on the play by their very fascination with it.

The basic outline, at least, of the legend is familiar to most readers, but some details of the full story are less well known. In trying to assemble a "full story" we must be careful to remember that our sources for Greek myth are many, and in some cases separated from one another by centuries; that we cannot always be sure when particular authors (including Sophocles) may be introducing innovations of their own; and that, in our quest for a single canonical or authoritative version of a myth or legend, we are imposing on the ancient stories a stricture that the ancients themselves did not impose. The demands of orthodoxy and narrative consistency that, for example, traditional Christian theology makes of its doctrines are alien to ancient Greek thought.

That said, we may attempt to piece together what the Russian formalists would have called a *fabula* for the Oedipus legend—that is, a more or less complete version of the story in chronological order of events—with the proviso that these events do come from a variety of sources, some actually postdating Sophocles' play.[10] The inventory for such a

---

9. The dramatic chronology, were one to follow the story from beginning to end, would be *Oedipus the King, Oedipus at Colonus, Antigone.*

10. In the broadest scope, such sources will include Homer, Hesiod, Pindar, the Attic dramatists and the scholia (ancient commentaries) on their plays, Thucydides, Pausanias, Diodorus Siculus, Apollodorus, Asclepiades, Hyginus, Palaephatus, Peisander, Nicolaus of Damascus, and even ancient vase paintings.

comprehensive *fabula,* using the Sophoclean texts as principal sources (and reflecting their theatrical nature), would go more or less as follows. I will number the items for subsequent ease of reference:

1. Laius, king of Thebes, visits the house of Pelops in Elis. There he becomes enamored of Pelops' son Chrysippus, and abducts him to Thebes. In return, Pelops curses him: Laius will die at the hand of his own child.

2. The Sphinx appears outside Thebes. This monstrous animal bars travelers from passing unless they can correctly answer her riddle: "What is it that goes on four legs in the morning, on two legs at midday, and on three legs in the evening; and when it has the most legs, then it is the weakest?" (See item 11 below.) Whoever cannot answer—namely, everyone asked—she chokes to death and devours (the word *sphinx,* from the verb *sphiggein,* means "choker").

3. Laius marries Jocasta, but they produce no children. He consults the Delphic oracle on this problem, and is warned by Apollo that should Jocasta bear him a son, that son will murder Laius.

4. Despite Laius' resolution not to have conjugal relations with Jocasta, she makes him drunk one evening and takes him to bed, thereby conceiving Oedipus.

5. When Oedipus is born, Laius pierces his feet and binds them together, and, following the ancient procedure for disposing of unwanted children, has him "exposed" on Mount Cithaeron.

6. A Corinthian shepherd finds the baby and presents him to Polybus and Merope, the king and queen of Corinth, who are themselves childless. They raise him as their own son, without telling him of his origin. (In Sophocles it is Jocasta who gives Oedipus to a Theban servant to dispose of; he, in pity, gives the baby to the Corinthian to take to Polybus and Merope. Sophocles' Jocasta herself tells Oedipus the version in no. 5 above; see item 18 below.)

7. In the flower of his youth, Oedipus is mocked by a companion with the taunt that Oedipus is not in fact the son of Polybus and Merope.

8. Oedipus goes to Delphi to consult the oracle, which gives him the prophecy that he will murder his father and have sex with his mother.

9. On learning this, Oedipus resolves never to return to Corinth, thinking of course that Polybus and Merope are his father and mother.

10. In his flight he comes to a crossroads in Phocis, where the roads lead to Daulia and back to Delphi,[11] and there he meets a procession: a

---

11. The nature, location, and possible symbolic value of this crossroads are more complex than one might guess. On the topic see Halliwell 1986b, Puhvel 1989, Johnston 1991, Rusten 1996.

herald, an older man in a horse-drawn wagon, and an entourage of atten-
dants. The first two make as if to thrust Oedipus off the road; a physical
conflict ensues, in which the old man horsewhips Oedipus. In return,
Oedipus kills him and (he says) all his men. Apparently, however, one
escapes (see item 19 below).

11. On his way to Thebes, Oedipus meets the Sphinx and correctly
answers her riddle: it is *anthrôpos,* the human being, who in its infancy
crawls on all fours; in the prime of life walks upright; and in old age leans
on a staff. At this the Sphinx, foiled, throws herself off a cliff.

12. Upon his arrival in Thebes, Oedipus is hailed as its savior, and—
since Laius has been found dead—is made its king and given the widow
of Laius, Jocasta, to be his wife.

13. Oedipus rules for a number of years, fathering four children upon
Jocasta: two sons, Eteocles and Polynices,[12] and two daughters, Antigone
and Ismene.[13]

14. Eventually—and here the stage action of Sophocles' *Oedipus the
King* begins—Thebes is beset with another calamity, this time a plague
that decimates its people, its livestock, its crops.

15. In despair the people of Thebes call upon their king, who had
earlier rid them of a plague of sorts, that of the Sphinx, to solve this new
riddle and save them once again.

16. Oedipus has already sent Jocasta's brother, Creon, to Delphi, to
inquire after the cause of this new plague. Creon, returning, announces
that the oracle has fingered the murder of Laius as the source of the *miasma,* or ritual defilement, that now afflicts the land. Oedipus immediately makes a proclamation: whoever knows any information about the
murder of Laius must immediately come forward; whoever suppresses the
truth must be banished. On the murderer(s) Oedipus lays a dreadful
curse.

17. Oedipus confronts the blind seer Tiresias with this latest message
from the Delphic oracle, and asks for elucidation. Tiresias at first demurs,
but is goaded by Oedipus into pronouncing that Oedipus himself is the
killer. Oedipus accuses Tiresias of scheming sedition against him with
Creon.

18. After the exit of Tiresias, Creon reappears, and a tense confrontation ensues; Jocasta then joins them and attempts to orchestrate a rec-
onciliation. When Creon exits, she tells Oedipus the story of Laius'

12. A version of their story is told by Aeschylus in *Seven against Thebes.* Which brother is
elder, and which younger, varies from version to version.
13. Their story is told by Sophocles in *Antigone.*

death, as recounted by the sole survivor of the conflict. (That is, she here recounts the events described above as item 3, the version of item 5 in which it is Laius who pierces the baby's ankles and has him taken away [cf. item 23], and a version of Laius' death that closely resembles that in item 10.)

19. Her mention of "a place where three roads meet" prompts Oedipus to ask for further details of Laius and the murder. Laius, she says, physically resembled Oedipus; and when Oedipus ascended the throne, the sole survivor of the conflict begged Jocasta to send him away as a shepherd. Oedipus now sends for this man, to hear his version of the story.

20. Oedipus tells Jocasta of the events described above as items 7–10. He singles out the plural, "thieves," in her version (item 18) of the killing of Laius: when Oedipus killed an older man at that crossroads, he says, he acted alone. If the shepherd corroborates her plural, then Oedipus will be exonerated.

21. Before the shepherd appears, a messenger arrives from Corinth with the news that Polybus is dead, and that Oedipus is heir to his throne. Oedipus expresses mixed feelings: sorrow at the death of Polybus; joy that he himself now runs no danger of killing Polybus; fear that he may yet find himself in incest with Merope. Hearing these sentiments, the messenger thinks to put Oedipus at ease by revealing that he need not fear about Polybus and Merope. Oedipus is not their blood kin: rather, he was adopted by them, having been taken to them as a baby by this very Corinthian messenger, who was then working as a shepherd. The baby Oedipus' ankles were pierced and bound together, and he was given to this Corinthian by a Theban shepherd, a servant of Laius.

22. Jocasta, more and more agitated as this narrative is spun out by the Corinthian messenger, pleads repeatedly with Oedipus to abandon his inquiry into these matters. When he refuses, she runs inside the palace.

23. Next the Theban shepherd is brought to Oedipus, and the Corinthian messenger identifies him as the man who had given him the baby Oedipus. Slowly, painfully, Oedipus extracts from the Theban shepherd his version of the story: it was *Jocasta* who had handed the baby over to him to be disposed of, because of the prophecies described in item 3 above (cf. items 5, 18); and he, the shepherd, took pity on the baby and gave him to this Corinthian.

24. Oedipus in anguish runs into the palace. Another messenger emerges from the palace to narrate to the Chorus the horrific events that have just taken place within (items 25, 26):

25. Jocasta, bewailing her lurid fate, has hanged herself.

26. Oedipus, coming in, finds her dead, unfastens the brooches from her robes, and gouges his own eyes with them to blind himself.

27. After items 25 and 26 are narrated, Oedipus reemerges from the palace, and sings a *kommos* (antiphonal ritual lament) with the Chorus.

28. Creon appears, and Oedipus humbles himself, asking Creon to banish him, to see to Jocasta's funeral rites, and to look after Oedipus' daughters, who are still young. Creon decides to wait for explicit instructions from the god Apollo, but takes the girls from Oedipus. (This is where our text of *Oedipus the King* ends; the Sophoclean version is continued in the posthumously produced *Oedipus at Colonus*.)

29. Oedipus is not, in fact, driven out immediately; Creon remains in the role of regent. Eventually it is decided to expel Oedipus, who meanwhile has finally become comfortable with his lot, but his sons Polynices and Eteocles, though now grown, do nothing to prevent his expulsion.

30. His daughters, however, remain loyal to him. Antigone attends him in all his wanderings; Ismene intermittently (and secretly) brings him important news from Thebes.

31. The Thebans have received an oracle from Delphi warning that the welfare of Thebes depends on where Oedipus will be buried after his death. Not wanting to receive him—the source of their previous *miasma*—back into Thebes itself, they nevertheless hope to maintain control over him just outside the boundaries of the *polis*.

32. Eteocles has ascended the throne of Thebes; Polynices, desiring to unseat him, has married the daughter of the king of Argos and is amassing an army to march against Thebes. But he has learned of the prophecy mentioned in item 31, and so he too hopes to gain control over the whereabouts of Oedipus.

33. (Here the stage action of Sophocles' *Oedipus at Colonus* begins.) At the end of his long life, after much wandering, Oedipus is led by his daughter Antigone to a grove sacred to the Eumenides in Colonus, a village near Athens, where he reveals that Apollo had, in addition to the baleful prophecies described in item 8, promised that Oedipus would find his final haven of rest in a precinct of the Eumenides.

34. A group of the old men of Colonus—the Chorus of this play—comes upon them. They warn him to move off the sacred ground (*temenos*) onto which he has unwittingly stepped. When they discover Oedipus' identity, they tell him in horror that he must leave the land. Oedipus asks to see Theseus, king of Athens.

35. Oedipus' other daughter Ismene arrives on the scene. She narrates the events described above in items 31 and 32. Oedipus resolves that the Thebans shall never gain control of him. He reveals the source of his anger against his sons, by narrating the events described in item 29.

36. The Chorus instructs Oedipus to make atonement to the Eumenides for trespassing on their holy precinct. Ismene goes to perform the ritual for him. The Chorus asks Oedipus to recount the horrifying events that led to his downfall. He protests that he is an innocent victim of fate.

37. Theseus arrives, and agrees to give Oedipus asylum from the Thebans should they come to take him away.

38. After the exit of Theseus, Creon arrives, and attempts to persuade Oedipus to return to Thebes with him. Oedipus refuses; Creon has Ismene and Antigone seized and sent away, and makes as if to take Oedipus as well. Theseus returns with men-at-arms and rescues Oedipus; he then pursues the Theban soldiers and brings back Antigone and Ismene. Theseus also brings word that Oedipus' son Polynices seeks a word with him. Oedipus is vehemently opposed to such a meeting, but Theseus and Antigone induce him to agree to it.

39. Polynices enters. He narrates the events described in item 32, promising that when Eteocles is overthrown, Oedipus will be reinstated in Thebes.

40. A blind prophet now, like Tiresias before him, Oedipus predicts that the siege of Thebes will fail, and that Polynices and Eteocles will kill each other; he curses Polynices to that death.

41. In a meeting with Theseus, Oedipus shows him where he, Oedipus, must die. Theseus must keep it a secret, and Oedipus, buried there, will be a talisman of good fortune for Athens—he who was once a *miasma* to Thebes. As he has cursed Polynices, he now blesses Theseus, and exits.

42. The Chorus prays that the gods of the dead will receive Oedipus. A messenger enters to tell his end: his daughters bathed him; Oedipus received from Theseus a promise to care for his daughters. All but Theseus retreated, and Oedipus disappeared; no one knows the exact spot except Theseus.

43. Theseus returns and refuses to let Oedipus' daughters know the exact spot where their father met his end. By keeping the secret, Theseus will keep his land safe forever.

℮

This, then, is a schematic account of the complete *fabula,* based primarily on Sophocles. Some intriguing variations may be gleaned from other sources: that the infant Oedipus was not taken to Cithaeron to be exposed, but was put in a chest and set adrift (like Perseus and Danaë, or like Moses in the basket); that Oedipus and Laius are both, independently, on the way to the Delphic oracle when they have their fatal confrontation; that the Sphinx was sent by Hera to punish Laius for his breach of hospitality (*xenia*) in abducting Chrysippus; that the Sphinx, alternately, was sent by Dionysus; that the Sphinx learned her riddle from the Muses themselves; that the Sphinx was actually an illegitimate daughter of Laius (!), who had learned from him a secret oracle given to their ancestor Cadmus at Delphi, and who herself ruled Thebes after Laius' death, using this secret "as a test to discourage claimants, until Oidipous came, having learned the prophecy in a dream";[14] that Jocasta is not the mother of Oedipus' four children; that she survives the cataclysmic event of his self-discovery; that Oedipus is not banished from Thebes, perhaps even that he does not blind himself. The exact moment of the Sphinx's appearance is also subject to variation: in some versions, this is not until the period between Laius' death and Oedipus' accession to the throne.

Narratologically, we may say that, in both the Oedipus plays of Sophocles, the *sjužet*—to use, once again, the Russian formalist term for the "narrative" that is extrapolated from the *fabula*—is produced (as a *sjužet* always is) by deliberate *selection* and *sequencing* on the part of Sophocles. In *Oedipus the King,* he omits items 1, 4, and the details of 2 and 11; displaces items 3, 5–10, 12, and 13; and prevaricates significantly upon item 5 until the climactic moment of the play. Particularly significant for the heightening of dramatic tension in the play is the suspension of item 23 until after the impact of item 21 is digested. In *Oedipus at Colonus,* he displaces items 29–32. Moreover, in both plays, a significant portion of the *sjužet* is presented, not in what Aristotle, in the *Poetics,* calls *mimesis*[15]—visual, onstage *representation* of the action—but as *diegesis,* that is, *narration* by a character or the Chorus. This no doubt reflects, in part, the dramaturgic constraints operating upon Sophocles and all playwrights of the fifth century B.C.E.; but it also has two marked aesthetic effects: first, it focuses the audience's attention on specific details of the narrated events, since the narration is necessarily limited and limiting; and second, it contributes to the audience's apperception of the speaker's character, since the events he chooses to tell (or to omit), and how he tells them,

---

14. Gantz 1993:498 (citing Pausanias 9.26.3–4).
15. See *Poetics* chap. 1–4, 1447a–1448b, and passim; also Kirby 1991b.

are themselves significant. We shall return to this matter of selection and sequencing when we discuss the *sjužet* of Pasolini's film version of the story.

When we begin our analysis of Sophocles' Oedipus plays, we find ourselves adrift on a boundless sea of interpretation. So much has been written on the topic that a comprehensive assessment is impossible.[16] I will confine myself in this chapter to aspects of the plays that I consider the most germane to a discussion of their relationship to Pasolini's screenplay and film. My discussion here, as in subsequent chapters, will occupy itself much with the terms "semiotics" and "semiosis." It is worth defining these at the outset, and as carefully as possible. By "semiosis" I mean, most simply, "the phenomenon of signification, of producing signs"; by "semiotics" I mean, most precisely, "the study of semiosis."[17] All of this has been the special area of study we associate with Ferdinand de Saussure on the Continent, and with Charles Sanders Peirce in the United States. I shall have more to say anon about Peirce's methodology in particular.

It may fairly be said that *Oedipus the King* is itself a study in semiotics: it is signs, and their interpretation, that set the story in motion from the very beginning. Laius is given a sign by Apollo at Delphi (item 3).[18] Oedipus is later himself given a sign at Delphi (8)—not the one he sought, namely, the answer to the question "Who are my parents?," though this question remains fundamental to the entire play. The place where three roads meet (10, 18, 19) serves as a sign for the killing of Laius. The riddle of the Sphinx (2) is a complex set of signs demanding interpretation, which no one can decode until Oedipus does so. Even then, he gives the answer "anthrôpos" (a human), not perceiving that the riddle is also a sign for himself—*Oidipous*, a quasi-homonym of *anthrôpos*: that is, the riddle of the Sphinx serves as a sign for the other cardinal question that

16. In the feeblest of gestures toward bibliographical recommendation, I direct the reader to the superb treatment in Knox 1957; the useful vademecum of Segal 1993; and the essays collected in O'Brien 1968, Gentili and Pretagostini 1986, and Bloom 1988. I also recommend chapter 8 of Goldhill 1986. For general treatments of Sophoclean tragedy, see, e.g., Bowra 1944, Whitman 1951, Knox 1964, Webster 1969, Reinhardt 1979, Winnington-Ingram 1980, Segal 1995. Important commentaries on the Greek text of *Oedipus the King* include those of Jebb 1893, Kamerbeek 1967, Longo 1972, and Dawe 1982; on *Oedipus at Colonus,* those of Jebb 1890, Ammendola 1953, and Kamerbeek 1984. A literal translation of *Oedipus at Colonus,* with notes and interpretive essay, is furnished in Blundell 1990; of *Antigone,* in Blundell 1998.

17. It is a common solecism to say "semiotic" when one means "semiosic," but I will try to distinguish between these two: by "semiosic" I mean "of or concerned with the process of semiosis"; for me, "semiotic" is the adjective for the second-order pursuit known as semiotics.

18. Indeed, the Presocratic philosopher Heraclitus said of Delphic Apollo that he "neither speaks [*legei*] nor hides [*kruptei*] his thought, but gives signs [*sêmainei*]" (fragment B93 Diels-Kranz).

Oedipus must answer: "Who am I?" Oedipus' marriage to Jocasta (item 12) is a sign of his royal position. The plague that besets Thebes (14) is a sign of the *miasma* that the killing of Laius has produced. The oracle that Creon brings back from Delphi (16), again, is a sign (though, once again, fraught with ambiguity). Jocasta's story (18) is a set of signs that must be interpreted against the version recounted by Oedipus himself (20) and by the old servant (23). The Corinthian messenger (21, 23) thinks that his message is a sign of good fortune for Oedipus, though in fact it signifies Oedipus' true parentage—and thereby his downfall. Oedipus' mutilated feet are a sign of his relationship to Laius and Jocasta, and, more generally, of his destiny; his name, Oidi-pous (< *oideô,* "swell"), means "Swollen-foot." Oedipus' self-blinding signifies how, though sighted, he was unable to "see" the truth about his own identity and his parentage, whereas Tiresias, though blind, had second sight and spoke the truth.[19]

As the play is about signs, so too it is about their interpretation: Oedipus prides himself on his ability to decode signs, particularly his solution of the riddle of the Sphinx, despite his lack of mantic skill:

> There was a riddle, not for some passer-by to solve—
> it cried out for a prophet. Where were you?
> Did you rise to the crisis? Not a word,
> you and your birds, your gods—nothing.
> No, but I came by, Oedipus who knew nothing,
> *I* stopped the Sphinx! With no help from the birds,
> the flight of my own intelligence hit the mark.
>   (447–453 = 393–398 Gk)[20]

Here he taunts Tiresias with the latter's supposed prowess in augury, the art of interpreting the significatory import of the flight of birds, and touts his own powers of inference as superior. Oedipus' semiotic abilities are again called upon by the people of Thebes, who implore him to decode the significance of the plague (with a view, of course, to its halt). When the facts surrounding the death of Laius begin to surface, Oedipus sets himself relentlessly to an examination of their semiosis. Certain signs—

---

19. Freud held that Oedipus' self-blinding was symbolic of castration. This, if true, would be equally semiosic.

20. English translations of Sophocles are for the most part taken, or adapted, from that of Fagles 1982. Line-numbers will be given both for his translation and for the original Greek text, the latter designated "Gk." Where line references are given to the Greek text only, the English translation provided is my own. The authoritative edition of the Greek text is now the Oxford Classical Text of Lloyd-Jones and Wilson (1990).

the triple crossroads, the physical appearance of Laius, the report of the sole survivor—prove crucial in the decoding of the fateful signification of this event. Once Oedipus infers that he himself was responsible for Laius' death, his interpretations of the plague-as-sign, of his own maimed feet, and of his relationship to Laius and Jocasta, are all but inevitable.

This semiosic activity carries over into *Oedipus at Colonus*. As soon as he is told he has come to a precinct sacred to the Eumenides, he exclaims:

> This is the sign [*xunthêma*], the pact that seals my fate. (55 = 46 Gk)

This too was given him as a sign by Apollo:

> When the god cried out those lifelong prophecies of doom
> he spoke of *this* as well, my promised rest
> after hard years weathered—
> I will reach my goal, he said, my haven
> where I find the grounds of the Awesome Goddesses
> and make their home my home. (106–111 = 87–90 Gk)

Ever the interpreter of signs, Oedipus instantly knows that he has come to his final resting place, for the location itself serves as a *xunthêma*, or sign, of that to him.

All language is, of course, by definition semiosic. The Greek text of *Oedipus the King*, however, insists repeatedly, in its very vocabulary, on the phenomenon of semiosis, and—particularly—on the human connection with semiosis: the language of cognition, intellection, and investigation is ubiquitous in the play. Verbs of seeking, looking for, finding, revealing, making clear, learning, teaching, forming judgments, and above all, knowing; nouns for intelligence, thought, and mind; and an adjective meaning "clear, precise," and by extension, "accurate, true" pervade the Greek text of the play.[21] By virtue of this sizeable mass of vocabulary, and its relentless recurrence in every scene of the drama, the audience is repeatedly, indeed constantly, redirected to the recognition of Oedipus as semiotician, for it is precisely in this capacity that he comes to grief: it is

---

21. (For this philological material I am indebted to the careful scholarship in Knox 1957. The line numbers in this note refer to the Greek text.) Forms of *zêteô* "seek": 110–111, 266; *skopeô* "look for": 68, 130–131, 291, 407, 952, 964; *tekmairomai* "form a judgment on the basis of evidence": 108–109, 915–916; *gnômê* "intelligence": 398, 608; *phrontis* "thought": 67, 170–171, 1389–1390; *oida* "know": 397, 415, 744–745, 1008, 1014, 1022, 1181, 1455; *heuriskô* "find": 68, 108–109, 120, 378, 440, 441, 839, 1026, 1050, 1106–1107, 1213, 1397, 1421; *phainô* "bring to light, reveal, make visible": 131, 132, 329, 452–453, 457–458, 710, 754, 1058–1059, 1184, 1382–1383; *saphês* "clear, precise" → "accurate, true": 285–286, 390, 439, 978, 1065, 1182; *dêloô* "make clear": 475–476, 497, 608, 792, 1041, 1287–1288; *didaskô* "teach": 38, 357, 554, 698, 839, 1009; *manthanô* "learn": 120, 545, 574, 576, 708–709; *nous* "mind": 371, 916.

because of his tenacious pursuit of the sign, and his determination for
interpreting it, that he brings tragedy down on his own head.

ℰ

I have dwelt at some length on the Sophoclean plays, and their insistence
on semiosis, for a reason that will soon emerge. The fact is that Pasolini
is one of the founding fathers of modern semiotic studies, and is indeed
an important interlocutor of Umberto Eco in this regard.[22] It has hitherto
been more chic to cite French theorists than Italian, but the time has
come for us to redress that balance.

In his essay, "Why That of Oedipus Is a Story," Pasolini writes:

> Let us suppose that Moravia might want to describe, as a charac-
> ter in one of his novels, Silvana Mangano [the actress who plays
> Jocasta in *Edipo re*]. . . . He would have to use a system of writ-
> ten/spoken symbols (our beloved Italian) [*un sistema di simboli
> scritto-parlati—il nostro bell'italianuccio*], adapting them to his own
> personal ideology. He would have to fashion them into a style
> system [*un sistema di stile*], wouldn't he? The symbols Moravia uses
> are signs by nature [*sono di natura segnica*],[23] . . . [Moravia] resolves
> the sign quality of the symbols and reconstructs in his imagina-
> tion—that is through his experience of reality—the living reality
> of Mangano. Thus the sequence is: Mangano in reality—trans-
> formation of this reality into sign-symbols—reconstruction of
> Mangano in reality. Is language then nothing but an intermedi-
> ary? . . . Of course we shouldn't lose sight of the fact that the only
> important element in this sequence is Mangano herself: through
> language one can pass only from reality to reality. . . . Never has a
> semiologist . . . described a person, for example Silvana Mangano,
> as reality with a voice of its own: *the real Mangano as language*. Se-
> miology has ranged over the whole of reality in its researches on
> specific languages, but it has not yet considered *the whole of reality
> as language;* thus it has not yet become a philosophy. . . . How
> would such a description of the reality of Mangano as language
> differ if, instead of being observed in life, she were observed on

---

22. A point made by de Lauretis 1980–1981. See, e.g., Eco 1968 : 112, 150–160.

23. Perhaps a better translation of "sono di natura segnica" would be "are of a semiosic nature," or even "have a semiosic character," since "signs by nature" could be taken to suggest that
the symbols Moravia uses—words—are *natural* signs; whereas it is more or less semiotic dogma
that languages are systems of arbitrary or conventional (not natural) signs.

the screen, that is as a figurative symbol of herself? . . . in substance
the semiology of the real Mangano as a figurative linguistic symbol would not differ very much. . . . It's at this point that . . . we
should have to begin to compare her reality as language in life and
her reality as a non-sign language in a particular film: that is the
reality, as far as I'm concerned, of Mangano-Jocasta.[24]

This remarkable text is significant for a number of reasons. First, it was
written in 1967, the year of the publication of Derrida's *De la grammato-
logie,* and thus well before the popularization of the Derridean "Il n'y a
pas de hors-texte" ("There is nothing outside the text"). Nonetheless,
Pasolini shows an awareness of the fact—subsequently more widely re-
cuperated from the writings of Charles Sanders Peirce—that the entire
universe is a nexus of signs (*"the whole of reality as language"*).[25] Second,
Pasolini explicitly moves beyond the sign-system that had, understand-
ably enough, preoccupied Saussurean semiology—verbal language—and
toward a recognition that film itself is fundamentally semiosic. Third, Pasolini here formulates an embryonic notion of two key Peircean semiotic
concepts: the *interpretant* ("[Moravia] resolves the sign quality of the symbols and reconstructs in his imagination—that is through his experience
of reality—the living reality of Mangano") and *unlimited semiosis* ("Thus
the sequence is: Mangano in reality—transformation of this reality into
sign-symbols—reconstruction of Mangano in reality . . . through language one can pass only from reality to reality"). In view of all this, we
need to take very seriously his assertion that "The cinema is 'semiologi-
cally' an audio-visual technique."[26]

It is difficult to ascertain the extent to which Pasolini is independently
arriving at these ideas, and the extent to which he is indebted for them
to Peirce, either directly or through his reading of Eco and other latter-
day theorists. There are however indications in his essays that he has
thought seriously about some of these ideas as formulated by Peirce.[27]
I would draw particular attention to his brief but dense "Table," which,
without once mentioning Peirce, is nonetheless deeply implicated with
Peirce's designation of three modes of being: Firstness, Secondness, and

24. Pasolini 1971a: 10–13 (emphasis in text).
25. Observed independently too by Bruno 1994, who writes: "Conceiving of the real and
cinema as systems of signs, inhabited by the trace of other signs, Pasolini inscribes them in a
process that eludes definition, and affirms endless textuality. . . . his semiotic research does not
seek to establish codes or to categorize, but rather to venture into the polyphony of an all-
encompassing signification" (93–94).
26. Pasolini 1971a: 5.
27. See, e.g., "The Rheme" and "The Code of Codes" (Pasolini 1988: 288–292; 276–283, in
particular p. 280).

Thirdness.[28] *Firstness* is concerned with phenomenal reality, in and of itself, and without regard to other contingencies, and as such occupies semiosically the realm of quiddity—the suchness of a thing *in ipso,* before
it signifies anything to someone or something else. *Secondness* is concerned with one's awareness of, or interaction with, Firstness: for example, when an apple is red, in and of itself, and apart from my apperception of it, that is Firstness; when the apple's redness is perceived by
me, that is Secondness. The concept of *Thirdness* is the most complex and
difficult, but it entails (among other things) the *consciousness* that Secondness has to do with Firstness. To return to our previous example, Thirdness would account for my awareness of my *perception* that that red round-
ish object *is* an apple, and for my ability to make generalizing inferences
about such signs: for instance, that this is a fruit, that fruits grow on trees,
and so forth. Thus Firstness has to do with phenomena and their qualities,
in and of themselves; Secondness has to do with facts about phenomena;
and Thirdness has to do with reflections or speculations upon phenomena
and the facts we perceive about them.

In returning to Pasolini's "Table," we find his tabulation of a series
of semiotic "codes" that inform human existence. His "Ur-code," or
"Code of Codes," corresponds to Firstness: "the savage in the presence
of an animal is in the presence of a 'sign' of that language. . . . both the
eaten animal and savage who eats it are part of the entire body of the
Existing or of the Real, physically without a break in continuity." [29] His
"Code of Observed (or Contemplated) Reality" corresponds to Secondness: "A man . . . can be a pure observer. . . . Perhaps he is not aware of
the detachment (*which is that of philosophy*): however, he lives the moment
of awareness through which *Reality presents itself as Objectivity.*" [30] His
"Code of Imagined (or Internalized) Reality" begins to move toward
Thirdness: "Observed reality can be internalized and projected onto the
screen of one's memory as recollection or as expectation. The illusion
that reality's objectivity is meant to be possessed, or conquered, or modified, or understood is accentuated, as is the illusion of its succession." [31]
Thirdness is further explored in his Codes of Represented Reality, of
Evoked/Verbal Reality, of Portrayed Reality, and of Photographed Reality. When we come to the "Code of Transmitted (Audiovisual) Reality"
and the "Code of Reproduced (Audiovisual) Reality," which seem to

28. Pasolini 1988:293–297; cf., e.g., Hartshorne and Weiss 1931–1958:1.23–26, 418–420;
Buchler 1955:75–78.
29. Pasolini 1988:293.
30. Pasolini 1988:293 (emphasis in text).
31. Pasolini 1988:293–294.

have to do primarily with television and cinema, interestingly, we find ourselves circling back to the Ur-Code: the "abstraction of television language,"[32] and, most of all, the abstraction of film-language (which he calls "cinema"),

> shades into the "*Langue*" of Lived Reality [i.e., Firstness].[33] Essentially its code is the Ur-code. . . . [Our awareness—Secondness— that there is a Code of Codes—Firstness—could only come about] through the awareness of the Language of Transmitted Reality and the Language of Reproduced Reality [Thirdness]. As one who sees himself for the first time in a mirror and realizes that he is always an image and not only in the mirror—not signified signifying "man," but signifying himself.[34]

In this remarkable fashion, Pasolini (a) accounts for the relationship of cinema to Firstness, Secondness, and Thirdness; (b) shows how, in cinema, Thirdness brings us (like the loops of a Borromean Knot)[35] back to Firstness and Secondness; and (c) forcefully makes his point that, by invoking Firstness, cinema has the peculiar power—possibly the unique power—of dissolving our mental distinctions between "reality" and the representation thereof. Hence his chronic insistence (despite objections to the contrary) that "reality" and its depiction in film are both sign-systems, and essentially sign-systems *of the same order.*

It would seem, despite his feverish theoretical work in the 1960s and early 1970s, and the subsequent reception thereof in the 1980s and 1990s, that Pasolini has not (yet) universally been taken seriously as a semiotician.[36] Teresa de Lauretis, writing in the early 1980s, said,

> But most of all—and on this nearly everyone agrees—Pasolini was not a semiologist. Here again, it seems, reality got in the way. Nevertheless he was deeply interested in semiology, for a time, and that interest, concurrent as it was with cinema, prompted his

32. As distinct from the "concrete 'television transmission'" (Pasolini 1988:296), which draws attention to itself as a mechanical medium, and thus to the viewer's distance from the quiddity of what is viewed.

33. *Langue* was Saussure's word for "language" in its totality as general (and unexpressed) potentiality, as opposed to *parole*, "speech" as a specific (expressed) instantiation of *langue*. In Pasolini's system, these would correspond roughly to *cinema* and *film* respectively.

34. Pasolini 1988:296 (emphasis in text).

35. For the metaphor of the Borromean Knot see Merrell 1995:39.

36. A notable exception is Aristarco 1977:109 (emphasis added): "L'intervention de la linguistique et de la sémiologie—*Pasolini est parmi les premiers à le soutenir*—est la seule chose qui puisse provoquer la disparition d'une telle ontologie et ouvrir *une recherche de caractère scientifique sur le cinéma.*"

interventions on questions of film theory which are still very much at issue today. Thus I would disagree with the assessment (made in 1974, however [by Antonio Costa]) that "Pasolini's theoretical writings on cinema are of little or no use for the development of a scientific semiology of the cinema, nor for film theory and/or film criticism." Or rather, I would disagree with the latter part of the statement, since "the development of a *scientific* semiology of the cinema, which never was Pasolini's concern, is no longer a concern at all: it is a moot case.[37]

What it takes to qualify as a semiologist, or to provide a "scientific" semiology (as opposed to an "unscientific" one), is not clear from this passage; nor is it clear whether de Lauretis, writing at that time, made a distinction between "semiology" and "semiotics" (she seems to use the two terms interchangeably in this essay). I, however, have elsewhere used the former term to refer specifically to the linguistics-based tradition that stems from the work of Saussure, and the latter to refer to the broader (and in my opinion, more useful) tradition we associate with Peirce.[38] And, using the two terms with these distinctions, I would say that it is just possible that the reason Costa and others[39] found no *semiological* use for Pasolini's theories was that these critics of Pasolini were more in the Saussurean tradition than the Peircean. It is no fault or shame to Saussure (a linguist by profession) that his system of "sémiologie" was firmly rooted in linguistics—was, essentially, a linguistic system, a method of analyzing the *linguistic* sign. But I take it as no coincidence that the greatest impact of Saussurean semiology has historically been felt in the realm of *literary* theory, particularly poststructuralism and especially deconstruction. Only very recently has the point begun to be made that the Peircean system, both because it did not originate as a mode of purely linguistic analysis and because it is not schematized according to the same narrow binarism as the Saussurean, is much the more versatile of the two.[40] It lends itself easily to fruitful application, not only in linguistic and literary

---

37. De Lauretis 1980–1981: 159 (emphasis in text). Her text includes a citation from Costa 1977:41.

38. See Kirby 1996b: 209 and n. 7.

39. De Lauretis (1980–1981: 165 n. 4) remarks that "that opinion was shared by many at the time." I imagine that some, at least, of those "many others" were influenced by Umberto Eco's critique (in *La struttura assente*) of Pasolini as of a "singular semiological naïveté" ("di singolare ingenuità semiologica," Eco 1968: 152). Nothing daunted, Pasolini responded to Eco's critique in his "Code of Codes" ("Il codice dei codici," Pasolini 1972: 277–284, translated in Pasolini 1988: 276–283).

40. The case for this assertion is convincingly made in Eco 1975, Merrell 1992, and Merrell 1995: 1–27.

analysis, but equally in sociology, politics, music, the plastic arts—indeed in the study of any human [41] behavior, not excluding film theory or film criticism.

To rephrase my point, then: I surmise that the reason Pasolini was given short shrift by *semiologists* was that, whether they realized it or not, he was in fact a (Peircean) *semiotician*. As such, he was (in this as in so many other ways) far ahead of his time. And, in the essay I have just cited, de Lauretis is already beginning to show a prescient awareness of this fact—and of the fact that his theories are worth a second look. By the time of the publication of *Alice Doesn't*, in 1984, she was ready to say that Pasolini's views on the relation of cinema to reality "appear to have addressed perhaps the central issues of cinematic theory." [42]

For Pasolini, cinema, while "la lingua scritta della realtà," is by no means confined to verbal language, nor of course to the writing of words: it is "translinguistic." It was part of Pasolini's own prescience to move beyond semiology as a mode of narrowly linguistic analysis, and to recognize that human life itself, in all its complexity, evinces semiosis:

> By living, therefore, we represent ourselves, and we observe the representation of others. The reality of the human world is nothing more than this double representation in which we are both actors and spectators: a gigantic happening, if you will. . . . [Cinema] *is, therefore, nothing more than the "written" manifestation of a natural, total language, which is the acting of reality.*[43]

That is to say, Pasolini's memorable description of cinema—"la lingua scritta della realtà"—is pregnant in every word. ◆ *Lingua,* yes, not only because Saussure's impact on the (post-)modern discussion of signs has been massive, but indeed because our spoken and written language is the sign-system with and by which we interact most extensively each day, so that it easily becomes a metaphor for semiosis in general; ◆ *scritta,* because (even at this early stage, before the jargon of the *Tel Quel* group had become widespread) Pasolini was able to conceive of nonverbal modes of signification as kinds of *écriture:* as de Lauretis says, "for Pasolini cinema is precisely writing in images, not to *describe* (portray) reality or fantasy, but

---

41.   Nor is it restricted to matters anthropological: the subfields of zoösemiotics and phytosemiotics deal with semiosis among animals and plants respectively.

42.   De Lauretis 1984:48 (in fact this chapter is a reworking of de Lauretis 1980–1981).

43.   Pasolini 1988:204 (emphasis in text). In her own translation of this passage, de Lauretis (1980–1981:163) renders "Vivendo, dunque, noi ci rappresentiamo, e assistiamo alla rappresentazione altrui" (Pasolini 1972:206) as "Thus in living, in practical existence, in our actions, 'we represent ourselves, we perform ourselves, and watch others representing-performing-enacting themselves [*rappresentare* in Italian conveys all of these].'"

to *inscribe* them as representations";[44] ♦ *realtà*, because, for Pasolini, cinema and life are both "languages" in the metaphoric sense I have just described. For Saussure, the object in the "real" world—the *referent*—is at one level of reality, while the *sign* (composed of signifier and signified) is at another; in the Peircean schema, sign, interpretant, and object are all parts of the triad of semiosis, and full credit is given to the fact that, in the chain of unlimited semiosis, what functions now as an object may later function as a sign; what now functions as an interpretant may next be scrutinized as an object in its own right. So too, for Pasolini, the signs of "actual" life and the signs of cinema are in some sense on equal footing: we generate signs in our daily existence just as they are generated on-screen, and we are spectators whether we are observing ourselves and those around us in life, or are watching a film.[45] Hence he can say, in another context, "So the question is: what is the difference between the cinema and reality? Practically none. I realized that the cinema is a system of signs whose semiology corresponds to a possible semiology of the system of signs of reality itself."[46]

These formulations are directly significant for a "reading" of *Edipo re,* not only because much of Pasolini's richest semiotic work dates from the same period as *Edipo re,* but also because here perhaps more than in any other film Pasolini is peering into the abyss of his own psyche: in *Edipo re* above all, the question of the connection between art and life is paramount. We can only speculate on the extent to which Sophocles—who had not, after all, read Freud—saw himself in Oedipus. Pasolini, on the other hand, saves us the trouble, by announcing roundly, "Edipo sono io."[47] Readers in the postmodern era are trained to separate gestures of authorial intent from readers' responses, and indeed from the demonstrable data of the text (including filmic texts); and, as we shall be reminded in chapter 2, authors are entirely capable of being disingenuous in the expression of their own intentions. Be all that as it may, Pasolini stated quite openly his intentions in making *Edipo re:* "When I made it I had two objectives: first, to make a kind of completely metaphoric— and therefore mythicized—autobiography; and second to confront both

44. De Lauretis 1980–1981:165 (emphasis added). Pasolini himself said, "Barthes, who has so widened the concept of 'writing,' should be profoundly jealous of my idea of cinema as 'writing'" (1988:231).

45. Pasolini's comments cited above are significant too for the theories of performativity now current in speech-act theory and gender studies. For a rudimentary bibliography, consult Austin 1962, Butler 1990, Parker and Sedgwick 1995.

46. Stack 1969:29. Cf. Pasolini 1988:228: "Reality is a language."

47. Roncoroni 1986:51, which continues: "In *Edipo* racconto il mio complesso di Edipo. Racconto la mia vita."

the problem of psycho-analysis and the problem of the myth."[48] Now *metaphor*, as Aristotle knew well, is quintessentially semiosic: in the metaphor *X is Y* (or *the Y of X*, the form it actually assumes more commonly in English),[49] the vehicle (here *Y*) serves as a *sign* for the tenor (here *X*). Thus Oedipus, in the metaphor *Edipo sono io*, is a sign for Pasolini himself.[50] Jocasta and Laius in the film (which is not, as we shall see, the same as "in the oedipal complex" as Freud envisions it) are signs for Susanna and Carlo Alberto Pasolini, Pier Paolo's parents—and not just dramatically, but visually: for Silvana Mangano is costumed, in the prologue of the film, in replicas of Susanna's clothes, copied from old photographs.[51] Some of the details of this family romance are well known: Pasolini had what he termed an "enormous, almost monstrous love for my mother," and a sense of "permanent, even violent tension" with his father, whom he describes as "overbearing, egoistic, egocentric, tyrannical and authoritarian." He makes the perceptive, paradoxical observation that "I always thought I hated my father, but recently . . . I realized that basically a great deal of my erotic and emotional life depends not on hatred for my father but on love for him."[52] And, in his essay on the film, "I have certainly never dreamt that I was making love to my mother. . . . If anything, I have dreamt rather of making love to my father."[53] This sheds light on his answer to a question, in an interview, where he was asked why the *Edipo re* gives "a lot more emphasis to the parricide than to the incest":

> If I remember right, the two have an equal importance in Sophocles' text. You've just pointed out that in my film the parricide comes out more than the incest, certainly emotively if not quantitatively, but I think this is fairly natural because historically I have always put myself in a relationship of rivalry and hatred towards my father, so I am freer in the way I represent my relationship towards him, whereas my love for my mother has remained something latent. . . . everything ideological, voluntary, active and practical in my actions as a writer depends on my struggle with my father.[54]

48. Stack 1969:120.
49. Martin 1993:762. For more on metaphor in antiquity, see Kirby 1997a.
50. Cf. Barthes 1964:5: "la *situazione* edipica (non già il puro aneddoto) ha ormai per noi il potere di una metafora, vale dire di una funzione" (emphasis in text).
51. Stack 1969:12; Schwartz 1992:507.
52. Stack 1969:13.
53. Pasolini 1971a:9—10.
54. Stack 1969:119—20.

As Oswald Stack, the interviewer, points out, "In the Prologue you made a very deliberate choice of having a scene where the father says to the baby: 'You're stealing my wife's love.' This is significantly outside the usual Freudian concept of the myth. In fact you're setting up good reasons for the baby to hate his mother."[55] In other words, in a typical Freudian scenario, Stack would presumably expect the son to fantasize about, and fear, his father's rivalry, whereas in the film, Laius' jealous animosity toward the infant Oedipus is portrayed as quite actual. This is not only a departure from Freud's reading of the Oedipus story,[56] on which account it is the child who directs his first impulses of violence and hatred toward his father, but also from the ancient presentation of the legend, in which Laius' first gesture of hostility toward the infant Oedipus is not prompted by feelings of "oedipal rivalry," but by fear instilled by a prophecy given by the Delphic oracle, and his second gesture of hostility—raising his riding whip against Oedipus at the crossroads—is done in ignorance of Oedipus' identity. Indeed, in both Sophocles' and Pasolini's versions, it is not even Laius who sees to the baby's disposal, although we are initially led to think so, but Jocasta (see again items 5, 6, 18 in our inventory of the *fabula*).

Another detail of this family romance is worth our notice. In the previous paragraph I spoke of the "son" fantasizing about "his father's" rivalry. This is one of the notorious aspects of Freud's approach to the oedipal complex: it is difficult to say how this is to be adapted to the case of daughters, or (for that matter) to children of either sex who are not heterosexual. This is not the place for an extended examination of Freud's assessment of same-sex love, but there is considerable evidence that the notion of a "pathological" homosexuality is not a Freudian, but a neo-Freudian formulation.[57] Be that as it may, Pasolini is manifestly reading Sophocles through neo-Freudian lenses, at a time when the pathological model was still universally in vogue, and it is fascinating to see how he goes about adapting and altering Freudian theory to his own purposes: he avows his intense love (desire?) for his father without disavowing the intensity of his attachment to his mother, and he gives no evidence of suspecting pathology in Oedipus, either in the film itself or in his discussions of it.[58] On the contrary, this film represents what might in the jar-

55. Stack 1969:120.

56. Freud 1953–1976:4.261–264. The relevant material is conveniently excerpted and translated in Edmunds and Dundes 1983:174–178.

57. See, e.g., Lewes 1988, Isay 1989.

58. Which is not to say that Pasolini did not have deeply conflicted feelings about his sexuality: on the one hand, we are told that he "spoke of homosexuality as something quite normal"

gon of today be called the "queering of Oedipus"—not, of course, by
rewriting the *fabula* so as to offer a homoerotic oedipal triangle, but (once
again, on the metaphorical level) by using Oedipus as a vehicle for which
Pasolini is the tenor.[59] In view of the possibilities, it is remarkable that
Pasolini did not exploit the Chrysippus motif of the original *fabula* (item 1,
and the variant in which the Sphinx is sent by Hera to punish Laius for
the abduction of Chrysippus). In connection with all this, however, we
should note a substantial innovation by Pasolini: in the epilogue of the
film, Oedipus is seen (in modern clothes) walking through the streets of
Bologna and Milan, led by Angelo, a young man. This is, of course, an
allomorph of item 33, in which Oedipus is led to the grove at Colonus
by his daughter Antigone. The homoerotic overtones of this innovation
would be difficult to ignore, even if Pasolini had not explicitly made for
us the connection between the aged Oedipus and the poet: "The Epilogue is what Freud calls the 'sublimation.' Once Oedipus has blinded
himself he re-enters society by sublimating all his faults. One of the forms
of sublimation is poetry."[60] And for Pasolini, of course, filmmaking was
the practice of poetry: "to make films is to be a poet"; "the language of
cinema is fundamentally a 'language of poetry.'"[61] So the analogy Sophocles : *Oedipus the King* : : Pasolini : *Edipo re* is further convoluted by the
pronounced metaphor of Oedipus as Pasolini. In connection with Sophocles, one is reminded of how, when asked in old age how he felt about
sex, the tragedian is said to have remarked that he was happy to have
broken free of it, like a slave who had escaped from a raving and savage
master.[62] All this obscures, however, the original meaning of "sublimation," which is "to elevate to the sublime." This is key for our interpre-

---

(Schwartz 1992:191); on the other, that he referred to his own sexuality as an incurable, deadly
disease ("una malattia inguaribile: mortale," Schwartz 1992:188). On his late repudiation of homosexuality—as philosophical position, if not as personal practice—see Lawton 1980–1981.

59. On this aspect of the film, see, e.g., Viano 1993:10–17, 173–186 ("the autobiography of
a homosexual," 180), and in particular, 178: "Pasolini chooses the Greek myth given primacy by
Freud as the motor of human development because it is the myth which contains a 'scientific'
explanation for his homosexuality." Cf. too Viano 1993:263–293 (on the *Trilogy of Life*).
    Perhaps the "queerest" oedipal anecdote of all is that recounted by Schwartz 1992:220–
227: Pasolini, arrested and put on trial in 1949 for "the corruption of minors" and "obscene acts
in a public place," embarked on a three-year nightmare of public disgrace. When the news
reached his parents, Schwartz tells us (p. 227), "Carlo Alberto raved, blamed Susanna for what
'her' son—'your homosexual son,' he is supposed to have said—had done. She took to her bed
for an entire day, and Pier Paolo lay at her side while they talked it through."
60. Stack 1969:129. Pasolini (1971b:9) refers to this innovation as the only radical departure
from the traditional version besides his version of the Sphinx episode; but see below. On the
Oedipus/Angelo sequence, see again Viano 1993:179–180.
61. Stack 1969:154; Pasolini 1988:172.
62. This anecdote is told in the first book of Plato's *Republic* (329b–c).

tation of the ending of the film, since, already in Sophocles' *Colonus,*
Oedipus is represented as becoming a chthonic divinity.[63] All doubt and
hesitation expunged, his former anguish and *miasma* burnt away, in his
final hours Oedipus becomes a tower of anger, of serenity, and of self-
assurance, as he makes the transition to nothing less than a new order of
being: from the end of his earthly, mortal existence springs the beginning
of his new status, for eternity, as demigod.

℮

In discussing his screenplay for *Edipo re,* Pasolini claimed himself to have
made "a special translation, which is very straightforward and faithful to
the [Sophoclean] original," excepting virtually only "the odd phrase
which I invented like for the Sphinx episode and one or two other
things."[64] Since the Sphinx episode—items 2 and 11 in our inventory—
is not mimetically portrayed in Sophocles' script, but only obliquely referred to by characters, this was of course unavoidable, unless Pasolini
were to resort to the same strategy for the Sphinx as he had in including
the exposing (item 5) in the Prologue: action without dialogue. Nonetheless, the celebrated riddle of the Sphinx (item 2), attested to not by
Sophocles but by other ancient sources, is not used by Pasolini:[65] instead,
the Sphinx in the film says to Oedipus: "There is a riddle in your life.
What is it?," to which he answers, "I don't know it. I don't want to know
it." The Sphinx says, "It's useless. Useless. The abyss into which you
thrust me is within you."[66]

63. Recognized by, e.g., Whitman 1951:195; Edmunds 1981:229; Henrichs 1983:95.
"Chthonic" deities (< Gk *khthôn* "ground," "earth") are those associated with the earth, and
thus with burial, death, and the underworld. Prominent among these were the Eumenides (a
euphemistic name for the Furies, who play a key role in the *Oresteia* of Aeschylus), and some
of the semidivine "heroes" of Greek legend. A number of famous figures of ancient legend and
history—including Helen, Theseus, and, interestingly, Sophocles himself—were elevated to the
status of *hêrôs* or "hero," a semidivine category for entities each of whom was attached to a specific geographic locale, where his or her shrine was located. The hero's bones were typically said
to be housed in the shrine. In Oedipus' case, of course, this could not have obtained, for reasons
made clear in the *Colonus* itself. His chthonic associations in that play, however, put him in close
resonance with the Eumenides, who were held to preside especially over matters of oaths, family
curses, and revenge (all issues of great import in the Theban plays of Sophocles).
64. Stack 1969:126.
65. "Non c'è dunque più traccia dell'enigma tradizionale" (Fusillo 1996:94).
66. The entire exchange—which is not in the published screenplay, but is found in the film
itself—is as follows: "C'è un enigma nella tua vita. Qual è?" "Non lo so. Non voglio saperlo."
"Ah, è inutile. Dimmi." "Non voglio vederti, non voglio vederti, non voglio sentirti." "È inutile, è inutile. L'abisso in cui mi spingi è dentro di te." (The version reported in Viano 1993:178,
182, "There is an abyss within you," represents an extreme compression of this. The version

In point of fact, the reader who sets Sophocles' script side by side with Pasolini's screenplay will find notable differences, in addition to the innovations already discussed. Pasolini, for one thing, expatiates in stage directions that dwarf even those of George Bernard Shaw. Our extant texts of the Greek tragedians, by contrast, give no stage directions, not even entrances and exits: everything must be inferred from the dialogue,[67] and modern editions of the tragedies sometimes vary substantially in the stage directions they supply. In addition to this, of course, the action in the play all takes place in one location—by reason of the obvious logistical restrictions—whereas in the film Pasolini exploits to the full the locative freedom that cinematography affords him. He has not made any real attempt to give his sets or costumes any substantive archaeological authenticity, and has dispensed altogether with the Chorus, which plays such a significant role in fifth-century Attic tragedy.

In order to give a clear sense of how Pasolini's plot compares with the Sophoclean, and with the received *fabula* as a whole, I offer the collation of events found in table 1. The scenes of the film are numbered as in the published screenplay, and the items of the *fabula* are numbered as in the inventory above. Scenes in the screenplay and/or film that have no ancient antecedents are indicated by an asterisk in the right column.

Pasolini, as can be seen from this tabulation, follows the chronological sequence of the *fabula* exactly, but leaves out items 1–4, 13, 22, 24–25, 28–32, and 34–43. He has also innovated rather more than his remarks about fidelity to Sophocles might suggest, and expanded on certain events (such as the lovemaking in scenes 30, 34B, 35–36, and the filmed version of scene 39, where Oedipus actually says "Madre" to Jocasta) in

---

cited by Fusillo [1996: 94] is closer to the actual film version, but still not exact.) Note too the paronomasia of *spingi* and *Sfinge*.

　　Literary critics typically see the Sphinx as a specular counterpart (evil twin, Jungian shadow) of Jocasta the mother—the dark side of the female principle, and the one that overtly assails Oedipus (as opposed to the clandestine assault on him by Jocasta during his infancy, and the covert *miasma* she offers him in adulthood). In view of this, it is interesting that—despite the grammatical gender of *Sfinge* (the French *Sphinx* is, by contrast, typically masculine) and the biological femaleness of the Sphinx in the legend, Pasolini's Sfinge is quite clearly male. Perhaps, then, this monster is a Doppelgänger, not of Jocasta, but of Oedipus himself, or perhaps the two are conflated: if so, the riddle posed by Pasolini's *Sfinge* may be read autobiographically. On such a reading, "L'abisso in cui mi spingi è dentro di te" takes on a sexual import, with overtones that extend even to the realm of the anatomical.

　　Fusillo 1996 describes the Sphinx as "una figura femminile . . . che parla con voce prettamente maschile" (93), and draws a connection between Sphinx and superego (94).

　　67. Obviously, in a single-performance production directed by the playwright, such directions will have been given in rehearsal. For more on matters of production, see, e.g., Taplin 1977, 1978; Wiles 1997.

Table 1. Collation of items in the Oedipus *Fabula* and scenes in
Pasolini's *Edipo Re*

SCENE	ITEM	SCENE	ITEM
1–6	★	33–34A	16
7–10	5–6	[34B–C][a]	★
11	7	34D	17
12–18	8	35–36	★
19–20	9	37	18
21–25	★	38–39	18–20
26	10	40	21
27[b]	11–12	41–42	23
28–30	12	[43][c]	★
31	14	44–45	~26, part of 27
32	15	46–48	~33

a. These scenes in the film are not in the published screenplay.
b. The first part of scene 27 includes an event not in the ancient tradition: Oedipus
   passes the blind prophet Tiresias, who is playing the flute. This is an important
   mirror-scene to scene 45, where the boy hands the blind Oedipus a flute.
c. This scene in the published screenplay was not included in the film.

a way that no ancient playwright would have thought of doing. As for the
items included by both writers, Pasolini has depended far more completely on mimesis than Sophocles, who (again, probably for logistical
reasons) relied on the diegetic mode for inclusion of a number of items,
and who also displaced certain items from their chronological sequence
(this, I think, for dramatic and not merely logistical reasons). And, of
course, Pasolini has included the striking framing-sequences at beginning
and end.

A very significant alteration comes at the end of scene 42 in Pasolini's
version. Here, after his conversation with the herdsman, Oedipus says,
"Tutto è chiaro . . . Voluto, non imposto dal destino": "Everything is
clear . . . willed, not imposed by destiny." [68] Of this line, Pasolini remarks:

68. Pasolini 1967:133; cf. Pasolini 1971b:97. My punctuation is significant: both the Italian
and the English editions of the screenplay include a comma after *imposto/imposed,* as if to say that
all was *willed by destiny* though not *imposed by destiny.* (Fusillo 1996:119 punctuates similarly.) This
is not, however, the way the line is delivered in the film itself: Oedipus is very clearly setting
"voluto" in opposition to "imposto dal destino." The punctuation in the citation from Stack's
interview reflects this. What is still not clear is the grammatical agent of *voluto:* willed by Oedipus
himself? Willed by Apollo (as opposed to an impersonal fate)? And, if the latter, how does "the
will of the gods" differ substantially from fate?

That is an absolutely mysterious phrase, which I have never been able to understand; but it is in Sophocles. The exact phrase is: "There, now all is clear, willed, not imposed by destiny." I cannot understand the phrase, but I find it wonderful, precisely because it is enigmatic and incomprehensible. There is a subtlety underneath which is hard to explain. There is something very clear in the phrase, I feel it could be explained, but I can't do it. Anyway, it's a verse from Sophocles which I lifted just as it stands.[69]

But in fact he has *not* lifted it "just as it stands": the reader will search the Sophoclean text in vain for such a line. At 1182 (Gk) Oedipus does exclaim, "Alas, alas, everything would come out clearly," this following on the heels of the herdsman's remark that "If you are the man he [scil. the Corinthian messenger] says you are, know that you were born ill-fated" (1180–1181 Gk). But the latter is a far cry from "willed, but not imposed(,) by destiny." In the lines that follow, other observations are made about the operation of fate: "What madness swept over you? What god, / what dark power leapt beyond all bounds, / beyond belief, to crush your wretched life?" (1435–1437 = 1299–1302 Gk); "My destiny, . . . what a leap you made!" (1448 = 1311 Gk). In these loci as well, however, destiny seems implacably in control. The passage that comes closest to balancing adjudication between the foreordination of Apollo and the work of his own free will is at 1467–1471 (= 1329–1332 Gk): "Apollo, friends, Apollo— / he ordained my agonies—these, my pains on pains! / But the hand that struck my eyes was mine, / mine alone—no one else— / I did it all myself!"[70] But he is speaking specifically of his self-blinding, not of the entire train of events preceding it.

It is very curious that Pasolini would insist so emphatically on the authenticity of this line, when only the first half of it is in Sophocles. That Pasolini would so radically alter the original text here, reminds us that perhaps the thorniest philosophical problem confronted in the Sophoclean version of *Oedipus the King,* and pointedly revisited in *Oedipus at Colonus,* is what we may call the Riddle of Fate: If destiny ordains our lot, what role (if any) is played in our lives by human will? This problem is, obviously, not confined to ancient Greek drama. Biblical theologians have long clubbed one another over the difficulties attendant upon Paul's explicit formulation of predestination in the ninth chapter of his Epistle

69. Stack 1969: 125–126. Fusillo 1996: 119 refers to Sophocles' line as "un verso . . . che Pasolini *amplifica* nella traduzione" (italics mine).

70. A similar balance is struck in the Hebrew scriptures: "In his heart a man plans his course, / but the Lord directs his steps" (Proverbs 16.9, NIV).

to the Romans. Problematically, even Paul can give the question no response except another question: "One of you will say to me: 'Then why
does God still blame us [scil., if he has predestined us to damnation]? For
who resists his will?' But who are you, O man, to talk back to God?"[71]

Sophocles presents the problem dramatically, of course, with reports
of repeated visits to the Delphic oracle—by Laius, by Oedipus, by
Creon—and revelations that the gods have ordained this awesome fate
for Oedipus before his conception. And it is made abundantly clear that
whatever Oedipus has done, he has done in ignorance: he did not know
the old man at the crossroads was his father or that the widowed queen
of Thebes was his mother; in fact he was doing everything he could think
of to prevent killing Polybus and having sex with Merope, the people he
had always thought of as his parents. This fact of ignorance is at the basis
of Aristotle's theory, in the *Poetics,* of *hamartia*—not a "tragic flaw" of
character, but rather a mistake of fact stemming from ignorance.[72] Indeed
Oedipus himself insists repeatedly on this in *Oedipus at Colonus:* he has
suffered, he says, "the worst horrors on earth, suffered against my will, /
I swear to god, not a single thing self-willed" (588–589 = 521–523 Gk),
and should thus be considered innocent: "I am innocent! Pure in the eyes
of the law, / blind, unknowing, I, I came to this!" (615–616 = 548 Gk).[73]

Pasolini's Oedipus, by contrast, when he has his first glimpse of the
blind Tiresias playing his flute, spins us a riddle of his own: "*I am listening
to what is beyond my destiny*" ("*Io ascolto ciò che è al di là del mio destino*").[74]
But what can this be? Sophocles himself, years before writing *Oedipus the
King,* had written:

> The power of fate is a wonder,
> dark, terrible wonder—
> neither wealth nor armies
> towered walls nor ships

71. Romans 9.19–20 (NIV). This passage is, of course, central to the Calvinist/Arminian
controversy, as it is also to much else in the history of Christian systematic theology.

72. *Poetics* 13.1453a. Else 1957 makes much of the fact that this ignorance is one of kinship
ties: not every killing is parricide, not every sexual encounter is incest; these designations depend
precisely on such bonds of kinship. On *hamartia* and its distinction from moral defect, see *Nico-
machean Ethics* 5.8.1137b 11 ff. The topic is well elucidated in Nussbaum 1986: 382–383.

73. Historically, it is important to keep in mind that the *Colonus* is Sophocles' last play, performed posthumously in 401 B.C.E.; *Oedipus the King* is of uncertain date, but antedates the
Colonus by twenty or more years. The composition of *Antigone* antedates that of both the others,
though its dramatic date is the latest of the three.

74. Pasolini 1967: 91; cf. Pasolini 1971: 56–57 (emphasis in text).

> black hulls lashed by the salt
> can save us from that force. (*Antigone* 1045–1050 = 951–954 Gk)

What is it, then, that can be said to stand beyond destiny?

For Pasolini, who has made *Edipo re* into his dreamlike oedipal auto-biography, there can be only one answer: maternal love. This answer is, in a sense, both given and not given in *Edipo re:* that is to say, it is made explicit verbally, but not on-screen. The text of the screenplay ends with an explicitly semiosic reference to the music that signifies the work and office of the poet, who is himself simultaneously sign for Sophocles, for Oedipus, and for Pasolini:[75]

Su quest'immagine, animata da un lieve, antico e inenarrabile vento, scoppia la musica del motivo da cui essa trae, subito, *un senso sconvolgente*—una ripetizione, un ritorno—un'immobilità originale nel muoversi vano del tempo—la misteriosa musica del tempo infantile—il canto d'amore profetico—che è prima e dopo il destino—la fonte di ogni cosa.[76]	The slightest breath of an ancient and inexpressible wind gives life to this pastoral scene; over its image flows that same musical theme, at once investing the surroundings with *its own disturbing meaning*—a repetition, a return—an original immobility in the vain movement of time—the mysterious music of childhood days—the love song of the prophet—older and younger than destiny itself—the source of all things.[77]

Here, in a text that in the Italian attains a lyricism of unsurpassed beauty, he returns to the idyll of his early childhood bliss with Susanna (*la misteriosa musica del tempo infantile—il canto d'amore profetico*), and solves the riddle of fate by placing that bliss of maternal love outside fate itself, as the sublime source of all things (*che è prima e dopo il destino—la fonte di ogni cosa*).[78]

---

75. "He plays the pipe, which means, metaphorically, he is a poet" (Stack 1969:129). Cf. Amengual 1976:99: "Pasolini est Œdipe, comme nous tous. Artiste e créateur, il est aussi Sophocle."

76. Pasolini 1967:143 (emphasis added).

77. Pasolini 1971b:104 (emphasis added).

78. Cf. Fusillo 1996:124.

CHAPTER 2

THE WORLD AS TEXT

&

Umberto Eco's *The Name of the Rose* as Semiotic Fiction

Poi ch'innalzai un poco più le ciglia,
vidi 'l maestro di color che sanno
seder tra filosofica famiglia.
—Dante, *Inferno* 4.130–132

*I*t would be difficult to imagine another book that could have simultaneously as much scholarly interest and as much popular appeal as
Eco's *Il nome della rosa*.[1] Given the preoccupation of certain characters in
the novel with abstruse matters of scholastic theology, its popular appeal
is more surprising still. A best-seller in Italy, France, and Germany, as
well as the United States, it has been translated into numerous languages,
including Catalan, Croatian, Greek, Icelandic, and Portuguese, and has
been made into a major Hollywood film.[2]

Others have noted the novel's focus on semiotics, including some of
the writers anthologized in *Naming the Rose: Essays on Eco's* The Name of
the Rose.[3] Eco himself was invited to contribute to the volume a response
to those collected essays, in which he remarks,

> I never suspected that my novel was so consistent with my research
> in semiotics, because I told my story by accepting a split per-

1. N.B.: *The Name of the Rose* is a detective novel of sorts, and readers who have not yet
completed the novel may want to do so before reading this chapter—not only because of "whodunit," but also because of other surprising revelatory turns of Eco's plot that must (by the very
nature of things) be discussed here.

2. The film (Twentieth-Century Fox, 1986) stars Sean Connery and Christian Slater. Given
the generally dismal results of novel filmizations, the success of this one is notable, but is the
result (in my opinion) of a wise decision not to attempt to mirror the semiotic implications of
the novel discussed in this chapter.

3. Inge 1988.

sonality, and I did not (consciously) try to put in my novel the
theories I had developed in my scholarly writings. I will admit,
though, that even the most schizophrenic personality cannot be as
split as that. A good reader can understand the relationships between my various books better than I can.[4]

Now I am not at all sure that such a disavowal, from a writer as wry and
ironic as Eco, ought to be taken as ingenuous. Be that as it may, what is
clear to all is that the novel, from cover to cover, does indeed explore the
nature of semiosis—beginning with its epigraphic inscription, *Naturalmente, un manoscritto:* "Naturally, a manuscript." This itself is susceptible
of a number of possible interpretations: (1) Naturally, Eco would present
his ideas in a manuscript, because he is a professional writer, and writing
(in its various forms—handwriting, word-processing, the publication of
books) is a relatively permanent and convenient medium for storing, re-
trieving, and disseminating information. (2) Naturally, *The Name of the
Rose* is in manuscript form, because the novel is set in a monastery, and
particularly concerns the monastery's library. Moreover, this (1327 C.E.)
was in the days before the invention of the printing press, when libraries
indeed could house "manuscripts" only in the strict sense of the word:
documents written (*scripti*) by hand (*manu*). (3) Naturally, given the
power of the written word, only a manuscript could cause all the mischief
that occurs in the course of the narrative. (4) Naturally, the novel would
be *about* a manuscript, a metatext if you will—and not just about any
random manuscript, but about a manuscript that is itself about semiosis—
Aristotle's *Poetics*—and about what that manuscript itself signifies.

It is difficult to say which, if any, of these possibilities is the most
plausible or the most attractive interpretation, in and of itself, of the epigraph. In point of fact, none of them is the likeliest: turning the page to
a sort of preface, we find that the editor (Eco?) describes his discovery of
an edition of (naturally) Adso's manuscript, from which he has suppos-
edly made the translation that is *Il nome della rosa.*

There are at least two things to be said about this: first, that the manuscript in question is lost, and unavailable to the editor even when he
journeys to Adso's monastery at Melk: "As the reader must have guessed,
in the monastery library I found no trace of Adso's manuscript" (1–2). In
this it mirrors the fate of the second book of Aristotle's *Poetics,* which—
in *The Name of the Rose* at least—was reported to have survived until the
end of the novel's narrative, at which point it was eaten, like the scroll in

---

4. Eco 1988a:xii. Hereafter, page references to this edition will be given, in parentheses, in
the text.

the vision of St. John the Divine, by the aged blind monk Jorge. Second, and again like the *Poetics,* this manuscript is fundamentally concerned with *semiotics*—with a discussion of the nature and effects of *representation.* In any case, it is that other manuscript—the precious, long-lost manuscript of the second book of Aristotle's *Poetics*—that provides the fulcrum for Eco's entire plot; and, naturally, it will be this manuscript that is our first conduit to the fount of Eco's semiotic inspiration in writing the novel. In this chapter I want to focus on this fact, and on the ancient sources of semiotic theory that underlie *The Name of the Rose.*

Every page of the novel is awash with semiosis. The latter is Charles Sanders Peirce's term for the phenomenon of signification, and it may be best to begin here with a very brief sketch of Peircean semiotics, both because (as I indicated in the previous chapter) I believe the Peircean system to be much superior to the Saussurean,[5] and because Eco's own writings on semiotics are themselves profoundly indebted to Peirce.[6] The primary texts—Peirce's semiotic papers[7]—are densely written and forbiddingly hermetic, and I think this is what explains why the staggering significance of Peirce's work has not been more broadly received before now. By the same token, I predict that the work of his epigones, in our own generation,[8] may rectify this problem, and that when this happens, Peircean semiotics will prove one of the most important philosophical developments of the twentieth century—indeed of modern times.

Not that semiotics is an entirely new system. Indeed it has its roots in classical antiquity,[9] when the ancient Greeks began to make philosophical inquiry about representation and signification in the phenomenal

---

5. Again I would draw my reader's attention to Merrell 1992 and Merrell 1995: 1–27. See also Eco 1975.

A word on technical terminology. As I mentioned in chapter 1, I use the word "semiotics" to mean *the study* (or *theory*) *of semiosis;* Ferdinand de Saussure had, at about the same time as Peirce, used the term "sémiologie" to mean approximately the same thing, and "sémiologie" was also used by Roland Barthes in his influential treatise on the topic (Barthes 1968). For a careful distinction between the two words see, e.g., Deely 1997: 83, 87 and n. 16.

To be excruciatingly faithful to Peircean orthography, it seems, we should be spelling the English noun "semeiotic," i.e., without an *s* and with another *e* (see Fisch, Kloesel et al. 1986: 321–322; Shapiro 1983 : x); this has not, however, been the orthography that has gained widest acceptance.

6. See, e.g., Eco 1976: 15–16; Sebeok 1997: xiii; Deely 1997: 99; Capozzi 1997: 218.

7. Largely collected in Hartshorne and Weiss 1931–1958. A new chronological edition of Peirce, far more complete than the *Collected Papers,* is slowly being published by the Indiana University Press (Fisch, Kloesel et al. 1981–). For first aid, one may consult the useful selection in Buchler 1955.

8. E.g., Merrell 1992, along with Merrell 1995, Parmentier 1987, and of course Eco 1976 and 1984a.

9. Or, on the account of Manetti 1993, even in ancient Mesopotamia. On Manetti's book see Kirby 1996b. On ancient semiotics see also Clarke 1990.

universe. They noted that, quite apart from the elements of material reality, we make signs (the Greek term was *sêma* or *sêmeion*) to represent
those things, and that we connect the signs with the things themselves by
mental apperception. While one or another of these three items—the
thing itself, our designation of it, or our conceptualization of thing and/
or designation—has, at various times in history, been the locus of particular scrutiny or anxiety,[10] we have not since antiquity succeeded in
dispensing with any of them; thus, even if only in their rejection, we
continue to find ways to deal with their demands on our thought.

Peirce's way was to propound a triadic relationship among the major
elements of semiosis: the thing itself, which he terms the *object;* the sign,
which (in addition to "sign") is called the *representamen;* and the mental
image we form connecting sign with object, which he calls the *interpretant.*[11] It is in this context that Peirce offered his famous definition of the
sign as "something which stands to somebody for something in some
respect or capacity."[12]

Any number of things may be a sign. If you see a red-and-white
striped pole twirling around outside a shop, you are entirely justified in
going in and asking for a haircut. If you put a kettle on the fire, and a few
minutes later it starts whistling, you can reasonably get your tea ready in
the pot and pour the water over it. If you are playing out in the yard, and
your mother puts her head out the back door and calls, "Dinner's on!,"
no one will be surprised if you run inside, expecting to eat. Each of these
things—the barber's pole, the whistling of the kettle, the call "Dinner's
on"—is a sign of one sort or another. That we recognize them as such is
testimony to the universal function of semiosis in our daily lives.

10. We see such anxiety (expressed evidently in playful form) as early as the fifth century
B.C.E., when the sophist Gorgias of Leontini is said to have written a work (now lost) entitled
On Nature, or On Not-Being. Other sources from antiquity report that this book proffered a threefold catena of arguments: (1) Nothing exists. (2) Even if something did exist, we could not know
it. (3) Even if we could know it, we could not articulate our knowledge. It should be immediately clear that each of these arguments focuses on one of our semiotic elements: respectively,
(1) the thing itself, (2) our mental apperception of it, and (3) our designation of it.

 Subsequent anxieties, particularly surrounding the apperception and representation of reality, have been explored by modern and postmodern writers on phenomenology and linguistics,
from Hegel and Husserl to Derrida.

11. These are roughly analogous to Saussure's terms (respectively): *referent, signifier,* and *signified.* For Saussure, however, the "sign" is a compound of signifier plus signified, mirroring (in
binary fashion) the referent. Peirce's ternary system both sets semiosis free from Saussure's primarily linguistic focus, as Merrell 1992 shows, and enables us to contemplate how signs and interpretants themselves may be considered as objects—thereby becoming susceptible of further
signification (by new signs) and further apperception (by new interpretants). This is what Peirce
called "unlimited semiosis."

12. Cited in Buchler 1955:99 (cf. Hartshorne and Weiss 1931–1958:2.227–229).

Semiosis, in the Peircean system, is not limited to signs of human devising. The fields of "zoösemiotics" and "phytosemiotics" explore the semiosis we find in the animal and plant worlds—for example, the wagging of a dog's tail, or heliotropic movement in certain flowers, respectively. Seen through this matrix, semiosis is the process of signification (and, in some sense, interpretation) that goes on, moment by moment, in every nook and cranny of the universe.

Peirce offers a tripartite categorization of signs. These are *icon, index,* and *symbol.* The icon bears some resemblance—for example, visual—to its object. A portrait of George Washington would be an icon representing the man Washington. The index, true to its name, indicates the object in some significant way: rising smoke, then, would be an index of burning fire. Of the three, the symbol has perhaps the most arbitrary relationship to its object: for example, the thirteen stripes on the U.S. flag represent the original colonies symbolically, but not iconically or indexically. Language, both spoken and written, is a system of symbolic signs.[13]

A key passage historically for the study of semiotics comes from the opening of Aristotle's deceptively short treatise, *On Interpretation:*

> Spoken sounds are tokens [*sumbola*] of experiences [*pathêmata*] in the mind [*psukhê*],[14] and written marks are *sumbola* of spoken sounds. And just as written marks are not the same for everyone, neither are spoken sounds; but what these are signs [*sêmeia*] of in the first place—*pathêmata* of the *psukhê*—are the same for all; and the actual things [*pragmata*] of which these *pathêmata* are likenesses [*homoiômata*] are also the same.[15]

All three elements of the Peircean triad are here: the token/sign (= representamen); the "actual thing" (= object); and the experience in the mind (= interpretant).[16]

---

13. The basic exception to this is perhaps onomatopoeic words, which might be said to have an (audial) iconic resemblance to the sonic "objects" they signify.

14. The word *psukhê* is particularly troublesome for translators; our derivative "psyche" might be thought viable, but it has become overladen with connotations of psychology and particularly, I think, of psychoanalysis, and these hinder rather than help. "Soul," perhaps the commonest translation, is in my opinion the least helpful of all here, freighted as it now is with ideas of Judeo-Christian theology that would have been entirely foreign to Aristotle and the other Greeks of his time. His treatise *Peri psukhês,* whose Latin title is *De anima,* is essentially a work of cognitive psychology. Hence I have settled, dubiously, on "mind."

15. *On Interpretation* 16a 3–8. My translation is adapted from that of J. L Ackrill in Barnes 1984.

16. Modern semioticians, however, find particularly useful the specifically triadic nature of Peirce's model. That is to say, no one element of the triad is more closely connected to the second than to the third; indeed at the center of the triad, according to Peirce, one finds

Not only are these doctrines central to the plot of *The Name of the Rose:* they are explicitly set forth in its pages, and from very early on. William of Baskerville, a "learned Franciscan" (13), has charge of the spiritual direction of the narrator, Adso of Melk, himself a Benedictine novice who serves as William's scribe. On the first page of his Prologue, Adso says:

> I prepare to leave on this parchment my testimony as to the wondrous and terrible events that I happened to observe in my youth, now repeating verbatim all I saw and heard, without venturing to seek a design, as if to leave to those who will come after (if the Antichrist has not come first) *signs of signs,* so that the prayer of deciphering may be exercised on them.[17]

That his language here is apocalyptic and biblical does not negate the fact that he is speaking of signs and their decoding—of semiosis, that is, and interpretation.

No sooner have they reached the abbey where the story takes place, than William executes an astonishing feat of inference, which he subsequently explains to Adso:

> "My good Adso," my master said, "during our whole journey I have been teaching you to recognize the evidence through which the world speaks to us like a great book. Alanus de Insulis said that
>
> > *omnis mundi creatura*
> > *quasi liber et pictura*
> > *nobis est in speculum*
>
> and he was thinking of the endless array of symbols with which God, through his creatures, speaks to us of eternal life. But the universe is even more talkative than Alanus thought, and it speaks not only of the ultimate things (which it does always in an obscure fashion) but also of closer things, and then it speaks quite clearly." (23–24)

"nothingness" (Merrell 1995:68–69), in which, he says, resides "unbounded freedom." This seems at least subtly different from Aristotle's formulation in a number of respects: (1) Aristotle's discussion is an explicitly linguistic one. (2) The (linguistic) signs he discusses are explicitly said to be signs of the *interpretants* themselves (if I may call them that), not signs of *objects*. (3) Moreover, he seems (in this passage at least) to be committed to a sturdier notion of objective reality than I think Peirce was. None of this detracts from the landmark nature of this semiotic analysis. I have no doubt that it powerfully influenced Peirce, who was (as his published writings show) a serious scholar of Aristotle.

17. Eco 1983a:11 (italics mine).

The world, for William, is a text to be read—a set of signs to be inter-preted. The message could not be expressed more clearly. (The Latin text here says, "Every creature of the world, / like a book or picture, / is for us a mirror.") A few pages later, Adso gets a lesson in interpretants worthy of Peirce himself:

> "[T]hat kind of print [i.e., a horse's footprint] expressed to me, if you like, the idea of 'horse,' the verbum mentis [i.e., 'word of the mind'], and would have expressed the same to me wherever I might have found it. But the print in that place and at that hour of the day told me that at least one of all possible horses had passed that way. So I found myself halfway between the perception of the concept 'horse' and the knowledge of an individual horse. And in any case, what I knew of the universal horse had been given me by those traces, which were singular. I could say I was caught at that moment between the singularity of the traces and my igno-rance, which assumed the quite diaphanous form of a universal idea. . . . And so the ideas, which I was using earlier to imagine a horse I had not yet seen, were pure signs, as the hoofprints in the snow were signs of the idea of 'horse' and signs and the signs of signs are used only when we are lacking things." (27–28) [18]

The primacy of *things* here, of course, makes this look like a nominalist, Ockhamist argument. The language itself, however, is palpably Augus-tinian, bringing to mind the opening of the second book of *De doctrina christiana,* where Augustine defines a sign as something that causes us to think of something *other than* what Peirce would call an interpretant—"something," he says, "beyond the impression the thing itself makes upon the senses." That is to say, a sign points to an object. "Thus if we see a track, we think of the animal that made the track." [19] It also brings to mind the speculative grammar of the mediaeval *modistae,* with their three modes—the *modi essendi* (being), *intellegendi* (thought), and *significandi* (signifying)—which may be said to correspond with some close concin-nity to Peirce's object, interpretant, and representamen, respectively. [20]

18. This passage is quite closely based on a passage in Voltaire's *Zadig;* see Eco 1983b: 208–209; DelFattore 1988: 78–80; Cohen 1988: 66–67.

19. These citations from Augustine are from *De doctrina christiana* 2.1 (in the translation of Robertson 1958). The point is worth making, I think, that Peirce's own semiotic theory must owe extensive debts to the formulations of Augustine and Boethius. In such capacity these au-thors, whose work has doubtless influenced Eco directly, will also have been indirect influences on Eco's work.

20. On speculative grammar see, e.g., Hunt 1980, Rosier 1983.

Not long after this, Adso meets the monk Salvatore, whose speech marks him as a most extraordinary man:

> Nor, for that matter, could I call Salvatore's speech a language, because in every human language there are rules and every term signifies ad placitum a thing, according to a law that does not change, for man cannot call the dog once dog and once cat, or utter sounds to which a consensus of people has not assigned a definite meaning, as would happen if someone said the word "blitiri." And yet, one way or another, I did understand what Salvatore meant, and so did the others. (47)

(The term "blitiri"—most accurately, *blituri*—is used by the ancient Greeks as onomatopoeic for the sound of a harp string; too, it is used, by such late-antique writers as Sextus Empiricus and Diogenes Laertius, as Aristophanes had used *tophlattothrattophlattothrat:* to signify meaningless sound.)

Salvatore is a linguistic, a semiosic monstrosity.[21] In that respect he is all of a piece with the bizarre and disconcerting events and people in the abbey. But Adso's observations on language here are reminiscent not only of the passage from Aristotle's *On Interpretation* quoted above, but also of his semiotic remarks in the *Posterior Analytics:*

> Again, how will you prove what a thing is? For it is necessary for anyone who knows what a man or anything else is to know too *that* it is (for of that which is not, no one knows what it is—you may know what the account or the name signifies when I say *tragelaphos* [i.e., "goatstag," a nonsensical term], but it is impossible to know what a *tragelaphos* is.[22]

The *Poetics* of Aristotle—or the extant "torso" of the text—takes up merely forty-seven small pages in the Oxford edition of Rudolf Kassel.[23] From hints in this extant portion, as well as from other ancient sources (including Aristotle's own *Rhetoric*), it is clear that there must have been a second "book," that is, another scroll containing the remainder of the

---

21. Veeser 1988:12–114, I should mention, sees Salvatore as a manifestation of the Bakhtinian "carnivalesque," and thus a salutary and beneficent presence in the narrative.

22. *Posterior Analytics* 2.7, 92b. My translation is adapted from that of Barnes (1984:1.152).

23. Kassel 1965 (a superb scholarly edition).

treatise; and most scholars conclude that it was here that Aristotle offered his complete analysis of comedy.[24] The second book of the *Poetics* is one of those manuscripts from antiquity that classical scholars would give their eyeteeth for, along with, say, the complete poems of Sappho and Pindar, the treatise *On the Chorus* written by Sophocles, the dithyrambs and tragedies written by Plato in his youth, or indeed the dialogues of Aristotle that won him such a gilded reputation as a prose stylist. But even without the missing second scroll, this tiny first book has exercised an influence on the study of Western belles lettres second perhaps only to that of the Bible—and certainly all out of proportion to its size. Murray Abrams aptly opines, "A history of criticism could be written solely on the basis of successive interpretations of salient passages from Aristotle's *Poetics*."[25] Its stock, like that of Aristotle himself, has risen and fallen with the times. To Dante he was the *Maestro di color che sanno;*[26] to Aquinas, of course, he was the key to the harmonization of Christian theology and classical philosophy. The particular ascendancy of the *Poetics* in literary criticism and theory, however, is an epiphenomenon we associate primarily with the Renaissance and the rediscovery of Greek literature.[27]

At the beginning of our own century the *Poetics,* while much cited, was not the object of much concentrated study even by classicists. Ingram Bywater, in England, published an edition of the Greek text of the *Poetics,* with commentary, that began to reverse this dismal state of affairs;[28] the Chicago Aristotelians—Richard McKeon, R. S. Crane, Elder Olson, and their school—attempted to found a whole school of literary criticism on the basis of Aristotelian philosophy;[29] in Italy, the perceptive and elegant work of Augusto Rostagni offered a firmer philosophical basis for reading the text of the poetics than classical scholars had previously had.[30] The publication, in 1957, of Gerald Else's massive *Aristotle's Poetics: The Argument*—despite its sometimes radical assertions—made English-speaking readers begin to see once again that this little document was, indeed,

---

24. In fact there are brief discussions of comedy in chapters 3, 4, and 5 of the *Poetics,* but nothing like the extended analysis of tragedy that the extant torso provides. A conjectural reconstruction of the second book is offered, brilliantly if quite controversially, in Janko 1984.

25. Abrams 1953:15.

26. *Inferno* 4.131.

27. On the influence of the *Poetics* on the Latin Middle Ages—in the translation by William of Moerbeke (1278) and the translation of Averroës' middle commentary on the *Poetics* by Herman Alemannus (ca. 1256)—see Lobel 1931, Minio-Paluello 1947, Kelly 1979, and Dahan 1980.

28. Bywater 1909.

29. See, e.g., Crane 1952. Chapter 3 of Leitch 1988 offers a useful profile of the Chicago School.

30. See, e.g., Rostagni 1945. Albeggiani 1934 had preceded this in Italy.

structured according to a coherent (and compelling) argument, and that Aristotle's observations about mimesis in general, and tragic drama in particular, might have more than merely antiquarian value. Since that time the importance of the *Poetics* has loomed ever larger in Western scholarship, on both sides of the Atlantic,[31] and the trend shows no sign of reversal.

There is much, then, that we cannot say about Aristotle's literary theory, because we lack the second book of the *Poetics*. What is clear from the extant torso, however, is that he sees *poiêtikê,* or "poetics," as part of a larger schema of artistic endeavor, all of which is founded on the phe-nomenon of *mimêsis,* which we may translate (poorly) as "representation" or "imitation" (or perhaps both);[32] that, moreover, he understands the poetics of tragic drama as a quintessentially *rhetorical* phenomenon;[33] and, in close connection with both these points, that the function of mimesis depends on its fundamentally *cognitive* and *semiosic* nature.[34] In the first three chapters, he situates drama in a much larger schema of the various art forms native to his place and time—painting, sculpture, music, and dance, for instance—and offers a systematic, even taxonomic, break-down, according to the medium, the mode, and the object of mimesis.[35] In the fourth chapter, he offers three particularly important observations on the nature of mimesis: it is *natural* to humans; it is *peculiar* to humans; and it is crucially implicated in the process of human *learning.* These as-sertions form part of his defense of mimesis against the scorching critique of it that had been made by Plato in the *Republic;* in the course of that defense, Aristotle grounds mimesis firmly in his theory of cognition and semiotics, offering it as not only acceptable but indeed essential to the human experience.

In the fifth chapter, Aristotle defines *to geloion,* "the laughable" or "the comic": "*to geloion* is a sort of error [*hamartêma*] and *aiskhos* [i.e., 'ugliness' or 'shame'] that is not painful or destructive, just as, clearly, a comic mask is something *aiskhron* [i.e., 'ugly' or 'shameful'] and

---

31. For the tiniest beginning of a scholarly bibliography on the *Poetics* since Else 1957, I would direct the reader to Lucas 1968, Dupont-Roc and Lallot 1980, Else 1986, Halliwell 1986a, Janko 1987, Belfiore 1992, Golden 1992, and Rorty 1992. Each of these books will of course contain further bibliography (that in Rorty 1992, based on Belfiore's, is particularly useful).

32. On mimesis in Plato and Aristotle, see Kirby 1991b, 1996a.

33. Demonstrated in detail in Kirby 1991a.

34. On this aspect of the *Poetics,* see above all the work of Leon Golden (e.g., Golden 1992).

35. For a schematic diagram of these three chapters of the *Poetics,* see the figure in Kirby 1996a: 33.

contorted, but without pain" (*Poetics* 5.1449a 34–37). His emphasis on *to aiskhron,* the "ugly" and "shameful," in contrast to *to kalon*—the "fine" and "beautiful"—together with his paradigm of the comic mask, leads me to believe that he is not here offering a comprehensive theory of humor, of everything that may cause us to laugh, but rather a distillation of what is comic about Attic Old Comedy, that is, comic drama as it was produced by Aristophanes and his ilk in the Athens of Socrates' day. Thus, for example, this definition explains why slapstick and bawdy jokes are funny, but not the rarefied humor behind linguistic paronomasia (unless that too depends upon being perceived as a mistake). It is apparent that Aristotle offered a more comprehensive theory of the humorous in the second book of the *Poetics,*[36] and it is this tantalizing supposition that fuels Eco's narrative. For Jorge of Burgos, who in the novel is well aware of what that scroll contains, is implacably opposed to a world where laughter is encouraged: "laughter is something very close to death and to the corruption of the body" (96). It is not surprising that Jorge is more a Platonist (or realist) in his metaphysics and epistemology than an Aristotelian (or nominalist): "as there is bad speech there are also bad images. And there are those that lie about the form of creation and show the world as the opposite of what it should be, has always been, and always will be throughout the centuries until the end of time" (79). The monk Benno, in conversation with William, reports a conversation that he has had with Jorge: "But Jorge added that the second cause for uneasiness is that in the book the Stagirite [i.e., Aristotle] was speaking of poetry, which is *infima doctrina* and which exists on figments" (111). At such times he sounds very like Socrates in the tenth book of the *Republic:*

> What about a joiner who specializes in making beds? Weren't we saying a short while ago that what he makes is a particular bed, not the type, which is (on our view) the real bed? . . . So if there's no reality to his creation, then it isn't real; it's similar to something real, but it isn't actually real. It looks as though it's wrong to attribute full reality to a joiner's or any artisan's product, doesn't it? . . . I think the most suitable thing to call him [scil. the painter who paints a picture of a bed] would be a representer of others' creations. . . . The same goes for tragic playwrights, then, since

---

36. Cf. Aristotle's *Rhetoric* 1.11.29, 1372a 1–2: "The laughable has been defined separately in the [books] on poetics"; 3.18.7, 1419b 5–6: "How many forms of the laughable there are, has been said in the [books] on poetics." The very plurals here underscore the fact that there were at least two scrolls to the *Poetics*—if indeed Aristotle is here referring to the *Poetics* and not (as some surmise) to other writings, such as his dialogue (now lost) *On Poets.*

they're representers: they're two generations away from the throne of truth, and so are all other representers.[37]

As we contemplate this counterpoint of philosophical subjectivities, we become aware that Eco himself is the site of a remarkable convergence: one of classical literature, of mediaeval culture, of the modern recuperation of antiquity, and of twentieth-century semiotic theory. *The Name of the Rose* is the result of this convergence, spun into narrative.

In a subsequent, highly charged conversation, William and Jorge engage in heated disputation over the propriety of laughter itself. The arguments on both sides not only echo various Aristotelian assertions, but highlight the semiotic nature of the discussion:

> "Laughter shakes the body, distorts the features of the face, makes man similar to the monkey."
>
> "Monkeys do not laugh; laughter is proper to man, it is a sign of his rationality," William said.
>
> "Speech is also a sign of human rationality, and with a speech a man can blaspheme against God. He who laughs does not believe in what he laughs at, but neither does he hate it. Therefore, laughing at evil means not preparing oneself to combat it, and laughing at good means denying the power through which good is self-propagating." (131)

Perhaps the most salient point scored by William is when he provokes, if not actual guffaws, at least a sneer from Jorge ("Jorge sogghignò," says the original text):

> "It is told of Saint Maurus that when the pagans put him in boiling water, he complained that the bath was too cold; the pagan governor foolishly put his hand in the water to test it, and burned himself. A fine action of that sainted martyr who ridiculed the enemies of the faith."
>
> Jorge sneered. " . . . A saint immersed in boiling water suffers

---

37. Plato, *Republic* 10.597a–e (cited in the translation of Waterfield 1993). Cf. also *Republic* 10.602c–607a, *Laws* 2.668a–b, and Kirby 1991b.

It is interesting to ponder how much Plato the learned reader might have known at this period—a reader, that is, who did not have access to the breathtaking holdings of Jorge's library (which is of course fictitious). The Plato of the Middle Ages was, above all, the Plato of the *Timaeus,* which they will have known in (partial) translations by Cicero and Calcidius, and later in Latin renditions of Arab versions. In addition to this, however, the *Phaedo*—of particular importance for the doctrine of the Forms—was translated ca. 1403 by Leonardo Bruni, and it seems there had been a least one earlier version.

for Christ and restrains his cries, he does not play childish tricks on the pagans!"

"You see?" William said. "This story seems to you offensive to reason and you accuse it of being ridiculous! Though you are controlling your lips, you are tacitly laughing at something, nor do you wish me to take it seriously. You are laughing at laughter, but you are laughing." (133)

William says Jorge finds the story "offensive to reason"—considers it a *hamartêma,* Aristotle might say—and not to be taken seriously: one could imagine this staged comically, in quasi-cartoon fashion, where even a boiling cauldron is "not painful or destructive." That is to say, this anecdote, as William relates it, is *geloion* in a squarely Aristotelian sense, and affects even Jorge as such, in spite of himself.

This heated exchange occurs fairly early in the novel—at Terce of the second day. It is not until the night of the seventh day, a few pages from the end in fact, that the full revelation is made: that the library's vast holdings have included the only extant copy of the second book of the *Poetics,* a fact Jorge had deliberately obfuscated earlier in the novel (p. 112), and that indeed Aristotle here formulates a comprehensive theory of humor, based on a semiotics of actions and speech. William translates aloud a paragraph of it (468)[38] and then, without reading further, speculates inferentially what the rest of it must say (471–472), including that "Aristotle sees the tendency to laughter as a force for good" (472). Jorge reveals that he fears and hates this book above all others because it is by Aristotle, whose influence on Christian thought Jorge finds pernicious and dangerous:

"Every word of the Philosopher, by whom now even saints and prophets swear, has overturned the image of the world. But he had not succeeded in overturning the image of God. If this book were to become . . . had become an object for open interpretation, we would have crossed the last boundary." (473)

It is not difficult to see in Jorge a villain of Grand Guignol proportions, the very negation of Eco's own deep admiration for Aristotle, and of his abiding faith in the salubrious power of laughter.[39]

---

38. In crafting this remarkable paragraph, Eco appears to have to relied on information in the so-called Tractatus Coislinianus, a tenth-century manuscript in the Bibliothèque Nationale in Paris, and perhaps on some remarks in Aristotle's *Rhetoric.* Janko (1984), as I have mentioned, believes that the Tractatus is a reliable epitome, or summary, of the second book of the *Poetics.* While he makes the case with powerful erudition, his thesis has not met with universal acceptance.

39. On the latter, one should consult, e.g., Eco 1984c, as well as the hilarious entries in Eco 1993 and 1994. See too de Lauretis 1981:79–89; Lattarulo 1985:96–99; Fuhrmann 1988:18–20.

One has so much to keep track of in reading this complex novel that one is likely to lose sight of certain historical details: one of these is the generally abysmal status of classical learning in Western Europe at this time. Most Greek texts were known scantily or not at all;[40] the vast repository over which Jorge has presided in this library would have been an oasis of unimaginable proportions, and the destination of every scholar in Europe, were its contents widely known. This, then, has implications for the details of the plot: one could not expect even the educated person (unless he had unlimited access to the treasures of this library) to know the works of Plato or Aristotle in Greek; the doctrines of the *Republic,* for example, would be largely mysterious to scholars of the period. On the other hand, Eco is intimately and subtly acquainted with all this material, and is exploiting it on a metanarrative level; he knows that his well-educated readers will know it too. There is, then, a contrapuntal interplay between the events and ideas that the characters in the story are involved with, and the subsequent history (including the history of ideas) that the reader of *The Name of the Rose* will know. Not least in this counterpoint, as we shall see, is the question of the putative sources upon which Eco has relied for his material, and the place the *Poetics* occupies in all this.

Semiosis, as I have already remarked, is conspicuous everywhere in *The Name of the Rose.* Eco makes it egregiously obvious that his characters are themselves named significantly. William of Baskerville, the detective of this story, is of course meant to make the reader think of Conan Doyle's *Hound of the Baskervilles,* and that great rationalist, Sherlock Holmes, who bases everything he does on the power of his human logic; also perhaps of William of Ockham, with whose famous Razor our William admonishes his assistant: "Dear Adso, one should not multiply explanations and causes unless it is strictly necessary" (91).[41] What is perhaps not immediately as clear is that his faithful sidekick, Adso, is meant to resonate with "Watson" (the monk's name is *Adson* in French).[42] And, of course, Jorge of Burgos, the blind librarian who plays such a crucial role in the story,

40. On the slow but exciting recuperation of Greek letters in the West, the reader may consult, e.g., Wilson 1992 and Grafton 1997.

41. On Ockham see Zecchini 1985:337–341; Miethke 198; Fuhrmann 1988:10–11. It appears that Ockham himself did not actually enunciate this principle per se; see Adams 1987.

42. Eco has himself published on Sherlock Holmes (Eco and Sebeok 1983). To make things even more complicated here, however, Eco has averred that the William/Adso relationship is meant to recall that of Serenus Zeitblom and Adrian in Thomas Mann's *Doktor Faustus* (Eco 1997:64). This multiplicity of resonances is typical rather than exceptional in Eco's fiction.

harks back (or forward) to Jorge Luis Borges, another blind librarian whose work as a writer of both fiction and nonfiction has made a decisive impact on Eco's own work.[43] Eco himself says,

> Everyone asks me why my Jorge, with his name, suggests Borges, and why Borges [i.e., Burgos?] is so wicked. But I cannot say. I wanted a blind man who guarded a library (it seemed like a good narrative idea to me), and a library plus blind man can only equal Borges, also because debts must be paid.[44]

I will attempt in what follows to demonstrate the nature of some of those debts.

In turning to Borges' story, "The Library of Babel,"[45] we immediately find where one of the seeds of *The Name of the Rose* was sown:

> The universe (which others call the Library) is composed of an indefinite and perhaps infinite number of hexagonal galleries, with vast air shafts between, surrounded by very low railings. From any of the hexagons one can see, interminably, the upper and lower floors. . . .
>
> Like all men of the Library, I have traveled in my youth; I have wandered in search of a book, perhaps the catalogue of catalogues; now that my eyes can hardly decipher what I write, I am preparing to die just a few leagues from the hexagon in which I was born. . . .
>
> The Library exists *ab aeterno*. This truth, whose immediate corollary is the future eternity of the world, cannot be placed in doubt by any reasonable mind.[46]

We have here, then, a huge library, equipped with air shafts, and including hexagonal galleries; and a narrator who traveled in his youth and is telling his tale now in old age. Moreover, we have a library functioning

---

43. Cf. the neat summation in Kellner 1988:9: "[J]ust as the Gospel attributed to John provides Adso his narrative opening, so the work of Borges may be taken as the best guide for readers of *The Name of the Rose*. . . . a central core of themes appears throughout Borges' work: his philosophical realism, his repeated discussion of roses, and his illusionism, which weaves the symbols of words, labyrinths, libraries, and mirrors."

On Borges' blindness, his work as a librarian, and his eventual appointment to the directorship of the National Library of Argentina, see the "Autobiographical Essay" in Borges 1978: 203–260.

44. Eco 1984b:27–28.

45. Collected in Borges 1964:51–58.

46. Borges 1964:51–52.

semiosically—representing the manifold, infinite universe itself.[47] This fertile metaphor, irresistible (I would imagine) for anyone as literary as either Borges or Eco, lends itself to all sorts of extensions: the human as reader or, perhaps, librarian; the quest for knowledge, and even life itself, as reading. The power to make a good metaphor is, as Aristotle says, dependent on the ability to see *likenesses* (*Poetics* 22.1459a 7–8)—that most semiotic of pursuits.[48]

All of this resonates powerfully with us when we turn to *The Name of the Rose,* whose narrative is spun by the now aged Adso, and whose very endpapers show a floor plan of the fateful abbey where this story takes place, including the Aedificium with its four *heptagonal* towers[49]—the Aedificium, on whose top floor is housed the library. This library is the jewel of the abbey:

> I know it has more books than any other Christian library. I know that in comparison with your cases, those of Bobbio or Pomposa, of Cluny or Fleury, seem the room of a boy barely being introduced to the abacus. I know that the six thousand codices that were the boast of Novalesa a hundred or more years ago are few compared to yours, and perhaps many of those are now here. I know your abbey is the only light that Christianity can oppose to the thirty-six libraries of Baghdad, to the ten thousand codices of the Vizir Ibn al-Alkami, that the number of your Bibles equals the two thousand four hundred Korans that are the pride of Cairo, and that the reality of your cases is luminous evidence against the proud legend of the infidels who years ago claimed (intimates as they are of the Prince of Falsehood) the library of Tripoli was rich in six million volumes and inhabited by eighty thousand commentators and two hundred scribes. (35)

But despite, or perhaps because of, the wondrous nature of this library, its floor plan is kept strictly secret:

> The library was laid out on a plan which has remained obscure to all over the centuries, and which none of the monks is called upon

47. Stephens (1983 : 13) says, "Eco's library thus reflects Borges' idea that the library is a semantic cosmos, a specular inversion of the medieval idea of *liber mundi,* of the cosmos as a book."

48. On Aristotle's concept of metaphor, and its connections with both semiotics and cognitive theory, see Kirby 1997a.

49. Heptagonal, as reflecting the spiritual perfection embodied in the number seven (Genesis 2.2–3, Psalms 119.164, Matthew 18.21–22, Revelation 1.4, 3.1)? Or is Eco simply one-upping Borges here?

to know. Only the librarian has received the secret, from the librarian who preceded him, and he communicates it, while still
alive, to the assistant librarian, so that death will not take him by
surprise and rob the community of that knowledge. And the secret seals the lips of both men. Only the librarian has, in addition
to that knowledge, the right to move through *the labyrinth of the
books,* he alone knows where to find them and where to replace
them, he alone is responsible for their safekeeping. . . . Only he
decides how, when, and whether to give it to the monk who re-
quests it; sometimes he first consults me. Because not all truths are
for all ears, not all falsehoods can be recognized as such by a pious
soul. . . . *A spiritual labyrinth, it is also a terrestrial labyrinth. You might
enter and you might not emerge.* And having said this, I would like
you to conform to the rules of the abbey. (37–38; italics mine)

The metaphors of library-as-world, library-as-labyrinth, and library-as-
mystery, like Peirce's unlimited semiosis, rebound indefinitely through
the novel: the library's catalogue, for instance, functions as a sign of the
library itself, and is equally universal, equally labyrinthine, and equally
mysterious to the uninitiated:

William asked how he could find out the names of the books kept
in the cases kept upstairs, and Malachi showed him, fixed by a
little gold chain to his own desk, a voluminous codex covered
with very thickly written lists. . . . "Splendid works. But in what
order are they listed?" He quoted from a text I did not know but
which was certainly familiar to Malachi: "'The librarian must
have a list of all books, carefully ordered by subjects and authors,
and they must be classified on the shelves with numerical indications.' How do you know the collocation of each book?"

Malachi showed him some annotations beside each title. I read:
"iii, IV gradus, V in prima graecorum"; "ii, V gradus, VII in tertia
anglorum," and so on. I understood that the first number indicated the position of the book on the shelf or gradus, which was
in turn indicated by the second number, while the case was indicated by the third number; and I understood also that the other
phrases designated a room or a corridor in the library, and I made
bold to ask further information about these last distinctions. Malachi looked at me sternly: "Perhaps you do not know, or have
forgotten, that only the librarian is allowed access to the library. It
is therefore right and sufficient that only the librarian know how
to decipher these things." (74–75)

The trope of the labyrinth, and its use as a sign for the acts of reading and interpretation, are deeply Borgesian, and not only because of the title of his anthology, *Labyrinths*. In another story, "The Two Kings and the Two Labyrinths"[50]—so minute I reproduce it here in full—two very different kinds of labyrinth serve equally malevolent purposes:

> Chroniclers worthy of trust have recorded (but only Allah is All-Knowing) that in former times there was a king of the isles of Babylon who called together his architects and his wizards and set them to build him a labyrinth so intricate that no wise man would dare enter inside, and so subtle that those who did would lose their way. This undertaking was a blasphemy, for confusion and marvels belong to God alone and not to man. With the passage of time there came to his court a king of the Arabs, and the king of Babylon (wishing to mock his guest's simplicity) allowed him to set foot in his labyrinth, where he wandered in humiliation and bewilderment until the coming of night. It was then that the second king implored the help of God and soon after came upon the door. He suffered his lips to utter no complaint, but he told the king of Babylon that he, too, had a labyrinth in his land and that, God willing, he would one day take pleasure in showing it to his host. Then he returned to Arabia, gathered his captains and his armies, and overran the realms of Babylon with so fair a fortune that he ravaged its castles, broke its peoples, and took captive the king himself. He bound him onto a swift camel and brought him into the desert. Three days they rode, and then the captor said, "O king of time and crown of the century! In Babylon you lured me into a labyrinth of brass cluttered with many stairways, doors, and walls; now the Almighty has brought it to pass that I show you mine, which has no stairways to climb, nor doors to force, nor unending galleries to wear one down, nor walls to block one's way."
>
> He then loosened the bonds of the first king and left him in the heart of the desert to die of thirst and hunger. Glory be to the Living, who dieth not.

Eco, in his *Reflections on the Name of the Rose,* gives a threefold codification of the labyrinth:[51] first, the classical Greek labyrinth, like that

---

50. Borges 1978:89–90.

51. Eco 1984b:57–58. See too Eco 1984a:80–84; and Mann 1988. On labyrinths generally see Peyronie 1988, and (in extenso) Doob 1990.

housing the Minotaur on Crete: "This kind does not allow anyone to get lost: you go in, arrive at the center, and then from the center you reach the exit. This is why in the center there is the Minotaur; if he were not there the story would have no zest, it would be a mere stroll." Second is "the mannerist maze; if you unravel it, you find in your hands a kind of tree, a structure with roots, with many blind alleys. There is only one exit, but you can get it wrong. You need an Ariadne's thread to keep from getting lost. This labyrinth is a model of the trial-and-error process." Thirdly,

> there is the net, or, rather, what Deleuze and Guattari call "rhizome." The rhizome is so constructed that every path can be connected with every other one. It has no center, no periphery, no exit, because it is potentially infinite. The space of conjecture is a rhizome space. The labyrinth of my library is still a mannerist labyrinth, but the world in which William realizes he is living already has a rhizome structure: that is, it can be structured but is never structured definitively.

(Thus we may say that the labyrinth of Borges' King of Babylon is of the type Eco calls mannerist, while that of the King of Arabia is, quintessentially, rhizomatic.)

The labyrinth, then, functions semiosically as a representamen of the modes of human thought: the classical labyrinth corresponding to the Aristotelian syllogism or *deduction,* reasoning from universals to particulars, with its formal nexus of major premise and minor premise leading ineluctably to the conclusion; the mannerist, to the process of *induction,* which reasons from particulars to universals, but which is never as certain as deduction; and the rhizomatic, to the nonlinear thought that is virtually the emblem of the postmoden era.[52] Perhaps we may also compare the rhizome to Peirce's third kind of reasoning, which he calls *abduction,* that is, the "first starting of a hypothesis and the entertaining of it, whether as a simple interrogation or with any degree of confidence";[53] his schematization of this is

> The surprising fact, C, is observed;
> But if A were true, C would be a matter of course,
> Hence, there is reason to suspect that A is true.[54]

---

52. It is no coincidence that we owe this metaphor of the rhizome to Deleuze and Guattari— two of the twentieth century's most dedicated enemies of the "tyranny" of linear thought. See Deleuze and Guattari 1976.

53. Cited in Buchler 1955:151 (cf. Hartshorne and Weiss 1931–1958:6.522–528).

54. Cited in Buchler 1955:151 (cf. Hartshorne and Weiss 1931–1958:5.189).

This mode of inference does not proceed in an orderly, linear fashion; as Eco himself says in *A Theory of Semiotics,* "At first glance abduction seems to be a free movement of the imagination, more endowed with emotion (more similar to a vague "intuition") than a normal decoding act."[55] Moreover, it is an extremely common pattern of human thought, and, in fact, one practiced conspicuously by William of Baskerville in *The Name of the Rose,* as for example in the passage (cited above) when he explains his hypothesis about the horse's footprints.[56]

The labyrinth, then, represents in its various forms the varieties of human cognition.[57] Beyond this, in its numerous turns and twists—in its multifarious mysteries—it may be taken as a sign of the world itself. This would be why the narrator in the Borges story recounted above opines that to build a labyrinth, as the King of Babylon did, is an act of blasphemy: to do so is to ape the demiurgic power of the godhead. This is also why, in *The Name of the Rose,* the two metaphors of library-as-world and labyrinth-as-world are so smoothly conflated. As James E. Irby writes in his introduction to Borges' *Labyrinths,* "The world is a book and the book is a world, and both are labyrinthine and enclose enigmas designed to be understood and participated in by man."[58]

The physical labyrinth of the library is, as Eco remarks, a mannerist maze; but the library as potentiality—the library as a source of potentially infinite intertextuality—is the quintessential rhizomatic labyrinth. Borges' mention of the "catalogue of catalogues," in his description of the library of Babel, brings to mind Italo Calvino's "system of systems" as discussed in *Six Memos for the Next Millennium* (on which see chapter 4 below); it also serves as an apt reminder of Peirce's "unlimited semiosis," which we discussed in chapter 1—the notion (again harking to the rhizome) that every interpretant can serve as the object of a new semiosic triad, and that every object is itself a sign in some sense, so that the whole universe flows backward and forward into itself semiosically.[59] Nowhere is this more vividly illustrated than in a library, where books cite other books, which cite other books, and so on ad infinitum.

Within a given novel, moreover, the reader is introduced to yet another form of labyrinth: the plot. These, too, can be of more than one

55. Eco 1976:1932. For more on abduction, see Eco 1983b.
56. Noticed too by Bennett 1988:123: "From the moment we meet him, he is performing abductions, and he consistently affirms his belief in the abductive process as leading to valid conclusions."
57. For more on the library and labyrinth as tropes for human memory, see Carruthers 1990.
58. Borges 1964:xix.
59. Floyd Merrell's conceit of the "chimerical octopus," enunciated in Merrell 1987:260 (and cited in Deely 1990:80–81), vividly illustrates the rhizomatic nature of unlimited semiosis.

sort. The paradigm of the rhizomatic novel-plot is, perhaps, Julio Cortázar's *Rayuela*,[60] which prints its chapters (as of course it must) in one order, and even numbers them sequentially, but also offers an alternative sequence in which these may be read, moreover suggesting that the reader may decide to read them in whatever order she likes.[61] The plot of *The Name of the Rose*, on the other hand—like that of every detective novel—is perforce linear. I say "perforce," because detective fiction is a sort of game between author and reader, in which "whodunit" must be susceptible of discovery, but not self-evident; in order to preserve this delicate balance, the clues must be presented as elements of the narrative in a certain temporal and logical sequence.[62] What certainly is rhizomatic in *The Name of the Rose*, however, is the tumultuous semiosis that over and over again confounds the *characters'* assessment of what is happening. Nothing is as simple or as linear as they would have liked it to be; life is not a series of apodeictic syllogisms. Rather the way in which we interact in the world, according to Peirce, is by the inferential process he calls abduction—which is, par excellence, rhizomatic. Even William himself comments to Adso on the lack of order in the universe as a whole (491–492).

Yet another story by Borges that is, I think, highly suggestive for our study—and which, moreover, brings us squarely back to Aristotle, the

60. Translated as Cortázar 1966. This remarkable book begins with a "Table of Instructions" in which it is acknowledged that "this book consists of many books" (because of the rhizomatic potential I have discussed). One of the possible ways of reading suggested by the author involves a "hopscotch" from one chapter to another, beginning (for example) with chapter 73 and then reading chapters 1, 2, 116, 3, 84, 4, 71, 5, and so on. Another alternative dispenses altogether ("with a clean conscience") with the reading of chapters 57–155.

61. I maintain that the tables of contents for Italo Calvino's *If on a Winter's Night a Traveler* and *Mr. Palomar* indicate that he invites his reader to take similar liberties with those texts.

The rhizomatic plot is the purview of what is known as "combinatory" literature. Extremely innovative experiments in this genre were conducted by members of the Oulipo group (to which Calvino also belonged); one thinks above all of Raymond Queneau in his *Cent mille milliards de poèmes*. (On Oulipo see, e.g., Motte 1986.)

Fiction of a combinatory nature found a much more populist (and young) readership in the 1980s and 1990s, in the interactive books that Bantam Books published by the score in their "Choose Your Own Adventure" series. Similar genres continue to enjoy great popularity on the World Wide Web, as any Internet search for "interactive fiction" will demonstrate. Many computer and console games are also based on comparable interactive principles. "First-person shooter" games such as *Doom, Half-Life,* and *Jedi Knight;* "role-playing" games such as *Baldur's Gate;* "adventure" games such as *Grim Fandango* and *Castlevania: Symphony of the Night;* and the so-called "god games," such as *SimCity* and *Pharoah,* all grant varying degrees of what one might call "narrative interactivity" to the player. Depending on the nature of the game, the sophistication and complexity of what one might call the "plot" will vary considerably.

62. Novels like Donna Tartt's *The Secret History* attempt to explode this convention by revealing the murderer on the very first page of the book.

Poetics, and the semiotics of mimesis—is "Averroës' Search."[63] It tells the story of Ibn-Rushd, or Averroës as he is better known, a twelfth-century Arab philosopher living in Spain, as he puzzles over the meaning of two mysterious words in the *Poetics.* In the Borges story we see him writing his commentary on Aristotle, a monumental work of philology on which he hopes to pin his scholarly reputation. It is clear that for Averroës, Aristotle occupies a spot of unparalleled veneration: indeed in the Arab tradition he was known simply as *al-Failesuf,* "the Philosopher."[64] Averroës aspires to interpret the Aristotelian corpus "as the ulema interpret the Koran,"[65] despite the fact that he knows neither Greek nor Syriac, and thus, as he reads the *Poetics,* he must work with a translation of a translation.

> Few things more beautiful and more pathetic are recorded in history than this Arab physician's dedication to the thoughts of a man separated from him by fourteen centuries. . . . The night before, two doubtful words had halted him at the beginning of the *Poetics.* These words were *tragedy* and *comedy.* He had encountered them years before in the third book of the *Rhetoric;* no one in the whole world of Islam could conjecture what they meant. In vain he had exhausted the pages of Alexander of Aphrodisia, in vain he had compared the versions of the Nestorian Hunain ibn-Ishaq and of Abu-Bashar Mata. These two arcane words pullulated throughout the text of the *Poetics;* it was impossible to elude them.
>
> Averroës put down his pen. He told himself (without excessive faith) that what we seek is often nearby, put away the manuscript of the *Tahafut* and went over to the shelf where the many volumes of the blind Abensida's *Mohkam,* copied by Persian calligraphers, were aligned. It was derisory to imagine he had not consulted them, but he was tempted by the idle pleasure of turning their pages. From this studious distraction, he was distracted by a kind of melody. He looked through the lattice-work balcony; below, in the narrow earthen patio, some half-naked children were playing. One, standing on another's shoulders, was obviously playing the part of a muezzin; with his eyes tightly closed, he chanted "There is no god but God." The one who held him motionlessly

63. Collected in Borges 1964: 148–155.
64. Cf. Kirby 1998a
65. The *ulamaa* (< *ilm,* "knowledge" or "science") are those who have done religious studies in sufficient depth to be able to pronounce upon fine details of Qur'anic application.

played the part of the minaret; another, abject in the dust and on his knees, the part of the faithful worshipers. The game did not last long; all wanted to be the muezzin, none the congregation or the tower.[66]

Later that evening, Averroës dines in the home of a Qur'anic scholar, where the discussion turns on roses:

> The conversation at Farach's home passed from the incomparable virtues of the governor to those of his brother the emir; later, in the garden, they spoke of roses. Abulcasim, who had not looked at them, swore that there were not roses like those adorning the Andalusian country villas. Farach would not be bought with flattery; he observed that the learned Ibn Qutaiba describes an excellent variety of the perpetual rose, which is found in the gardens of Hindustan and whose petals, of a blood red, exhibit characters which read: "There is no god but the God, Mohammed is the Apostle of God." He added that surely Abulcasim would know of those roses. Abulcasim looked at him with alarm. If he answered yes, all would judge him, justifiably, the readiest and most gratuitous of impostors; if he answered no, he would be judged an infidel. He elected to muse that the Lord possesses the key to all hidden things and that there is not a green or withered thing on earth which is not recorded in His Book.[67]

The latter passage may be no more than a remarkable coincidence, including as it does both a disquisition on roses and a dangerous scholastic theological disputation; but the former is centrally on point: a scholar with a ravening hunger for Aristotle, occupying himself with the significance of the *Poetics,* and wondering about the nature of mimesis in drama. Irony of ironies, he gives himself—if he only knew it—the answer to his own conundrum: "what we seek is often nearby." For, just below his balcony, children are at that very moment engaged in mimesis: in a *dramatic representation* of the Muslim call to prayer. Not realizing that here, right under his very nose, is the solution of the mystery he ponders in the *Poetics,* he goes back to his writing.

A memoir by Eco himself is remarkable for its resonances, whether by chance or design, with this story by Borges.[68] Eco describes rummag-

66. Borges 1964:148–149.
67. Borges 1964:150.
68. Eco 1997:69–70. Eco himself declares, "This story too has nothing to do with a possible interpretation of my book" (70), but, as I have already indicated, I am quite reluctant to take such a denial at face value.

ing through the books in his home library, and finding there a sixteenth-century edition of the *Poetics* by Riccoboni, whose existence he had forgotten for decades. Having begun cataloguing his collection of rare and antique books, Eco sat down to write a formal description of this volume as well; in so doing, he found himself rewriting, almost word for word, the description of the Aristotle manuscript that he had written in *The Name of the Rose*—a book whose pages were stuck together, as with a sticky paste: "I had in my hands, in printed form, the manuscript I described in my novel. I had had it for years and years at my reach, at home. . . . by a sort of internal camera I photographed those pages, and for decades the image of those poisonous leaves lay in the most remote part of my soul, as in a grave." [69] Here, then, we see Eco standing by his bookshelves, just as Averroës had stood by his; Eco, however, makes the discovery that Averroës does not: "what we seek is often nearby." Sometimes, it would seem, what we have forgotten may even seek us. In any case, if Eco has not written this memoir in conscious (and playful) reminiscence of the Borges story, he has participated in yet another extraordinary coincidence connected with *The Name of the Rose*.[70]

The hunger for the *Poetics,* a now-lost manuscript; the yearning for philosophical knowledge; the attempt to understand Aristotelian doctrine. One further aspect of Borges' story is central to *The Name of the Rose,* and that is that mimesis itself is a quintessentially *semiosic* phenomenon: it is the means whereby we *imitate* or *represent* something, be it human action (Aristotle's stipulation for *drama*) or something else. Hence the children enacting the call to prayer are engaged, not only in drama, but also (and ipso facto) in semiosis: one child *represents,* or *signifies,* the minaret; another, the muezzin; another still, the congregation of the faithful. It is this crucial recognition—that mimesis is semiosic—that is fundamental to Eco's philosophical and narrative project, so much so that he could hardly have chosen another text of Aristotle to make his point as well. *Naturalmente: un manoscritto.*

69. Eco 1997:70.
70. Eco 1997 recounts a number of such coincidences. He lists four such on page 64 alone, but skirts the issue by attributing these (following the schema delineated in Eco 1990) to the intention of the *text* and not to that of the *author.*

FRESH AIR FROM HELICON

⁊⁊

The Neo-Latin Verse of Joseph Tusiani

> O, Latin's a dead language,
> As dead as dead can be;
> First it killed the Romans,
> And now it's killing me!
> — *Student chant*

I have placed this chapter at the midpoint of the book to highlight the fact that Joseph Tusiani is notably different from all the authors considered here in at least three ways: first, in that all the other works studied in this book are in prose;[1] second, because Tusiani is the only one of these five authors not to make a life for himself in Italy—a historical detail of some import for this chapter, in fact;[2] and third, because the language of the poetry considered in this chapter is Italian in only the most historical sense: Tusiani composes in Latin.

Many of those who were subjected to Latin instruction in school have less than fond memories of the experience. The problem, as far as I can diagnose it, is at least threefold: first, Latin is a difficult language to learn, and that means it is difficult to teach; an instructor of Latin has that much taller an order to fill. Second, Latin teachers at the high-school level, at any rate, sometimes seem disposed to use the teaching of grammar as an exquisite form of punishment or torture; in such cases students come away with a particularly bitter taste in their mouths. Third, it is a dead language, and that exacerbates its difficulty. But "dead" in this sense does

---

1. Although, as already mentioned, Pasolini was early known as a poet, both in Tuscan and in the difficult Friulan dialect.

2. Umberto Eco has traveled and taught extensively in the United States; I should point out, too, that Italo Calvino was born in Cuba, and lived for about a decade in France. But both of them, like Pasolini and Calasso, have rooted their lives and careers in Italy.

not mean what many take it to mean, namely, "boring" or "useless": rather it indicates that there is no living race that uses Latin as its native tongue. It survives, of course, in its offspring—the whole family of Romance languages, including—*in primis*—Italian. But language cannot be understood apart from culture, any more than any culture can be interpreted fully without a close scrutiny of its language.

In view of the obstacles I have enumerated, it is remarkable that as many succeed in learning Latin as still do these days. Some achieve a certain level of reading ability, perhaps make their way through some Caesar or Cicero, or (more likely in recent decades) some poetry, say Catullus, Ovid, or Vergil. But reading knowledge, being essentially receptive, is a far cry from active (or "generative") fluency in a language. And this is the crucial point about a dead language: a student of Italian, French, or Spanish can go to Italy, France, or Spain (or New York, Québec, Miami) and interact with native speakers of those languages; but the learning of an ancient tongue like Latin depends, for most people, on memorization and reading. Some who go on to advanced study will take a course in the composition of Latin prose, but even these (for the most part) do not afterward make regular use of that skill. Fewer still may attempt to study the composition of Latin verse in the meters used by the ancient authors: this is extremely difficult, demanding as it does the capacity to compose under severe formal constraints. So this calling is high, and its practitioners are few.

The achievement of Joseph Tusiani, then, in crafting a considerable number of neo-Latin poems according to the most rigorous stipulations of ancient metric, is remarkable.[3] By "neo-Latin" I mean the use of the Latin tongue since the final demise of its use as a living language in mediaeval Europe. After that time it remained in use as a scholarly lingua franca for (what was then) convenience in the international communication of academic research; even well into this century it was permissible to submit a Ph.D. dissertation at Harvard either in English or in Latin "of a good style."[4] But there is also a long tradition of neo-Latin poetry from the Renaissance on; some of the greatest poets in the West, including Petrarca, Ariosto, and Milton, have produced a sizeable body of such verse. Tusiani stands in that proud lineage, and like these postclassical poets has woven both the classical tradition and his personal Christian devotion into the fabric of his poetry.

---

3. Many of his poems have appeared in journals or anthologies, but over and above these Tusiani has published six volumes of his own Latin verse (Tusiani 1955, 1984, 1985, 1989, 1994, and 1998). Tusiani 1989:53–58 offers an extensive bibliography of his Latin verse.

4. Waggishly, one loves to imagine a dissertation that was rejected on stylistic grounds.

It would be a vast undertaking to offer a detailed assessment of Tusiani's entire Latin corpus, but in the course of this chapter I will provide
some basic analysis of a representative selection of the poems. As the writing of such verse requires considerable skill (and training), so too their
proper appreciation demands some technical competence on the part of
the reader; I will try in particular to draw attention to some of the elements of their composition that are part and parcel of the craft of these
poems. I will also provide translations of the passages I discuss, since
Tusiani's Latin œuvre is not yet as broadly known as it should be.

The first topic to be addressed is the nature of *quantitative verse*. In
the poetic tradition to which most of us are accustomed, meter is based
on the regulation of patterns of stressed and unstressed syllables: thus
Tennyson's

> To strive, to seek, to find, and not to yield

is recognizable as "iambic pentameter" because it consists of five "iambs,"
that is, five feet in the pattern {∪ / } (one unstressed syllable followed by
one stressed). So for us, meter is a function of *ictus,* the "beat" or "pulse"[5]
of verbal rhythm.

In the classical metric this was not so. While the ancients recognized
the presence of rhythmic stress in language, this was a separate concern
from that of meter per se. Quantitative meter, as its name implies, is based
on the *quantity*—long or short—of each syllable. A long syllable may be
so by *nature* (if it contains a long vowel or a diphthong) or by *position* (if a
vowel, even a short one, is followed by certain combinations of consonants). These combinations typically occur in recognized groups of two,
three, or four syllables, known as *feet*. Each metrical foot has a name:
{∪ − } iamb, { − ∪ } trochee, { − − } spondee, { − ∪ ∪} dactyl, {∪ ∪ − }
anapaest, and so forth. One or more feet may be taken as the basic unit
of a line of verse, and that unit is known as a *metron*. Thus the classical
"iambic trimeter" is made up of three metra, each metron composed of
two iambic feet. In certain kinds of lyric verse a more complex combination of syllables is used as a single-metron line. Most types of line have
a place where word-end is statistically common; this is called a *caesura* (or,
when it coincides with foot-end, *diaeresis*).[6]

5. "Pulse" is the term preferred by L. P. Wilkinson in his excellent book on metrical, pro-
sodic, and sonic effects in Latin (Wilkinson 1963).

6. The field of classical metrics is an extremely recondite and complex one, to which these
cursory remarks can hardly be called an introduction. For more information the reader might
consult Rosenmeyer et al. 1963 (a good basic introduction) and West 1982 (the ne plus ultra). For
those who read French, Koster 1936 is still very useful.

To compose Latin verse in the classical style, then, above and beyond a basic knowledge of the accidence and syntax of the language, one must

(a) know the quantity of each syllable used;
(b) be able to position these in a sequence that will (i) be semantically intelligible, and (ii) yield the desired pattern;
(c) be familiar with the metrical patterns themselves, which are governed by strict rules of composition;
(d) know which vocabulary is deemed more appropriate for prose than for verse (and vice versa).

Finally, the classical literature is by nature a deeply allusive one, and it would seem odd to compose classicizing verse without tapping into the rich mother lode of that tradition. That is to say, just as Catullus or Horace or Vergil would not compose without constant reference to their Greek and Roman predecessors, so now one would expect neo-Latin poetry to resonate with the entire classical tradition.

These are some of the constraints under which Tusiani has worked; and an awareness of them can only double and redouble the reader's appreciation of his poetic achievement.

FUNUS IN HORTULO ("A FUNUS IN THE GARDEN")[7]

Meter: elegiac couplets. The couplet is built of two lines of unequal length: a dactylic hexameter plus what is somewhat misleadingly called a "pentameter," itself made up of two "hemiepes" { $-\cup\cup-\cup\cup-$ } or their metrical equivalent, with a strong diaeresis between them. (For more on the dactylic hexameter, see below on *Naenia*.) A single elegiac couplet might be used for an epigram or witty saying, or for a lapidary inscription; as a regular meter for extended verse it was adopted by Hellenistic Greek poets like Callimachus, more or less in conscious reaction against the epic style of Homer and Hesiod, who used pure dactylic hexameter. Latin poets emulating or reacting to the Hellenistic Greeks— one thinks particularly of Catullus, Propertius, Tibullus, and Ovid— favored the elegiac couplet.

The genre to which this poem formally belongs is the *thrênos* or funeral lament; but the subject of the lament is a squirrel, who was alive

7. *Classical Outlook* 62 (Dec.–Jan. 1984–1985): 61; also in Tusiani 1985:27. *Funus* typically means a funeral ceremony, but it can also refer to a death, or the dead body itself. I have preferred to maintain this polysemy, rather than translate the word. *Hortulus,* a diminutive form, indicates that the garden is a small one.

only yesterday (*tam vivus heri,* 2). It thus claims as its ancestor Catullus 3, which laments the death of Lesbia's pet sparrow:[8]

> Lugete, o Veneres Cupidinesque
> et quantum est hominum uenustiorum:
> passer mortuus est meae puellae,
> passer, deliciae meae puellae,
> quem plus illa oculis suis amabat.   5
> nam mellitus erat suamque norat
> ipsam tam bene quam puella matrem,
> nec sese a gremio illius mouebat,
> sed circumsiliens modo huc modo illuc
> ad solam dominam usque pipiabat;   10
> qui nunc it per iter tenebricosum
> illuc, unde negant redire quemquam.
> at uobis male sit, malae tenebrae
> Orci, quae omnia bella deuoratis:
> tam bellum mihi passerem abstulistis.   15
> o factum male! o miselle passer!
> tua nunc opera meae puellae
> flendo turgiduli rubent ocelli.

> Weep, o you Venuses and Cupids,
> And all mortals of refinement:
> My girlfriend's sparrow is dead,
> My girlfriend's darling sparrow,
> Whom she loved more than her own eyes—
> For he was sweet as honey, and knew his own mistress
> As well as a girl knows her mother,
> Nor would he move from her lap,
> But jumping about hither and thither,
> Always and only to his mistress would he chirp.
> Now he travels the road of shadows
> To that place from which, they say, there is no return.
> Curses on you, evil shadows

---

8. That poem is not, however, in elegiacs but in hendecasyllabics, a meter used by Tusiani in his "Ad Pascolium poetam" and "Occasus simplex" (Tusiani 1989: 12, 36). The text of Catullus I have quoted here is that of Thomson 1978; the English translation is my own.

    Catullus was himself already working in a genre of sorts; the Greek Anthology includes some epitaphs for pet animals (see, e.g., nos. 189–216). Ovid would subsequently compose a parodic *thrênos* for the parrot of his mistress Corinna (*Amores* 2.6).

Of Orcus,[9] you who devour all lovely things:
You have robbed me of so lovely a sparrow.
O evil deed! O wretched little sparrow!
Thanks to you, now my girlfriend's
Swollen little eyes are red with weeping.

This poem maintains a delicate balance between the high, somewhat mannered sorrow of the funeral lament, on one hand, and the comic application of such formality to the death of a pet bird.[10] In the Catullan collection as it is currently constituted, it follows another, slightly shorter poem,[11] in which the poet describes the intimate and affectionate relationship between his girlfriend and the bird. (Poem 2, like number 3, is also parodic of a more serious genre, this time of the hymn to a divinity.)

Tusiani depicts the comings and goings of the squirrel as affectionately as Catullus does those of his sparrow:

> . . . ad me
>   Gressibus ambiguis expediebat iter
> Horrescensque manu mota remeabat in herbam
>   Inde resumpturus cautum iter ad spolia

> he would pick out his way toward me in tentative steps,
> and, terrified when I moved my hand, he would scamper back
>   into the grass
>   thence to make once again his cautious journey toward the
>   spoils. (9–12)

Whereas (like Gounod's "Funeral March of a Marionette") Catullus' poems can be read as having a comic tone, however, Tusiani's is decidedly more serious. Not only is the death of the squirrel read as emblematic of mortality—

> Te terrebam egomet multum qui terreor a te
>   Cuius finis ait finem hominis similem

---

9. I.e., the Underworld; sometimes personified (cf. Hades).

10. I set aside, for our purposes, the alternate interpretation of the *passer* as a comic code for the postcoital phallus, which dates back to Angelo Poliziano in the Renaissance, and which has drawn both kudos and complaint. See, e.g., Adams 1982:32–33 and nn. Even without this interpretation, the poem clearly has a comic overtone to it.

11. We must also, for now, shelve the textual problems attending on Catullus 2 and 2b: it appears either that the former is a complete poem of ten lines—in which case the text will still probably need some emendation—or that it is separated from the latter, a 3-line fragment, by some lacuna.

> I used to frighten you greatly, I who am greatly frightened by you
>> whose death imports that a human's end is the same (13–14)[12]

—but, on a more concrete level, the narrator also shrinks back with that ancient revilement that we feel in the face of death:

> Laetus heri ardebam caudam palpare pilosam,
>> Nolo hodie pavidus tangere corpus iners.
> Parce mihi. Pala parvum tumulabo cadaver,
>> Parve sciure, tuum. Me metus acer habet.

> Yesterday I was happy and eager to touch [your] furry tail;
>> today I fear to touch [your] still body.
> Spare me. With a spade I will bury your small corpse,
>> little squirrel. Sharp fear holds me in its grip. (15–18)

So, despite what could have been an inconsequential or frivolous topic, the poem has by its ending reached a very serious tone.

HORA LITOREA ("SEASIDE HOUR")[13]

Meter: glyconics $\{ \times \times - \cup \cup - \cup - \}$ alternating with asclepiadeans $\{ \times \times - \cup \cup - - \cup \cup - \cup - \}$. These complex metrical patterns were taken up from Greek lyric verse by Roman poets such as Horace. (An × marks "anceps" [Lat. "ambivalent"], a spot where the poet may use either a long or a short syllable.)

The poem wastes no time in evoking the hypnotic power of the ocean:

> Hymnos aequora cantitant,
>> Aures qui insolito murmure leniunt.
> Felix in sabulo sedens,
>> Cantu caeruleo, cymba velut vaga,
> Longinquam ad magicam insulam
>> Nunc lente vehor a criminibus procul.

> The waters are singing hymns
>> that soothe the ears with their exotic murmur.
> [I am] sitting on the sand, happy
>> at their cerulean song, like a wandering skiff

---

12. By its position, *multum* can be read to modify either *terrebam* or *terreor* (a construction known as *apo koinou*); accordingly I have translated it as modifying both.

13. *Vita Latina* [Avignon], no. 104 (Dec. 1986): 41.

> to a far-off magic isle,
>   now I am slowly taken, far from evil. (1–6)[14]

The narrator, naturally enough, is powerfully affected by this intoxicating ambiance:

> Procedens ita ad aureas
>   Oras, ad regiones sine nomine,
> Nil in mente habeo nisi
>   Istam qua rapior musicam amabilem.
> Quando—cogito—et unde ego
>   Audivi similes harmonicos sonos?
>
> Heading thus for golden
>   shores, for nameless regions,
> I have nothing in my mind but
>   this lovely music by which I am taken away.
> When, I wonder, and whence
>   have I heard such harmonies? (7–12)

The music, it turns out, is a token or foretaste of the life to come:

> Haec est musica quae venit
>   A tellure ubi pax regnat, ab insula
> Longinqua et magica et mea
>   Quae aeternum mihi erit deliciae et domus.
>
> This is the music that comes
>   from a land where peace reigns, from an island
> far-off, and magical, and my own,
>   that will be forever my delight and home. (17–20)

One is reminded by the tenor of these lines of the refrain to Baudelaire's "L'invitation au voyage":

> Là, tout n'est qu'ordre et beauté,
> Luxe, calme et volupté.

In fact, as early as Hesiod's *Works and Days* we find the legend of the land of the Hyperboreans, that magical region "beyond the North Wind"

---

14. *Cantitant* is a frequentative verb form (literally "singing and singing"), superbly appropriate here for the endless rhythm of the surf. *Aequora* is a term, restricted to poetic contexts, for the waters of the ocean. *Insolito*, here translated "exotic," is literally "unaccustomed." *Cantu caeruleo* might be read as an ablative of means, modifying *vehor* ("I am carried along by their cerulean song"). *Criminibus* is a technical (legal) term in classical Latin, referring not to crimes but to formal criminal charges; I have preferred to translate it in the most general sense here.

where all is peaceful and sublime. Certainly Homer's Odysseus tasted such respite, in his visits to Calypso and to the Phaeacians. But for him these were merely way stations on his journey, not *domus,* and certainly not *aeternum.* Tusiani has something rather different in mind, I surmise, an imagery redolent of the millenarian prophecies of Isaiah and Jeremiah:

> You shall have singing
>> as in the night when a holy feast is celebrated;
> and gladness of heart,
>> as when one goes up with flutes
> to the mountain of Yahweh,
>> to the rock of Israel. . . .
> Then will justice dwell in the wilderness,
>> and righteousness abide in the fruitful field.
> And the effect of righteousness will be peace,
>> and the result of righteousness, quietness and trust forever.[15]

For Tusiani's work is profoundly Christian, as I have already remarked and as we shall again see, and depends for its richness (like Thomist theology) upon an intimate fusion, or synthesis, of classical and biblical ideas.

LINGUA LATINA ("THE LATIN LANGUAGE")[16]

Meter: a five-line stanza made up of four glyconics (as in *Hora litorea*) and a pherecratean $\{ \times \times - \cup \cup - - \}$.[17]

For a Latinist to write a poem about the Latin language is analogous to Schubert's setting to music Franz Schober's lyrics "An die Musik"; and the tone of Tusiani's poem is in some respects similar to Schober's; but the length of Tusiani's poem is greater than Schober's, and the range of its imagery is broader. The opening personification moves to more abstract metaphor:

> O Latina loquela, tu
>> Lex et ars mihi pura.

> O Latin language, you
>> are pure law and art to me. (4–5)

---

15. Isaiah 30.29, 32.16–17. Cf. Jeremiah 31.12–14. (The translation is my own revision of the Revised Standard Version against the Hebrew.)

16. *Melissa* [Brussels] 21 (Nov. 1987). (Also in Tusiani 1989:47.)

17. An interesting collateral work is Tusiani's apostrophe to the Italian language, "Lingua materna," published in his collection of Italian verse (Tusiani 1992). The tone of that piece, as might be surmised from the title, is more intimate, less formal.

The Latin language is such that it is on the one hand powerful, fearful, great and commanding (*potens, metuenda . . . / magna et imperiosa,* 1–2) and, on the other, gentle:

Me doces sonitu sacro
Arborum fremitus leves
Et maris melos intimum,
Siderum harmoniam vagam
    Noctis in patula umbra.

By your sacred sounds
you teach me the soft rustling of the trees
and the secret song of the sea,
the wandering harmony of the stars
    in the outspread shadow of night. (11–15)

Here the well-known *topos* of the "music of the spheres" is invoked, but Tusiani's connection of this with the knowledge of *language* is, I think, a poetic innovation.[18] By the transitive power of language the poet is placed in intimate touch with the natural world, and thereby tuned in harmony with the rest of humanity:

Audio omnia corda quae,
Ut cor istud, amant diem,
Corda quae, velut hoc meum,
Flent diem fugientem ab his
    Dulce olentibus oris.

I hear all the hearts that,
like this heart,[19] love the day,
hearts that, like this my own,
mourn the day as it flees from these
    shores of sweet fragrance. (16–20)

The final stanza equates by metonymy the nation Rome with its language:

18. Gefurius discussed the music of the spheres in his *Practica musica* of 1496. For more on the topic, see (among many others) Job 38.7; Psalms 19.1; Plato, *Republic* 10.617b; Dante, *Paradiso* 13.25–30; Shakespeare, *The Merchant of Venice* 5.1.58–63; Sir Thomas Browne, *Religio medici* 2.9; Milton, *Paradise Lost* 5.177; Wordsworth, "On the Power of Sound" 12; James 1993; Durán 1997.

19. The demonstrative *istud* here seems ambiguous to me. The grammars teach that it refers to something near the addressee but not near the speaker (as *hic* refers, conversely, to something near the speaker but not near the addressee). By that rule *cor istud* should refer to the addressee's heart; but I read it as the narrator's (making *ut cor istud* congruent with *velut hoc meum* in the next line).

Roma, amorem animae meae
Concinis. Celebratio
Gloriae optima amor mihi est.
Roma-Amor, mihi plus vales
    Servitudine mundi.

Rome, you sing the love
of my soul. The celebration
of glory is my greatest love.
Rome/Love, to me you are more powerful
    than the slavery of this world. (21–25)

Here Tusiani plays on the ancient association of Venus with Rome, underscored by the palindromic relationship between the Latin name for Rome (ROMA) and the Latin word for love (AMOR).[20] The designation of Venus as tutelary divinity of Rome had been particularly exploited by Lucretius, in the opening of *De rerum natura,* and was picked up by Vergil in the narrative of the *Aeneid.*

QUINQUE POEMATA IOSEPHI TUSIANI ("FIVE POEMS OF JOSEPH TUSIANI")[21]

This set of five includes *Naenia, Cantiuncula vespertina, Hypnosis aprilis, In ascensu Domini,* and *Caeli interpres,* each of which is discussed below.

Naenia ("Lullaby")[22]

Meter: dactylic hexameter. This is (even by classical standards) a very ancient meter, dating back to the *Iliad* and the *Odyssey*—Greek epic poems of the eighth century B.C.E. As the name implies, each line is made up of six dactyls { $- \cup \cup$ }, each of which may be replaced by its metrical equivalent, the spondee { $- -$ }. The origin of this meter seems to be Indo-European but not specifically Greek, so it was not the most natural meter even for Greek poets. Its adoption for Latin verse by such poets as Ennius and, later, Catullus, Lucretius, Vergil, and Ovid, was itself a tour de force.

In this ten-line poem, lines 1, 5, 8, and 9 are heavy with spondees: in fact, they all conform to an almost purely spondaic pattern, the only dactylic foot in each of them being the fifth, where (we are told) the classical poets avoided a spondee except in rare cases. The effect of all these

20. On the word "Amor" as the mystical name of Rome, see Stanley 1963.
21. *Hermes Americanus* 6 (1988): 4–6.
22. Also in Tusiani 1989:16.

spondees is to slow the movement of the verse; when, by contrast, Homer wants to describe the boulder of Sisyphus rolling back down the hill, for example, he uses a line of pure dactyls to suggest its speed (*Odyssey* 11.598). But the slower movement here is appropriate for a lullaby. The speaker is weary of the long abrasion of life (*longa . . . vexamina vitae,* 1) and calls for music to lull him to sleep,

> Ut mater lenta lenta dulcedine nato
> Cantat naeniolam . . .

> like a mother who, in slow, slow sweetness,
> sings a little lullaby to her baby . . . (5–6)

The distinction of light and dark is blurred here, as both are called upon, together with joy, to slip over the speaker's eyes (*loquere de lumine et umbra / Una laetitia supra labentibus oclos,* 3–4); his desire is for "sweet dreams" (*somnia dulcia,* 7). But at the end of the poem, the immemorial equation is drawn between sleep and death:[23]

> Lalla me . . . Cupio dormire . . . mori . . . est . . . dormire . . .

> Sing me to sleep . . . I wish to sleep . . . to die . . . is . . . to
> sleep . . . (10)

and here, significantly, the fifth foot, elsewhere in the poem always dactylic, is now a spondee. The poem makes significant use throughout of alliteration (*Lalla . . . lalla, longa,* 1; *Musica, multiplici,* 2; *sopi suadente susurro,* 2; *Lalla . . . leviter, loquere . . . lumine . . . / laetitia . . . labentibus,* 3–4; *Cantat . . . precando, / Candida . . . canta,* 6–7; *Lalla . . . lalla . . . languore,* 8).

Cantiuncula vespertina ("Little evening verses")

Meter: the same five-line stanza employed in *Lingua latina.* The first line of each stanza is the last of the one preceding it; this links them by a rhetorical device known as *klimax* (or *gradatio*), which gives cohesiveness to the material it entails, by means of its own intertwined structure (A → B, B → C, C → D); but it also (as the name implies) lends a sense of climax to the final unit (C → D, or sometimes simply D).[24]

---

23. Death (*Thanatos*) and Sleep (*Hupnos*) were brothers in the ancient mythology; a famous calyx crater in the Metropolitan Museum of Art, painted by Euphronios, shows the two of them carrying away Sarpedon after his battle with Patroklos in the Trojan War. (There is also a black-figured lekythos, decorated by the Athena Painter, and housed in the Staatliche Museen, Berlin, that depicts the same scene.)

24. On *klimax* (Latin *gradatio*) see, e.g., *Rhetorica ad Herennium* 4.34–35; Quintilian *Institutio oratoria* 9.3.54–57; and Kirby and Poster 1998.

The title alone could hardly prepare us for what is to come in this surprising poem. Its narratee is the personified Love, and its first stanza opens the theme of sorrow and evil in the world:

> Me pudet cecinisse, Amor,
> Dona laetitiae tuae:
> Terra adhuc lacrimas habet
> Et minacior advenit
>   Umbra noctis amara.

> I am ashamed to have sung, Love,
> of the gifts of your joy: [25]
> the earth still has sadness
> and more threatening comes
>   the bitter shadow of night. (1–5)

(Note particularly the term *umbra,* which has been echoed from the preceding poem in the set, although there it was not explicitly connected with evil.) This notion is elaborated in the lines that follow, along with some delineation of its effects:

> Umbra noctis amara iam
> Labitur super ultima
> Serta, et acre silentium
> Muta reddit et irrita
>   Vatis intima verba.

> The bitter shadow of night
> now falls upon my newest
> garlands, and a bitter silence
> strikes mute and powerless
>   the inmost words of the poet. [26] (6–10)

The final stanza ties up these threads—the crepuscular note, the address to Love, and the theme of evil in the world:

> Cum die pereunte, Amor,
> Fac viri pereat scelus

---

25. By a figure known as *hendiadys* (Greek for "one by means of two"), "the gifts of your joy" may be taken to mean "your gifts of joy" or "your joyous gifts," though this genitival construction is actually most common in Semitic languages.

26. *Vates* is a powerful and pregnant term; it can mean "prophet," and in such contexts as the present one, it has the sense, not merely of "poet," but of "prophetic bard." No doubt Tusiani is fully aware of these connotations, and indeed exploiting them here; cf. also on *Caeli interpres* below.

> Grant, Love, that along with the fading day
> the evil of man may disappear[27] (16–17)

If we are to take Tusiani's corpus as exhibiting some metaphysical or theological consistency, then I think we can say that the personified Love turns out, in this stanza, to be the very godhead; for there is none other in the Christian universe that is competent to expiate sin, and the theme "God is love" is prominent in the Christian scriptures (see especially 1 John 4.8). The God/Love equation also has pagan antecedents, as we see in Hesiod (e.g., *Theogony* 120) and Plato (above all in the *Symposium*).

Hypnosis aprilis ("Enchantment of April")[28]

Meter: glyconics (as in *Hora litorea*) plus a single final pherecratean (see under *Lingua latina.*).

This piece is an invocation to the personified Spring. The lilting gly-conic meter is sustained by the repetition (in different positions in the line) of the words *dulciter* "sweetly," *canticum* "song," and *ultimum* "last" (i.e., "latest," "newest," as in *Cantiuncula vespertina*). The stock scenery of spring is invoked (*foliis tuis,* "with/in/by your leaves," 2; *omnibus tremulis rosis,* "with all the quivering roses," 5; *rivulis refluentibus,* "as the streams [thaw and] flow once again," 9).[29] Tusiani's interest in color and *chiaroscuro* finds voice here:

> Et coloribus omnibus
> Nunc per orbem ineuntibus
>
> and as all the colors
> are now coming in throughout the world (6–7)

and, as elsewhere in Tusiani's verse, the adjective *candidus*—literally, "white" or "gleaming"—has a richly metaphoric sense here, in its appli-cation to the song that is invoked (12; cf. *In ascensu Domini* 16).

---

27. My translation "man" is not an intended (or indeed unintended) sexism; the typical Latin word for "humans" (or the human race) is *homines*. But Tusiani here has used the word *vir* which means, specifically, a male adult. Doubtless this choice was partly determined by the exigences of the meter, though it may also have been influenced backward by the traditional English usage of "man" and "mankind" in the sense of "the human race." The word *nostrum* ("our") would both fit the meter here, and avoid charges of gender-specificity, if that were a desideratum. But Latin-speaking cultures—both classical and mediaeval—have been unflinchingly androcentric.

28. Also in Tusiani 1989:34. *Hypnosis,* from Greek *hupnos* (see on *Naenia* above), seems to be a relative neologism; it does not appear to date from the classical or mediaeval period in either Greek or Latin. I would translate it, most literally, as "putting to sleep." This poem's repeated references to *cantica*—"songs," possibly "incantations"—draw attention to its magical under-current.

29. The distinction between the ablative of means and the ablative absolute is blurred here, particularly in lines 5 and 9.

This desired song is no mere diversion or distraction, however; in fact it is perhaps not to be thought of as ordinary music, as its presence will presage the presence of the numinous:

> Canticum ultimum amabile
> Dulciter cane quod meos
> Impleat sonitu dies,
> Ah, dies aliter sine
> Musica, sine murmure
> Ullius deitatis in
> Me . . .

> [O Spring,] sing sweetly
> your latest lovely song
> so that it fills my days with sound,
> ah, days otherwise without
> music, without any
> murmur of divinity in
> me . . . (13–19)

As in the first, second, and fifth pieces of this collection, music not only figures prominently here but takes on a larger symbolic (spiritual) significance.

In ascensu Domini[30]

Meter: dactylic hexameter (as in *Naenia*). The title should not be translated "On the ascension of the Lord"—that would require *De ascensu*—but rather, in the ecclesiastical style, "[Composed] for [the feast of] the Ascension of Our Lord."

The argument of the poem is shaped around an antithetical distinction, enunciated in the first line: *Ascendit Dominus: cur non ego, servus, ad astra?* ("The Lord has ascended; why have I, [his] slave, not [ascended] to the stars?").[31] The antithesis is elaborated and explicated in the lines that

---

30. Also in Tusiani 1989:30.

31. *Servus* is the Latin Vulgate translation of New Testament Greek *doulos,* which the influential King James Version (1611) renders "servant." But while this translation has become traditional, the reader should note that *doulos* and *servus* in the classical period both meant "slave," and a slave was technically considered property—not an autonomous individual, but a chattel of his or her master. In Pauline theology *doulos* is used in its own metaphorical antithesis: the pagan is a "slave" to sin; in salvation the Christian is "set free" from this tyranny, but thereby becomes the *doulos*—slave—of God (see, e.g., Romans 6.6–22). Hence I have translated Tusiani's *servus* as "slave" here.

Anxiety about the resurrection of the dead, like anxiety about the return of Christ with which it is associated, is a biblical topos. Cf. 1 Corinthians 15.12–24, 50–55; 2 Peter 3.3–10.

follow: *Alae sunt Domino, sed servo est ardor eundi* ("The Lord [has] wings, but his slave, the pain of going," 4).[32] The vast gulf separating the human from the divine, the Lord from his servant, is the backbone of this binary opposition.[33] But at the end of the poem, the antithesis is dissolved:

> ... Ascendere noli,
> Nunc sine me noli tua quaerere candida regna.
> Annos extremos tibi notos hic remorare,
> Ibimus et tandem coniunctim ad sidera digna.
>
> ... Do not ascend,
> do not now without me seek your shining realms.
> Linger here until the end of the years known to you,
> and at last together we will go to fitting stars.[34] (15–18)

Thus is the servant exalted to the station of his master, thus the promise of resurrection and transfiguration fulfilled for the faithful, thus the bride of Christ united with the divine bridegroom.[35] The use of the unusual adverb *coniunctim* draws attention to the peculiar intimacy of this union. And the phrase *sine me* in line 16, "without me," is a skillfully crafted echo of *sine servum* in line 2. The echo involves wordplay, however, since in line 2 *sine* is not the preposition, but an imperative of the verb *sinere*, "allow":

> Forti cum Domino sine servum ascendere victum,
> Liber et ille erit in caelo. . . .
>
> Allow the conquered slave to ascend with his mighty Lord,
> And he will be free in heaven. . . . (2–3)

Caeli interpres

Meter: elegiac couplets (as in *Funus in hortulo*).

The opening proclamation, *Caeli interpres sum*, "I am the interpreter of heaven"—that is, an augur or prophet who interprets divine omens— is in fact the theme of the poem overall. Focused self-reflexivity about

32. *Ardor*, lit. "burning," is used by Lucretius (3.251) as an antonym of *voluptas*, "pleasure." Perhaps in our passage it has a very physical connotation—the heat that brings sweat. With a genitive (as here, *eundi*) it can also mean "passion" in the sense of "passionate love [for]."

33. This antithesis is common in Greek poetry, and particularly salient in Pindar; see, e.g., Pythian 10.27, Isthmian 7.43–44.

34. I.e., "the stars we deserve." *Sidera* is sometimes used as a metaphor for fame; here *sidera digna* may be taken to mean "appropriate glory"; or perhaps *digna* "worthy, deserving" is to be read as a transferred epithet modifying "we."

35. See Luke 1.52, 9.48, 14.7–11; 1 Corinthians 15.20–24; Revelation 21.1–3.

one's craft is a *topos* of ancient poetry at least as early as Pindar,[36] but here
Tusiani is actually combining this poetic gesture with another, even more
ancient: the invocation of the Muse. The opening lines of both the *Iliad*
and *Odyssey,* which are reckoned the oldest works of Western literature,
appeal to the goddess for aid and inspiration in singing the epic. At one
point, when about to detail the massive Catalogue of Ships, Homer (in
an extended passage) renews his invocation, and explains why:

> Tell me now, you Muses who have your homes on Olympos.
> For you, who are goddesses, are there, and you know all things,
> and we have heard only the rumour of it and know nothing.
> Who then of those were the chief men and the lords of the
>   Danaans?
> I could not tell over the multitude of them nor name them,
> not if I had ten tongues and ten mouths, not if I had
> a voice never to be broken and a heart of bronze within me,
> not unless the Muses of Olympia, daughters
> of Zeus of the aegis, remembered all those who came beneath
>   Ilion.[37]

Right at the beginning of the Western tradition, then, we find an
explicit and conscious stipulation of the poet's privileged role in the divine order—more specifically, of the connection of the poet (as *vates*)
with the numinous. But Tusiani's poem is sung from a different rhetorical posture than Homer's: there is no trace of supplication or invocation
here. Rather, its imperative is addressed to the reader (*Audi me,* "hear
me," 2) and its promise and claim are of competence to interpret the
Divine Music (*musica prima Dei,* "the first music of God," 4):

> Adloquor omnes qui cupiant cognoscere quae sint
>   Gaudia supremae magnifica harmoniae

> I speak to all who desire to know what are
>   the magnificent joys of the Supreme Harmony. (7–8)

Once again we find ourselves in the realm of the sublime music of the
spheres.

Were these lines dated to the classical period, and found by them-

---

36. See the beginning of Nemean 5, "I am no sculptor, fashioning statues / to stand motion-
less, fixed to the same base" (trans. Frank Nisetich); and of Horace, *Odes* 3.30.1 (writing at the
end of his first three books of odes), "I have completed a monument more lasting than bronze."
Tusiani engages in further poetical self-reflection in "Secretum" (Tusiani 1989:33).

37. *Iliad* 2.484–493 (trans. Richmond Lattimore). For more on the rhetorical significance of
the invocation of the Muse in Homer and Hesiod, see Kirby 1992a.

selves, one would probably brand them a fragment—perhaps the introduction to an important longer poem, the pieces of which became de-
tached in the vicissitudes of time. These eight lines certainly give promise
of the vatic delivery of some crucially significant information. And yet
we find them published, in the late 1980s, as a complete poem, and moreover as the end of a collection of five (*Quinque poemata Iosephi Tusiani*). I
am tempted to read them, therefore, as a kind of *sphragis* or "seal" on this
set of poems,[38] or—more extensively—as a comment on Tusiani's poetry
taken as a whole. In such light, they become an interpretive lens through
which the entire *corpus tusianicum* may be seen as no mere collection of
jottings, but rather a metaphysical commentary that elucidates the work
of God. On such a reading, the position of *Caeli interpres* immediately
following *In ascensu Domini* is then a strategic one.

The last pentameter line (8) shows in its form an elegance and perfection of Horatian proportions: *Gaudia Supremae magnifica Harmoniae.* Syn-
tactically it is a synchysis in ABAB formation, with *magnifica* modifying
Gaudia, and *Supremae* modifying *Harmoniae;* at the same time, the adjec-
tives (*gaudia, Harmoniae*) and nouns (*Supremae, magnifica*) are in chiastic
(ABBA) arrangement. And the whole verse is composed purely of these
four words, two in each hemistich, thus with a strong syntactic pull across
the metrical diaeresis. It is difficult to express the level of mastery that
such an exquisite line of verse represents.

Ver moribundum ("Dying spring")[39]

Meter: dactylic hexameter (as in *Naenia*).

The poem is couched in an apostrophe to Spring personified; in its
eleven lines it is overall a meditation on the swift passage of time.

Tu quoque, Ver, moreris, tu tam pretiosum et odorum?

You too, Spring, die, you who are so prized and fragrant? (1)

This theme was popular among the ancient poets, particularly as applied
in a "gather ye rosebuds" context: the most famous example of the latter,
of course, is Horace's *carpe diem* (*Odes* 1.11.8)—"pluck the day," that is,
make the most of opportunity.[40] But Tusiani's theme is not this, as we
shall see.

---

38. On the *sphragis* in ancient Greek poetry, see Ford 1985.

39. *JACT Review* [London] (ser. 2) no. 5 (Summer 1989): 3.

40. It should be noted that the usual translation, "seize the day," yields a rather more violent
image than Horace's own diction does.

In fact Horace is, in at least two other poems, the proximal source for
Tusiani's emblem of the coming (and ephemerality) of spring. The first,
Ode 1.4, was written and published early in Horace's poetic career:[41]

> Soluitur acris hiems grata uice ueris et Fauoni,
>   trahuntque siccas machinae carinas,
> ac neque iam stabulis gaudet pecus aut arator igni,
>   nec prata canis albicant pruinis.
>
> iam Cytherea choros ducit Venus imminente luna,   5
>   iunctaeque Nymphis Gratiae decentes
> alterno terram quatiunt pede, dum grauis Cyclopum
>   Vulcanus ardens uersat officinas.
>
> nunc decet aut uiridi nitidum caput impedire myrto
>   aut flore terrae quem ferunt solutae;   10
> nunc et in umbrosis Fauno decet immolare lucis,
>   seu poscat agna siue malit haedo.
>
> pallida Mors aequo pulsat pede pauperum tabernas
>   regumque turris. o beate Sesti,
> uitae summa breuis spem nos uetat inchoare longam;   15
>   iam te premet nox fabulaeque Manes
>
> et domus exilis Plutonia; quo simul mearis,
>   nec regna uini sortiere talis
> nec tenerum Lycidan mirabere, quo calet iuuentus
>   nunc omnis et mox uirgines tepebunt.   20

> Harsh winter is melting away in the welcome change to spring
>   and zephyrs,
>   winches are pulling down dry-bottom boats,
> the cattle no longer like the steading, the ploughman does not
>   hug the fire
>   and meadows are not white with hoar-frost.
>
> Venus of Cythera leads on the dance beneath a hanging moon,
>   and the lovely Graces, linking arms with Nymphs,
> shake the ground with alternate feet while burning Vulcan
>   tends to the grim foundries of the Cyclopes.

---

41. Texts of Horace are taken from the edition of Shackleton Bailey 1985. The translation of
1.4 is adapted from that in West 1995: 19–21.

Now is the time to oil the hair and bind the head with green
    myrtle
or flowers born of the earth now freed from frost;
now too it is time to sacrifice to Faunus in shady groves
    whether he asks for a lamb or prefers a kid.

Pale death kicks with impartial foot at the hovels of the poor
    and the towers of kings. O fortunate Sestius,
the brief sum of life does not allow us to start on long hopes.
    You will soon be kept close by Night and the fabled shades

and Pluto's meagre house. When you go there
    you will no longer cast lots to rule the wine
nor admire tender Lycidas whom all the young men
    now burn for, and for whom the girls will soon be warm.

The other ode dates from much later in Horace's career, coming as it does from his fourth book of *Odes,* and thus having been published in or after 13 B.C.E. This one, Ode 4.7, A. E. Housman regarded as the most beautiful poem in Latin; his translation, though not minutely accurate, is too famous not to include here:[42]

Diffugere niues, redeunt iam gramina campis
    arboribusque comae;
mutat terra uices et decrescentia ripas
    flumina praetereunt.

Gratia cum Nymphis geminisque sororibus audet   5
    ducere nuda choros:
immortalia ne speres, monet annus et almum
    quae rapit hora diem.

frigora mitescunt Zephyris, uer proterit aestas
    interitura, simul   10
pomifer autumnus fruges effuderit; et mox
    bruma recurrit iners.

damna tamen celeres reparant caelestia lunae:
    nos ubi decidimus
quo pius Aeneas, quo Tullus diues et Ancus,   15
    puluis et umbra sumus.

42. Text in Housman 1939.

quis scit an adiciant hodiernae crastina summae
    tempora di superi?
cuncta manus auidas fugient heredis, amico
    quae dederis animo.   20

cum semel occideris et de te splendida Minos
    fecerit arbitria,
non, Torquate, genus, non te facundia, non te
    restituet pietas.

infernis neque enim tenebris Diana pudicum   25
    liberat Hippolytum,
nec Lethaea ualet Theseus abrumpere caro
    uincula Pirithoo.

The snows are fled away, leaves on the shaws
    And grasses in the mead renew their birth,
The river to the river-bed withdraws,
    And altered is the fashion of the earth.

The Nymphs and Graces three put off their fear
    And unapparelled in the woodland play.
The swift hour and the brief prime of the year
    Say to the soul, *Thou wast not born for aye.*

Thaw follows frost; hard on the heel of spring
    Treads summer sure to die, for hard on hers
Comes autumn, with his apples scattering;
    Then back to wintertide, when nothing stirs.

But oh, whate'er the sky-led seasons mar,
    Moon upon moon rebuilds it with her beams:
Come *we* where Tullus and where Ancus are,
    And good Aeneas, we are dust and dreams.

Torquatus, if the gods in heaven shall add
    The morrow to the day, what tongue has told?
Feast then thy heart, for what they heart has had
    The fingers of no heir will ever hold.

When thou descendest once the shades among,
    The stern assize and equal judgment o'er,
Not thy long lineage nor thy golden tongue,
    No, nor thy righteousness, shall friend thee more.

> Night holds Hippolytus the pure of stain,
>   Diana steads him nothing, he must stay;
> And Theseus leaves Pirithöus in the chain
>   The love of comrades cannot take away.

Both of these poems, it will be seen, juxtapose the notion of the change of season with the brevity of human life. The first one, however, moves simply from winter to spring, and then abruptly[43] changes registers to speak of the inexorability of death (*pallida Mors*). The second, by contrast, cycles through the movement of the seasons, promising eternal renewal and rebirth—for the year, that is; for the individual person, of course, he says, there is no coming back from the underworld. In this, Horace himself seems to be echoing a famous sentiment of Catullus (poem 5.4–6), who urges his beloved to live and love with him while they can:

> soles occidere et redire possunt;
> nobis, cum semel occidit breuis lux,
> nox est perpetua una dormienda.

> Suns may set and rise again;
> for us, once our brief light goes out,
> then comes the big sleep.[44]

Tusiani's very notion of a *ver moribundum* is something of an oxymoron, since spring is the beginning of the yearly cycle of vegetal growth, the time when winter—itself a prime symbol of death—finally passes away, and life seems to regenerate itself after a period of paralysis. So to speak of the death of Spring is both powerful and, at first, confusing. But what is the "death" of spring but the onset of summer, when the year is in full flower? Thus Tusiani sees figured in the inevitable movement from spring to summer, in Spring's "serene death," his own progress toward eternal life:

> . . . ecce serena
> Morte tua vehor ad vitam immortalem ineuntem:

> . . . See, by your serene
> death I am drawn toward eternal life as it arrives. (8–9)

Here, as in *Hypnosis aprilis,* the spring season is redolent with spiritual symbolism, and draws the narrator's attention toward the divine.

43. Cf. the famous marginal note made by W. S. Landor in his copy of Horace here: "*Pallida mors* has nothing to do with the above."
44. Lit., "there is one long night to be slept through."

NAENIA GARGANICA ("RHYME OF GARGANO")[45]

Meter: dactylic hexameter (as in *Naenia*).

This poem includes a number of features we have already seen in other samples of Tusiani's Latin verse: The opening vocative, here addressing the *naenia* itself; the explicit references to natural settings: *ab odora valle remota*, "from a far-off fragrant valley," 1; *ut plaga vento / Arsa refecta est*, "as a seared plain is refreshed by a breeze," 3–4; the riot of flowers in 8–9, *violae et spiramine menthae / Involvor, mollisque thymi croceaeque genistae*, "I am wrapped in the scent [lit. "the breathing-in," a vivid term] of violets and mint, of soft thyme and yellow broom." Here too we find music treated as a main topic, and that distinctive juxtaposition of the senses that is tantamount to elision: *Quomodo dulce melos fieri fragantia possit / Ignoro* ("I do not know how a sweet tune can become a fragrance," 6–7). But this poem differs from *Naenia*[46] in that it is not, itself, a *naenia*—a lullaby or nursery rhyme—but rather (one might say) a meta-*naenia:* it is a meditation on the nature and effect of the *naenia,* on its power of refection and inspiration in the face of a crushing *Weltschmerz:*

> . . . Nescio cur, sed musica moesta
> Me renovat terraeque facit tolerabile pondus.

> I do not know why, but sad music
> renews me and makes the weight of earth bearable. (4–5)[47]

The piece ends with a masterful juxtaposition: the penultimate line is composed, simply, of the comforting repetitions characteristic of a real *naenia: Blandula naenia, me, bona naenia blandula, sopi* ("sweet little chant, lull me, good and sweet little chant," 10),[48] while the last line is, by contrast, a gem of sophisticated Latinity: *Urbis ne piceas respirem auras miserandae* ("lest I breathe the dark breezes of the piteous city," 11). Here the verb (*respirem*) is in the exact center of the line; "piteous" and "city" are at its extremities; and "dark" and "breezes" flank the verb. Thus the syntactic structure of the line is ABCBA, a feat made possible by the highly inflected nature of the Latin language, but still no easy achievement

45. *JACT Review* (ser. 2) no. 5 (Summer 1989): 3. "Gargano" is a reference to the poet's birthplace in Italy.

46. And, for the same reason, from another, "Naenia gallinacea," published in the *Classical Outlook* 62 (Dec.-Jan. 1984–1985), along with *Funus in hortulo.*

47. One is reminded by this comment of Jessica's remark in *The Merchant of Venice* (5.1.69): "I am never merry when I hear sweet music."

48. The verse is of seventeen syllables; that is, there has been no substitution of spondees for dactyls anywhere in the line. This is, actually, statistically rather unusual in dactylic hexameter, and thus serves to draw attention metrically to the line.

within the confines of a single dactylic hexameter. As I have said, it stands
in striking contrast to the lulling repetitions of line 10; and in its contrast
of the fragrant valley with the squalid city, it harks back to a romanticized
image of the countryside that is typical of Hellenistic bucolic verse.

PHOTOGRAPHEMA MARITIMUM ("SEASIDE PHOTOGRAPH")[49]

Meter: elegiac couplets (as in *Funus in hortulo*).

I have chosen to include this poem because, unlike the others here, it
represents something no classical author, however prescient or ahead of
his or her time, could achieve: the description of some phenomenon of
the modern industrial world. It is by no means Tusiani's only foray into
such uncharted territory;[50] but within its small (four-line) compass it
problematizes one of the issues central to an endeavor like Tusiani's: what
falls within the boundaries of appropriate subject matter for such verse?
The question of *how* to write is, one might say, almost decided ipso facto
by the decision to emulate classical models in meter, diction, and syntax. But given only the other poems hitherto discussed, the reader might
naturally infer that Tusiani had also restricted himself to topics one could
encounter in the poetry of Theocritus or Horace. This is in fact hardly
the case, as *Photographema maritimum* shows:

> Unda tacet subito, subito tacet hora diurna:
> > Sistunt ecce simul tempus et Oceanus.
> Alta voce puer ridet ludens in harena
> > Atque eius risus tota creata tenet.

> Suddenly the wave is silent, suddenly the hour of the day is
> > silent;
> > look, at the same time Time and Ocean stand still.[51]
> In a high voice[52] a boy laughs as he plays on the sand,
> > and his laugh holds all created things.

An undiscriminating reading of the poem would regard it as entirely
conventional: a description of a picture of a boy playing at the beach. Its
technical designation is *ekphrasis,* the literary description of a work of

---

49. *Melissa* 8 (1985): 10. Also in Tusiani 1989:13.

50. See, e.g., "BAR dictus, locus iste . . . "(Tusiani 1989:50).

51. *Sistunt* is not merely "are standing still," which would be *stant,* but most exactly "come to
a halt." Tusiani's choice of verb indicates the instantaneous nature of this pause, which I shall
discuss below.

52. *Alta* can refer either to pitch or to volume, though here I am inclined to read it as the
latter. But "loud" sounds jarring in this context.

visual or plastic art. Any ancient artist could conceivably have painted such a picture, and any poet described the image.[53] But Tusiani's theme is, I take it, almost postmodern in its attention to the technological instantaneity of photography: the fact that, in a wink of the camera's eye, the film records exactly what was in the camera's field of view at that moment. This is indeed insisted upon in the first two lines, the second of which repeats the elements of the first in chiastic (ABBA) order. I think we can safely say that the nature of this insistence is different from any that one could possibly find in an ancient *ekphrasis,* because in any of the artistic media available to the ancients, such as painting, drawing, engraving, or sculpture, the actual execution of such a visual image would require the lapse of a certain amount of time. This is *not* entirely analogous to the time required to develop and print a photograph: in photography, the image per se may be captured in a fraction of a second, and—even when all due allowance is made for the photographer's artistic involvement in the composition, lighting, focus, etc., of the image—what is in the photograph, finally, mirrors what was in the field of view more directly than any handmade image could do. In the older visual arts, the hand moves, *in time,* in response to an image in the mind of the artist. That is to say, in these arts, there is a conceptual element that perforce mediates between the item depicted and the depiction. (Semioticians, as we might infer from the information in chapter 2, would say that the painter actually paints, not an unmediated object, but the *interpretant* of that object.)

The second couplet focuses not on the act of artistic creation or purely on the subject matter, but on a "reading" of the photograph. It turns out that this is not an unpeopled seascape, like one of Hokusai's magnificent woodcuts; the water and shore are in fact a backdrop for a human figure. We are not told the details of the boy's play, but one activity—his laugh—is singled out for semiotic significance: *eius risus cuncta creata tenet.* I would draw attention to the significance of Tusiani's decision to concentrate on laughter, which includes an auditory as well as a visual element. By this ruse he has dissolved the freeze-frame element of the first couplet, and (at the same time) extended the reader's sensory input beyond the visual and silent. One should note too that *tenet* is itself an ambiguous term: it could mean "comprises," or "holds [in place]"—that is, at the sound of his laughter, everything stands still (tying the second

---

53. Cf. for example Ovid's description of the decorations on the doors of the Palace of the Sun at *Metamorphoses* 2.11–12.

couplet to the first). This polysemy of the Latin vocabulary is a great source of poetic richness for the skilled wordsmith.

℮

A number of salient characteristics are common to the poems I have discussed in this chapter. Among these I would draw particular attention to (a) Tusiani's use of sensory description, and within this realm (i) his preoccupation with light and darkness, (ii) the *topos* of music (including—here not strictly a *sensory* phenomenon—the music of the spheres), and (iii) an acute awareness of the beauties of nature; (b) the power of life and death; and (c) devotion to God. Indeed it would be difficult to imagine a more elemental list than this. Also, it is a striking fact that many of the poems are couched in vocatives: that is, the narratee is explicitly insisted upon, often in the opening line, in the second person. This last item, though evinced also in Tusiani's English and Italian verse, I find particularly significant in his Latin, for this is a mode of poetry that today—by its very reconditeness, its cultural remoteness, and its severance from living speech—runs the risk of inordinate distance from its reader.[54] Here above all Tusiani makes an effort to reach for effective connection, rhetorical engagement, in his discourse.

One might well ask why a poet would elect to express himself in this difficult and increasingly obscure language, thereby severely limiting a poem's potential readership. One explanation, explicitly biographical, finds the answer in Tusiani's own life as a man of two worlds, two cultures. He himself wrote (fittingly enough, in Latin):

Saepe, praesertim in horis tristitiae animum obfuscantis, me ipsum interrogo ad causas explorandas, cur etiam nunc, in fine vigesimi saeculi ac vitae meae, carmina mea Latina pangam. . . . Hoc nunc est aenigma: utra lingua est vere mea? Tusca an Anglica? Quis sum ego—omnis homo an duo hominis aliena dimidia? Et	Often, especially in hours of soul-darkening sadness, I question myself, so as to look into the reasons why even now, at the end of the twentieth century and of my life, I compose my Latin poems. . . . This is the riddle: which language is truly mine, Italian or English? Who am I: a whole man, or two strange halves of a man?

---

54. I have discussed the rhetorical connection between narratee and reader in Kirby 1992b.

ubi sunt radices meae? Lingua	And where are my roots?
Latina unicam fortasse praebet	The Latin language provides
solutionem illusionemque su–	perhaps the only solution—
premam. Aut fortasse, ut de se	and the supreme illusion. Or
dicebat Quintus Ennius, mihi	maybe, as Quintus Ennius said
quoque tria corda in pectore	of himself, "I also have three
sunt.[55]	hearts in my breast."

Latin, then, on this reading, is the language of the third heart: caught in the pendulum swing between his birth culture and his adopted, Tusiani reaches back to a more ancient heritage, invoking a deeper magic. This is a powerful rationale, given his personal history. As Paolo Giordano maintains, "It can safely be said that the majority of writing done by immigrant authors is explicitly autobiographical in nature." [56] Giordano describes a dream recounted by Tusiani in his autobiography, in which he and his mother are

> in a long corridor bathed with a blinding white light, with many doors on the sides and one door on each end; one marked "Exit," the other "Entrance." They begin walking towards the door marked "Exit." When they arrive, he notices that it now says "Entrance" and that the sign on the door at the opposite end of the corridor has changed accordingly to "Exit." [57]

Finally his father, who in actuality had died years earlier, appears and tells them to follow him: he knows where the exit is. They follow, but the dream is interrupted at that point, and Tusiani is awakened without ever discovering how to get out of the tunnel.

Thus, for Giordano, the resolution of Tusiani's problem of national identity

> is his awareness of being suspended between two worlds, his acceptance of his biculturalism, for which, instead of seeing himself as not belonging to either one or the other world, he can accept

55. Quoted in Sacré 1994:178–179. The English translation that follows is my own. I have emended the *duo homines* of Sacré's text to *duo hominis;* the sentence is a clear paraphrase of Tusiani's oft-quoted lines from *Gente mia:* "Two languages, two lands, perhaps two souls . . . / Am I a man, or two strange halves of one?" (Tusiani 1978:7; ellipsis in text.) Tusiani's mention of Ennius seems to be a reference to Aulus Gellius *Noctes atticae* 17.17.1: Quintus Ennius tria corda habere sese dicebat, quad loqui Graece et Osce et Latine sciret ("Quintus Ennius used to say that he had three hearts, because he could speak Greek, Oscan, and Latin").

56. Giordano 1994a:60.

57. Giordano 1994a:80–81.

himself as being the man of "two languages, two lands, [. . .] two [socio-cultural] souls," which he has previously questioned in his poetry.[58]

And this, as I have said, is a powerful answer to the question, Why Latin verse? But the simplest answer is, For love: love of the old forms, love of the rigor and clarity of the classical models, love of the accumulated literary tradition of thousands of years. But love also of the world around him, of daily life and the wonders of the created order, of his fellow creatures in this latter-day world, and (not least) of the Creator that he discerns in all this. For all these reasons, it seems, Tusiani is moved to take wing in the rarefied (and rarely traversed) air of Helicon.

58. Giordano 1994a:82.

RHETORICAL VALUES ANCIENT AND MODERN

꒜

Hermogenes' *On Types of Style* and Italo Calvino's
Six Memos for the Next Millennium

Le style est l'homme même.
—Georges-Louis Leclerc de Buffon, *Discours sur le style*

$\mathcal{E}$very great culture, it seems, makes its mark on human history in some
particular way, and ancient Greece was certainly no exception in this regard. In envisioning the great flowering of Athenian cultures in the fifth
and fourth centuries B.C.E., the visually-minded will perhaps think first
of the magnificent sculpture and architecture of that era. There are, however, two institutions—themselves closely linked—that are, if possible,
even greater legacies of this period: democracy and rhetoric.[1]

The Athenians themselves developed a radical democracy of a sort,[2]
and it appears to be because of this that Athens saw the world's first systematic study of, and instruction in, the art of effective verbal communication. This they termed "rhetoric."[3] While Aristotle is said to have
claimed that the "inventor" of rhetoric was the Presocratic philosopher
Empedocles,[4] it is generally thought that the first teachers of rhetoric in

---

1. For the profound connection between these two, see especially Ober 1989.

2. Athenian democracy, we must hasten to add, had its own complications, limitations,
and imperfections: the Athenians did not, for example, scruple to enslave other human beings;
women were far from equal to men; and (if we may believe Thucydides) they had a vigorous
and sometimes brutal program of imperialism in the Mediterranean.

3. On the possible origins of the Greek word *rhêtorikê*, from which our word "rhetoric"
comes, see Schiappa 1990, O'Sullivan 1993.

4. Attested in, e.g., Quintilian, *Institutio oratoria* 3.1.6; Diogenes Laertius, *Lives of the Philosophers* 8.57.

Greece—whom we term sophists—came from Sicily. Ancient traditions tell us that Corax and his pupil Tisias were the first to write handbooks (*tekhnai*) of rhetoric.[5]

This brings me back to the word "rhetoric" itself. Sadly, in our day it is modified more often than not by the adjective "empty": our culture is incurably suspicious of rhetoric, which is often thought of as bombast, flummery, or verbal sleight of hand. This opinion was shared by some ancients as well, although there were many in classical antiquity who took it seriously and indeed prized it. Not counting the deprecatory sense, we tend to use the word in three different ways, which are worth setting out in some detail, since these meanings shed light on the ancient conceptions as well.[6]

The first meaning, which we may term rhetoric$_1$, is equivalent to "discourse" itself. In this sense, rhetoric is communication recognized for its suasive force. The sentence "his rhetoric was sincere" uses the word in this way. The second meaning, which we may term rhetoric$_2$, is theoretically one step removed from rhetoric$_1$: it is what we might also call "metarhetoric." Rhetoric$_2$ is the *study* of rhetoric$_1$, in the most purely scientific or philosophical sense. The third meaning, which we might term rhetoric$_3$, covers a threshold-region between rhetoric$_1$ and rhetoric$_2$; rhetoric$_3$ is what I call "potential discourse." While this involves mental assessment, it is no longer in the purely theoretical or philosophical realm occupied by rhetoric$_2$: potential discourse is the study, or teaching, of communication specifically with a view toward praxis. Under this heading, then, come the handbooks of rhetoric that seem to date as far back as Corax and Tisias. The word *tekhnê*, typically translated "art," takes on in Plato the meaning of a skill or competence that is accompanied by the ability to give an account of its governing principles. Hence, by metonymy, *tekhnê* even in antiquity came to mean a *handbook* that explained the principles of an art. Such *tekhnai* may have in some cases been no more than collections of memorable examples—a *tekhnê* on introductions may, for example, sometimes have been a compendium of interesting or effective introductions—but, over time, they came to be repositories of systematic explanation and codification.

Different writers in different *tekhnai*, of course, codified rhetoric in different ways. Later classical rhetoricians are accustomed to speaking of

5. On Corax and Tisias, see, e.g., Kennedy 1963 : 58–61; Kennedy 1994 : 32–34; Cole 1991b.

6. The various definitions offered in Cole 1991a differ somewhat from those given here, and fit closely with his densely argued position.

the five "parts" of rhetoric: *invention,* or the "finding" of argument; *arrangement,* the art of ordering ideas and topics, and of composing the various sections of an oration; *style,* the effective use of diction (choice of words) and composition (the aesthetic arrangement of words in a phrase or sentence); *memory,* the art of memorizing the oration for presentation; and *delivery,* the presentation itself, which covered gesture as well as language. These are the five parts of rhetoric as we know them from, say, the *Rhetorica ad Herennium,* Cicero, and Quintilian. They do not, however, seem as a list to date back to the Greek classical period: the pseudo-Aristotelian *Rhetoric to Alexander,* attributed to Anaximenes, focuses primarily on invention and arrangement; Aristotle's *Rhetoric* treats invention, style, and arrangement (in that order), and mentions delivery, but does not address it in detail.[7] Nor does the *Rhetoric* treat of memory. The ancients attributed to the poet Simonides not only a prodigious memory, but also a system of memorization,[8] which eventually came to be taught in the rhetorical schools. The sophist Hippias is also reputed to have taught mnemonic technique.[9]

Invention has to do primarily with what the speaker is going to say: what are his topics and arguments. Aristotle forever changed the face of rhetorical instruction by breaking this down into the three *entekhnoi pisteis* or "artistic means of persuasion": *êthos,* the (perceived) good character of the speaker as she speaks; *pathos,* the emotion(s) aroused in the audience by the speaker; and *logos,* the use of logical argument in the speech, whether inductive or deductive. Other theorists developed systems of *stasis theory,* which enabled the speaker to concentrate on whatever might happen to be the point at issue.

Arrangement may well have been one of the earliest elements of rhetorical instruction: the sophists seem to have concentrated on teaching their pupils to attend to the *moria logou,* or "parts of the oration," teaching them at least sometimes by example.[10]

Style is to invention as form is to content. It was perhaps inevitable that, as the use of persuasive language became formalized, experts would attend to the aesthetics of the situation; and stylistic beauty may be said to have a suasive force all its own. Hence classical rhetoricians focused

---

7. The earliest Greek treatise on delivery seems to have been the work of Aristotle's star pupil, Theophrastus, but it is unfortunately no longer extant.

8. See, e.g., Aristotle *De anima* 427b 18 ff.; Cicero *De oratore* 2.352 ff.

9. For Hippias, see the testimonia in 86 A 2, 5, 11, and 12 (Diels-Kranz).

10. On the Aristotelian vs. the sophistical traditions in rhetorical instruction, see especially Solmsen 1941.

their stylistic instruction on matters of what they called *diction* (the careful choice of words) and of *composition* (the most beautiful and effective disposition of the words chosen). The history of rhetoric shows that there is a tendency to move, over time, from a concern with issues of invention to a concern with issues of style. This is concomitant, it would seem, with a shift of focus from the oral to the written: a phenomenon of "slippage" recently identified in Italian as *letteraturizzazione*.[11] I am not sure that this ought to be regarded as an irreversible tendency; it seems that *letteraturizzazione* may be a cyclical phenomenon, or possibly a result of periodic vacillation between two poles. Those who are stylistically absorbed are more form-oriented, while those who are inventionally absorbed are more content-oriented.

Be all this as it may, even in antiquity there were whole *tekhnai* written on matters of style. Over time, there evolved a number of indices for rhetorical style; these may be broadly categorized as *kinds* of style and *virtues* of style. In Aristotle's *Rhetoric* (3.2–12), we find the embryonic form of a theory of style that takes account of both these categories. Theophrastus seems to have elaborated the theory of the virtues of style, under the headings of Clarity, Correctness, Ornament, and Propriety.[12] In Cicero we find a clear schematization of the kinds of style under the headings of Plain, Middle, and Grand, and furthermore a correlation of each of these with a particular purpose: to prove, to delight, and to move.[13] Demetrius' *On Style* harmonizes the two schemata; he elaborates four good kinds of style—Plain, Elevated, Elegant, and Forceful—and four corresponding vices—Aridity, Frigidity, Affectation, and Unpleasantness. In the Demetrian system the vices are conceived of, one might say, as virtues *manquées*.[14]

Assuming that the kinds of style will be deployed as appropriate to the subject matter, the theorist may turn to the particular contemplation of one or another of the virtues of style. This is the tactic of Pseudo-Longinus, whose powerful essay *On the Sublime* derives that virtue *(hupsos)*

---

11. For this concept see especially Kennedy 1999:3. He adopts the term from Florescu 1971.

12. The Theophrastan virtues of style are referred to by Cicero in *De oratore* 3.37 and *Orator* 79. The disappearance of Theophrastus' writings is a great loss to us; for more on his work see Mayer 1910; Grube 1952a and 1952b; Kennedy 1957; and Fortenbaugh 1985.

13. See Cicero's *Orator* 20–21, 69, 106–109, etc. Douglas 1957 shows how Cicero correlated the three kinds of style *(genera dicendi)*—plain, middle, and grand—with the "duties of the orator" *(officia oratoris)*: to teach, to charm, and to move, respectively.

14. See Demetrius *On Style* 36. The importance of this treatise—apparently not by Demetrius of Phalerum—is not to be underestimated. Its date, and probable sources, are keenly disputed; see, e.g., Solmsen 1931; Grube 1961; and Kennedy 1963:286.

from five sources: nobility of soul, powerful emotion, rhetorical figures, noble language, and a general effect of dignity.[15] In the same category we might place the late Greek rhetorician Hermogenes of Tarsus, among whose extant works we find one entitled *Peri ideōn*.[16] And this is a treatise that I want to discuss in some detail, because a ready familiarity with its contents will well prepare us for understanding what Italo Calvino is attempting to accomplish in *Six Memos for the Next Millennium,* the book he was working on at the time of his death.

ℰ

Hermogenes' *Peri ideōn* might aptly be subtitled "Seven Memos for the Postclassical Orator." Born in about 161 C.E., he was an oratorical child prodigy; Philostratus, who (along with Eunapius) is our primary source of information on the Second Sophistic, tells us that the emperor Marcus Aurelius came to hear him speak.[17] Hermogenes was evidently enamored of the style of the Athenian orator Demosthenes, to the extent that the Demosthenic style was Hermogenes' touchstone for excellence; all seven *ideai* of style may be found in Demosthenes' orations.[18]

It seems that Hermogenes knew, and may have modeled his *Peri ideōn*

---

15. *On the Sublime* 8.1. Which is not to say that this author gives no attention to "vices" of style; see, e.g., *On the Sublime* 3–5. The best introduction, with commentary, for *On the Sublime* is that of Russell 1964.

   The Greek word *hupsos* literally means "elevation" or "height"; it is thus closely related conceptually to the Latin *sublimis,* "lifted-up."

16. The standard edition of the Greek text is that of Rabe 1913. Wooten 1987 (from which my English citations of Hermogenes are taken or adapted) provides an excellent translation, with notes; see also the perspicuous discussion of Hermogenes in Wooten 1983:22–42.

   N.B.: an alternate title for Hermogenes' work is *Peri ideōn logou.* This is not easy to translate: *logos* is tremendously polysemous, and in rhetoric can mean a simple utterance, an entire oration, a story, a specific line of reasoning, or the use of enthymeme considered generally. Here it may mean "language" or "oratory"; yet another title found in some ancient manuscripts is simply "Hermogenes' Rhetorical Handbook." *Idea* is of course one of Plato's words for his famous concept of the Forms; but it can designate a species, sort, or class of things, and is etymologically related to the Greek word for "see"; the notion was probably that by examining a thing's appearance, one might determine its nature. So the title of Wooten's translation, *On Types of Style,* should not be taken to associate Hermogenes' work with the *kinds* of style, but rather with a number of *species* of good style. On the manuscript evidence for the title of the work, see Rabe 1913:xxi–xxiii.

17. Philostratus *Lives of the Sophists* 2.577. On the Second Sophistic generally see Kirby 1996c, and the bibliography collected there.

18. See, e.g., Hermogenes 215 (section numbers in Hermogenes are actually the page numbers in the Greek edition of Rabe 1913; these may be found in the margins of Wooten 1987).

Table 2. Schema of Hermogenes' *Peri ideôn*

1. CLARITY	*Saphêneia*
Purity	*Katharotês*
Distinctness	*Eukrineia*
2. GRANDEUR	*Megethos*
Solemnity	*Semnotês*
Asperity	*Trakhutês*
Vehemence	*Sphodrotês*
Brilliance	*Lamprotês*
Vigor	*Akmê*
Abundance	*Peribolê*
3. BEAUTY	*Kallos*
4. RAPIDITY	*Gorgotês*
5. ETHOS	*Êthos*
Simplicity	*Apheleia*
Sweetness	*Glukutês*
Subtlety	*Drimutês*
Modesty	*Epieikeia*
6. SINCERITY	*Alêtheia*
Indignation	*Barutês*
7. FORCE	*Deinotês*

on, a similar system of twelve stylistic *ideai* included in the so-called "Aristides Rhetoric," a compend dating from the second century C.E.[19] We may conveniently represent the schema underlying Hermogenes' work in tabular form (see table 2). This list immediately shows its classical pedigree.

◆ *Clarity,* with its subheadings of purity and distinctness, harks back to the Aristotelian demand that one strive for a style clear and free of ambiguity.[20] It was (along with correctness, ornament, and propriety) to become one of the Theophrastan virtues of style. In the postmodern era, with the valorization accorded to indeterminacy, blurred distinc-

19. Greek text in Schmid 1926. See also Schmid 1917–1918, and Kennedy 1972:628–632. Kennedy (1972:629 and n. 34), following Schmid, attributes the "Aristides Rhetoric" to Basilicus of Nicomedia.

20. *Rhetoric* 1404b 2, *saphê einai;* and 1407a 32, *mê amphibolois.*

tions, and inscrutability, its stock may be seen to have been devalued somewhat; but ancient considerations of language were fairly teleological, and it was clear to the Greeks that public discourse (whether in the courtroom, the political assembly, or for a ceremonial occasion) needed to be clear to be effective. This is not, of course, to say that they placed no value on purposeful obfuscation; but such discourse was known as an *ainigma* or "riddle."

Hermogenes says that clarity is derived from two sources: *purity* and *distinctness*. By "purity" he seems to mean not moral purity (or the appearance thereof), but rather the use of "common, everyday thoughts that occur to everyone" (227). This resonates with Aristotle's concept of *kuria kai oikeia,* or prevailing meanings and ordinary terminology (*Rhetoric* 3.2.6).[21] "Distinctness" (*eukrineia*) means, literally, "clear judgment," and, Hermogenes tells us, has the function of determining "what aspects of the case the judges should consider first and what second, and to make that clear to them" (235). (His description of the audience as "judges" betrays the preëminently judicial environment in which such oratory flourished.) As such, distinctness is organically linked to rhetorical *invention:* the matter of what one is going to say, and the rhetorical arguments that will be advanced in order to say it. We shall return to this significant linking of style with invention in our discussion of Calvino.

♦ *Grandeur,* in its various manifestations, is not perhaps to be sought above all else—simplicity, after all, is a subheading of ethos or character—but it is redolent of the Sublime of Pseudo-Longinus.

Hermogenes does discern a special link between grandeur and clarity—this, because "the very clear can seem trite and commonplace" (241). He uses the words "majesty" (*ogkos,* literally "bulk" or "mass") and "dignity" (*axiôma,* derived from *axios,* "worthy") apparently as synonyms for grandeur. "Solemnity" can contribute to grandeur because "Solemn thoughts are those concerning the gods" (242); in fact the word *semnos* can mean "revered" or "holy." (It can, however, also mean "pompous," which is the danger in adopting solemnity in discourse.) "Asperity" is Wooten's translation for *trakhutês,* literally "ruggedness" or "roughness." Here, as with solemnity, Hermogenes connects style with invention: "The thoughts that are typical of asperity are those that involve some open reproach" (255). It uses metaphoric diction (258) and brevity of phrase (259); sounds should clash and prose rhythms ought to be irregular (259). "Vehemence" is used to express thoughts involving criticism and

---

21. For more on *kuria kai oikeia,* see Kirby 1997a.

refutation (260). Vehemence and asperity, taken together, give some index of class- or caste-consciousness on the part of Hermogenes: whereas asperity is recommended in the critique of persons more important than the speaker, vehemence is for use against those less important. The approaches are similar; vehemence may be produced by using apostrophe (262) and may have a deictic quality (263). "Brilliance" is marked as particularly important in engendering grandeur; the Greek word, *lamprotês*, depends from the same metaphor as the English, as both have to do with effulgent light. In such a style, the speaker must seem confident (265), direct, unhesitating, and noble (266); it employs figures such as denial (*anairesis*), the "fresh start" (*apostasis*), and disjunction (*asundeton*) (267), and typically longer clauses (268), as opposed to the shorter ones of asperity. "Vigor" is *akmê* in Greek, which Wooten renders "florescence." Literally "height," it is the source of our English "acme." This aspect of style is close in thought and method to asperity and vehemence (270), but the figures that create it, such as apostrophe, refutation (*elegkhos*), and irony, as well as its native clauses, cadences, rhythms, and word orders, are like those characteristic of brilliance and ethos (271–272). "Abundance" may be considered in polarity with "purity" (277); it consists in the addition of "something extraneous to the subject matter of the speech (278, 281). The Romans would call this *copia* or *amplificatio*. It has no single native diction, but may involve syntactic parallelism (284–285), and figures such as enumeration (*aparithmêsis*), repetition (*epanalêpsis*), cryptic implication (*emphasis*), partitioning (*merismos*), and others (287–295).

♦ *Beauty,* like clarity, is one of those values that we may associate with the traditional cultural legacy of the West (and indeed, even more intensely, with that of the East). That the arts should exhibit beauty was perhaps taken for granted until our own century; the Greek word for "ornament" or "adorning," *kosmos,* is the same as that for "order" (as opposed to *khaos,* "chaos"), and this polysemy indicates something of the premium the Greeks placed on order.

Beauty, for Hermogenes, is closely connected with symmetry and harmony, and proportion; here his analogy is to the limbs of the body (297), reminding us that at least since Plato,[22] classical theorists compared the well-formed discourse to a living body—an organic whole with all its parts. Perhaps significantly, Hermogenes is willing to say that there is no specific thought intrinsic to beauty (298); in this instance style is set

22. See *Phaedrus* 264c.

free from invention. The diction used to produce beauty is the same as
that used for purity; it will come from the use of figures such as balanced
phrases (*parisôsis*), repetitions at the beginnings or ends of phrases (*epanaphora* and *antistrophe*), climax, and others (299–306), and will typically
use moderately long clauses that avoid hiatus (307–308). Too much solemnity is to be eschewed (309–311). In sum, this kind of beauty is
closely aligned with what Hermogenes calls the "carefully wrought style"
(*epimeleia*, 296). It is to be distinguished from the grace and charm that
come from "simplicity" and "sweetness," which contribute to ethos, as
we shall see.

♦ *Rapidity* is of course an index of virtuosity, but Hermogenes also op-
poses it expressly to flatness and carelessness (*aneimenon kai huption*, 312).
Rapidity depends basically on "the use of short clauses that develop the
thought quickly"; word order, cadences, and prose rhythms also come
into the picture (312). Figures such as parenthesis, interweaving (*epi-
plokê*), *asundeton* (which we saw in connection with brilliance), slight
variation (*exallagê*), *epanaphora* (which we saw in connection with
beauty), and others, will play a role in creating rapidity (314–317). This
form of style is only minimally connected with diction (312); Hermogenes does recommend the use of shorter rather than longer words (319).
As for word order, here hiatus should be especially avoided (319), since
hiatus will slow the speaker down. This was a practical issue, not only for
the orator delivering a spoken oration, but also for the ancient reader,
who typically (if not always) read aloud.[23] The rhythm of the prose should
be based on the trochee (– ∪)—appropriately enough, the "running"
foot (*trokhaios*, 319–320).

♦ In speaking of *ethos,* Hermogenes reminds us that oratory is, first and
foremost, an art of spoken language; only secondarily (by the function of
letteraturizzazione) do we investigate the rhetoricity of written texts. We
should keep in mind that this is not, however, a strictly modern phenomenon: while Hermogenes was himself apparently an orator of considerable power, he is also a connoisseur of the written text; born centuries after Demosthenes, he knows the latter's orations only because they
survived in published editions.

Ethos, then, can be conveyed in written discourse as well as in spo-

---

23. On reading in antiquity, see Balogh 1927, Hendrickson 1929, McCartney 1948, and
Knox 1968.

ken. The rhetor's good character, or *perceived* good character, was what Aristotle called "the most powerful mode of persuasion" (*Rhetoric* 1.2.4. 1356a 13). For Hermogenes, ethos means both "the revelation of character that necessarily appears throughout the whole speech" and "that which is naturally combined with the other styles" (321). It proceeds from a number of elements. "Simplicity" is similar in origin, diction, figures, and syntax to purity (322–329). "Sweetness" and grace are "intense forms of simplicity" (329). Sweetness is created by the use of mythical elements, the description of pleasures that are not shameful, amorous thoughts, personification, and the use of poetic dialect and epithets. It employs the figures characteristic of simplicity and purity, and the word order characteristic of beauty (330–339). "Subtlety" is an approach typical of simplicity (339). "Modesty" is mainly a product of thought, and "is created whenever anyone states that of his own free will he is aiming at less than he could attain," or when someone of great stature compares himself to someone of lowly rank; it may use the figure of purposeful omission (*paraleipsis*), or may cultivate an apparently simple, artless style (345–352).

◆ *Sincerity* is connected with speech that is *endiathetos*, "unaffected" or "spontaneous,"[24] but also with that which is *empsukhos*, "animated" (we might translate this "heartfelt"). Its subcategory of "indignation" (364–368) seems akin to this latter phenomenon. Sincerity is obviously a near relation of ethos, as is seen by the fact that Hermogenes points out its kinship to simplicity (352–353). The natural and quasi-spontaneous interjection of ideas, like the appearance of spontaneity in the expression of emotion, gives the effect of sincerity (354–359). For similar reasons, the use of rough or vehement diction may contribute to this stylistic effect. The figures that contribute to sincerity include apostrophe, perplexity (*diaporêsis*), self-interruption (*aposiôpêsis*), and self-correction (*epidiorthôsis*) (360–363). The syntax, word order, and prose rhythms that are typical of asperity are also useful in sincerity, unless one is attempting to arouse pity, in which case one would hew more closely to simplicity (363).

◆ *Force*—an attempt to translate the thoroughly untranslatable *deinotês*— is characterized by the proper use of the other six kinds of style: knowing what to do, and when. This term, *deinotês*, has a celebrated past:

24. *endiathetos*, from *en* + *diatithêmi* "arrange in," has in some contexts the meaning "innate" or "deep-seated."

deinos legein was a fifth/fourth-century colloquialism for being particularly skilled in rhetoric.[25] Literally *deinos* means "terrible," "fearsome" (as in "dinosaur," "terrible lizard"); today we use the words "terrific" and "awesome" with a colloquial force similar to that of *deinos* in classical Athens.

A forceful speech, according to Hermogenes, may or may not seem to be so (372). Pericles, the great Athenian leader, was forceful "because he used a certain kind of style when and as it should be used" (373). The thoughts that engender *deinotēs* may be paradoxical, profound, compelling, or cleverly contrived (373–374); stylistic approaches that create grandeur may also create force, but the figures, word order, and other elements appropriate here are those appropriate to solemnity, vigor, brilliance, and abundance (375). "And this, I think, is the essence of great and consummate knowledge: to know when to use an appropriate style and to be able to use it" (378).

𝑒

Six Memos for the Next Millennium is actually a set of five lectures on a group of related topics: Lightness, Quickness, Exactitude, Visibility, and Multiplicity. (Calvino died on 19 September 1985, before he could compose the sixth one, Consistency.) He calls each of these topics "values"[26] and imputes some virtue to each, but (as we shall see) in such a way that this imputation need not exclude the opposite value. It is worth working through his list, value by value, and remarking on each.

◆ *Lightness* came to have value for Calvino as a result of his own growth as a writer of fiction, when he found himself "becoming aware of the weight, the inertia, the opacity of the world. . . . I felt that the entire world was turning into stone" (4). But we are not to equate lightness simply with frivolity: "there is such a thing as a lightness of thoughtfulness, just as we all know that there is a lightness of frivolity. In fact, thoughtful lightness can make frivolity seem dull and heavy." Calvino suggests that "lightness" is a way of looking at the world based on phi-

---

25. See for example Sophocles *Oedipus the King* 545; Plato *Symposium* 198c, *Euthydemus* 304d, *Protagoras* 341a–b. The quality of *deinotēs* is discussed by Dionysius of Halicarnassus (*Thucydides* 23) and by Pseudo-Longinus (*On the Sublime* 12.4, 34.4); and the forceful (*deinos*) style is one the four praised by Demetrius (see especially *On Style* 240–301).

26. Calvino 1988:45. Esther Calvino reports, in her introductory "Note on the Text," that Calvino had toyed with some other titles, including the terms "Literary Values" and "Literary Legacies."

losophy and science, as mediated by the writer's art (10) His exemplars here are Ovid and, rather surprisingly, Lucretius:

> In both Lucretius and Ovid, lightness is a way of looking at the world based on philosophy and science: the doctrines of Epicurus for Lucretius and those of Pythagoras for Ovid (a Pythagoras who, as presented by Ovid, greatly resembles the Buddha). In both cases the lightness is also something arising from the writing itself, from the poet's own linguistic power, quite independent of whatever philosophic doctrine the poet claims to be following.[27]

Seen from this perspective, "lightness" calls to mind the *leggerezza* embraced by Aldo Palazzeschi in his philosophical program of *controdolore*,[28] and perhaps also Milan Kundera's *Unbearable Lightness of Being*. In connection with the latter, it is significant that Kundera has now also written a novel called *Slowness*.

Going on to discuss Italian literature, Calvino invokes Cavalcanti and Dante as representatives of two opposite literary tendencies: the former, of one that "tries to make language into a weightless element that hovers above things like a cloud"; the latter, one that "tries to give language the weight, density, and concreteness of things, bodies, and sensations" (15). Calvino cites a passage from Boccaccio which gives an anecdote about how Cavalcanti, the "austere philosopher," is set upon by the mischievous *jeunesse dorée* of Florence, who decide to pick a quarrel with him among the tombs along the Corso degli Adimari. Cavalcanti, surrounded, leaps nimbly over one of the great tombs and escapes. As Calvino remarks,

> What strikes me most is the visual scene evoked by Boccaccio, of Cavalcanti freeing himself with a leap "sí come colui che leggerissimo era," a man very light in body.
>
> Were I to choose an auspicious image for the new millennium, I would choose that one: the sudden agile leap of the poet-philosopher who raises himself above the weight of the world, showing that with all his gravity he has the secret of lightness, and that what many consider to be the vitality of the times—noisy, aggressive, revving and roaring—belongs to the realm of death, like a cemetery for rusty old cars.[29]

27. Calvino 1988:10.
28. On Palazzeschi and *leggerezza,* see Tamburri 1990, especially 143–146.
29. Calvino 1988:12.

Dante, of course, if I may paraphrase Quintilian on Cicero, is the name, not of a man, but of eloquence.[30] There is certainly no other single writer who can challenge his primacy as the embodied voice of Italian culture, at least in poetry. No poet has ever attained such primacy without what the Greeks called *ogkos,* the Romans *grauitas*—that is, the weightiness that lends dignity. For Calvino, then, Dante plays Prospero to Cavalcanti's Ariel:

> When Dante wants to express lightness, even in the *Divina Commedia,* no one can do it better than he does, but his real genius lies in the opposite direction—in extracting all the possibilities of sound and emotion and feeling from the language, in capturing the world in verse at all its various levels, in all its forms and attributes, in transmitting the sense that the world is organized into a system, an order, or a hierarchy where everything has its place. To push this contrast perhaps too far, I might say that Dante gives solidity even to the most abstract intellectual speculation, whereas Cavalcanti dissolves the concreteness of tangible experience in lines of measured rhythm, syllable by syllable, as if thought were darting out of darkness in swift lightning flashes.[31]

◆ *Quickness* is recommended as a thing of intrinsic beauty. Here Calvino begins with a brief legend of Charlemagne, told by the French romantic writer Jules Barbey d'Aurevilly, which is notable not only for its terseness but (within that) for its thematic coherence around a single motif, a magic ring, "a series of events that echo each other as rhymes do in a poem" (35). Here we learn what it was that most drew Calvino to the traditional folktale in his making of the *Fiabe italiane:* it was not, he says, loyalty to an ethnic tradition, or nostalgia for the literature of his childhood, but rather "because of my interest in style and structure, in the economy, rhythm, and hard logic with which they are told. In working on my transcription of Italian folktales as recorded by scholars of the last century, I found most enjoyment when the original text was extremely laconic" (35–36). This recollection induces him to make some observations on the relativity of narrative time to actual time—a topic studied at length by Gérard Genette in his *Narrative Discourse.*[32]

To help explain the beauty of quickness, Calvino borrows from the

---

30. Quintilian 10.1.112: *non hominis nomen sed eloquentiae.*
31. Calvino 1988:16.
32. Genette 1980 (see in particular chaps. 1–3: "Order," "Duration," and "Frequency").

Zibaldone di pensieri of Leopardi: "Speed . . . is most pleasurable in itself; that is, for the vivacity, the energy, the strength, the sheer life of such a feeling. Indeed it almost gives you an idea of the infinite—elevates the soul, fortifies it" (41). The idea of strength is central here: the virtue of quickness in literature entails not simply brevity but also a kind of grace. Calvino himself goes on to say that

> mental speed cannot be measured and does not allow comparisons or competitions; nor can it display its results in a historical perspective. Mental speed is valuable for its own sake, for the pleasure it gives to anyone who is sensitive to such a thing, and not for the practical use that can be made of it. A swift piece of reasoning is not necessarily better than a long-pondered one. Far from it. But it communicates something special that is derived simply from its very swiftness. . . . Quickness of style and thought means above all agility, mobility, and ease." (45–46)

Calvino's emblem for this virtue is the Roman god Mercury. But he recognizes that this principle implies its opposite, which we might term deliberateness, and which he personifies in the god Vulcan: "Implicit in my tribute to lightness was my respect for weight, and so this apologia for quickness does not presume to deny the pleasures of lingering" (45–46). For Calvino, Mercury and Vulcan represent the two inseparable and complementary functions of life: "Mercury represents *syntony,* or participation in the world around us; Vulcan, *focalization* or constructive concentration" (53). Under the circumstances, it is probably no coincidence that "focalization" is a technical term used by narratologists to designate "the perspective in terms of which the narrated situations and events are presented; the perceptual or conceptual position in terms of which they are rendered."[33] In his narratological observations on time, under the sign of Vulcan, Calvino comments among other things on strategies of repetition and of digression as ways of *slowing down time* in the text.

The chapter ends with a Chinese tale that embodies, in a single marvelous stroke, the principles both of deliberateness and of quickness:

> Among Chuang-tzu's many skills, he was an expert draftsman. The king asked him to draw a crab. Chuang-tzu replied that he needed five years, a country house, and twelve servants. Five years later the drawing was still not begun. "I need another five years," said Chuang-tzu. The king granted them. At the end of these ten

---

33. Prince 1987:31, s.v. "focalization." See also Genette 1980:189–194; Bal 1985:100–118.

years, Chuang-tzu took up his brush and, in an instant, with a
single stroke, he drew a crab, the most perfect crab ever seen.[34]

♦ In the chapter on *exactitude,* as in the previous one, Calvino employs
the medium as part of the message; that is, he begins by attempting a
precise definition of literary exactitude, subdivided under three headings:
first, the precise planning of the work in question; second, the evocation
of clear, incisive, memorable visual images; and third, precision of language. This precise categorization of ideas was called by the Greek rhetoricians and philosophers *diairesis,* "division"; by the Romans, *partitio*
or "partition." In the case of exactitude, as with lightness, Calvino's
own apperceptions have troubled him, and he expresses his misgivings in
memorable metaphors: as he "felt that the entire world was turning into
stone," so too he fears that

> a pestilence has struck the human race in its most distinctive
> faculty—that is, the use of words. It is a plague afflicting lan-
> guage, revealing itself as a loss of cognition and immediacy, an
> automatism that tends to level out all expression into the most
> generic, anonymous, and abstract formulas, to dilute meanings, to
> blunt the edge of expressiveness.[35]

Only literature, it seems, can cure this linguistic plague, and in literature,
exactitude is a powerful antidote. Even the rhetorical effect of *il vago,*
which in Italian can mean not only "vague" but also "lovely," "attractive," turns out to depend upon "a highly exact and meticulous attention
to the composition of each image, to the minute definition of details, to
the choice of objects, to the lighting and the atmosphere, all in order to
attain the desired degree of vagueness" (59–60). Art, in such a case, con-
ceals art.

This virtue of exactitude appeals to Calvino as the common goal of
two different types of knowledge: one is the exploration of "the mental
space of bodiless rationality," that is, by theoretical abstraction; the other
path "goes through a space crammed with objects and attempts to create
a verbal equivalent of that space by filling the page with words, involving
a most careful painstaking effort" (74). It is a measure of Calvino's own
formidable powers in this chapter that he makes considerable progress in
both these directions, without sacrificing his own lightness or quickness
in the process.

34. Calvino 1988 : 54. For more on Chuang-tzu, see, e.g., Watson 1968, Palmer et al. 1996.
35. Calvino 1988 : 56.

◆ With *visibility* we come to the genesis of images, of imag/ination itself. Here Calvino is concerned not only with how an artistic project is conceived of by the artist, but also with how it is received by the audience. He sketches out, in its briefest contours, a semiotics of imagination: "We may distinguish between two types of imaginative process: the one that starts with the word and arrives at the visual image, and the one that starts with the visual image and arrives at its verbal expression" (83). These, of course, are the mechanisms at work in the typical rhetorical schema of rhetor/logos/audience, a schema that is (as Calvino knows) applicable to literature and even to cinema.[36] For the artist, Calvino surmises, visual imagination precedes verbal expression (86); he corroborates this from his own experience as a writer:

> In devising a story, therefore, the first thing that comes to my mind is an image that for some reason strikes me as charged with meaning, even if I cannot formulate this meaning in discursive or conceptual terms. As soon as the image has become sufficiently clear in my mind, I set about developing it into a story; or better yet, it is the images themselves that develop their own implicit potentialities, the story they carry within them. Around each image others come into being, forming a field of analogies, symmetries, confrontations.[37]

In discussing the stimulation of the imagination of the audience (or reader), we are on ground well trodden by the classical rhetoricians; it was traditionally called *enargeia* (or *phantasia*) in Greek, *euidentia* in Latin.[38] In book 3 of the *Rhetoric*, Aristotle discusses what he calls *pro ommatôn poiein*, or "bringing before the [audience's] eyes": this, like metaphor, is a source of *asteia*, or "urbanity," and is to be used in oratory to trigger a cognitive link for the audience—to promote understanding.[39]

In the creation of fiction, as in oratory, the artist strives to bring the audience not simply to understand a concept—if that were the only requirement, exactitude might fill the bill—but at times *to see an image just as the artist sees it*. As with other values that he fears are threatened, in the case of visibility as well Calvino feels constrained to speak in terms of a

---

36. Just how this may be so is considered at length in Kirby 1992b.

37. Calvino 1988:88–89.

38. *Enargeia:* Hermogenes 343; *phantasia: On the Sublime* 15. The fullest treatment in Latin (under the name *euidentia*) is in Quintilian 4.2.63, 6.2.32, 8.3.61. I suspect it is not by chance that Calvino begins his chapter with a discussion of *fantasy*.

39. *Rhetoric* 3.10–11, 1410b–1411b. On Aristotelian *asteia,* and metaphor in particular, see Kirby 1997a.

"value to be saved," so as "to give warning of the danger we run in losing a basic human faculty: the power of bringing visions into focus with our eyes shut, of bringing forth forms and colors from the lines of black letters on a white page, and in fact of *thinking* in terms of images" (92, emphasis in text). In response to this danger, he envisions a "pedagogy of the imagination" that will protect this fundamental human faculty (92). And the skilled writer must understand what is visible, not only to the audience, but also to the fictional characters:

> The poet has to imagine visually both what his actor sees and what he thinks he sees, what he dreams, what he remembers, what he sees represented, or what is told to him, just as he has to imagine the visual content of the metaphors he uses to facilitate this process of visual evocation. (82–83)

In our own imaginative memories we might recur to Sophocles' figure of Tiresias, the visionary who—even in his blindness—sees what truly needs to be seen.

◆ *Multiplicity* in the textual sense is, as one might imagine, multiple in kind:

> There is such a thing as the unified text that is written as the expression of a single voice, but that reveals itself as open to interpretation on several levels. . . . there is the manifold text . . . on the model of what Mikhail Bakhtin has called the "dialogic" or "polyphonic" . . . There is the type of work that, in the attempt to contain everything possible, does not manage to take on a form, to create outlines for itself, and so remains incomplete by its very nature. . . . There is the type of work that in literature corresponds to what in philosophy is nonsystematic thought, which proceeds by aphorisms, by sudden, discontinuous flashes of light. (117–118)

Stylistically speaking, all this is akin to Hermogenes' concept of abundance, which is discussed under the heading of grandeur.[40] Roman rhetoricians termed this *copia,* and spoke in terms both of *copia rerum,* "abundance of topics" or fecundity of imagination; and of *copia uerborum,* that "abundance of words" which results in ease and eloquence of expression.

But the principle of multiplicity has its most far-reaching implications in the kind of metaphysics espoused by thinkers such as Carlo Emilio Gadda, whose view of the world as a "system of systems" is adduced by

40. See Hermogenes 277–296.

Calvino. Such a view, which Calvino labels "encyclopedism" (106), seeks "to represent the world as a knot, a tangled skein of yarn; to represent it without in the least diminishing the inextricable complexity or, to put it better, the simultaneous presence of the most disparate elements that converge to determine every event" (106). Literature, then, is to be set the task of "weaving together the various branches of knowledge, the various 'codes,' into a manifold and multifaceted vision of the world" (112).

č̃

These five "values" are, I suggest, all values one would first and foremost prescribe for the dancer: lightness, quickness, exactitude, are all crucial if one is to achieve what is called "grace" in dance; visibility is, of course, central to any event of stage performance; and multiplicity, as Calvino sketches it out, is the faculty of drawing the many into the one—no less important for the compelling performance. It is interesting that the same Greek word, *skhêmata,* was used to refer both to the various figures of a dance and to the configurations of language in prosody, diction, and thought.[41]

In light of the principle of multiplicity, one would like to see what Calvino would have done with *consistency,* the sixth, unwritten memo. I would not be surprised to find that he had conceived of it as something of a counterbalance, an anchor to the barque of multiplicity; for the very possibility of valorizing such "literary values" as he has enumerated here depends from a kind of consistency. But I shall have further speculation to offer about this sixth memo shortly—an attempted (re)construction of what position Calvino might have taken on consistency in his sixth lecture, had he lived to complete it.

č̃

It should immediately be clear that Calvino's work has a close kinship with that of Hermogenes: they are both rhetorical treatises enumerating and elaborating various aspects of style in formal language. Moreover, in certain instances they are treating identical topics. There are, by the same token, some differences between them, subtle as well as obvious, and these demonstrate inevitably that Calvino, like Hermogenes—like all of us—is a child of his age.

41. Dance: Aristophanes *Peace* 323, *Wasps* 1485; Euripides *Cyclops* 221; Xenophon *Symposium* 7.5. (Isocrates 15.183 refers to the exercise routines of athletic training as *skhêmata.*) Language: Plato *Ion* 536c; Aristotle *Rhetoric* 1401a, 1410b; Cicero *Brutus* 141; Quintilian 9.1.11.

I spoke earlier of the phenomenon of *letteraturizzazione*. To a certain extent, one is inclined to consider Hermogenes' (postclassical) treatise historically in light of this tendency. Yet it is not that Hermogenes' system takes no account whatever of invention; on the contrary, he regularly mentions the "thoughts" that are appropriate to this or that style. On the whole, however, the purpose of the treatise is undeniably to focus on style per se.[42] Calvino's work, on the other hand, seems to hover between questions of style and those of invention—as if, for the new millennium, he wants to urge an emphasis different from that of the age we are leaving behind, one in fact closer to the older (classical) values that gave the palm to invention.[43] As for the oral/written dichotomy, this was already an issue in Hermogenes' own time—the contrast between oral discourse and the written text. But I find it especially ironic that Hermogenes presents his ideas in written form, for training in oration, while Calvino intended first to present his ideas in oral form, as observations on writing.

Calvino's work is, in a sense, like the salmon swimming upstream: in an adventurous mood, one might term it *antiletteraturizzazione,* an endeavor to undo the effects of this slippage. Over and over again he insists upon the intricate connection of style with invention. See, for example, his remarks on Cavalcanti: "there is a lightening of language whereby meaning is conveyed through a verbal texture that seems weightless, until the meaning itself takes on the same rarefied consistency" (16). And this should not surprise us, because he conceives of literary invention as itself intricately connected with the profoundest of cognitive and philosophical formulations: "There remains one thread, the one I first started to unwind: that of literature as an existential function, the search for lightness as a reaction to the weight of living. . . . I am accustomed to consider literature a search for knowledge" (26). Time and again he intimates that his agenda are not merely stylistic but inventional and indeed metaphysical:

> This talk is refusing to be led in the direction I set myself. I began by speaking of exactitude, not of the infinite and the cosmos. . . .
> I think that this bond between the formal choices of literary composition and the need for a cosmological model (or else for a general mythological framework) is present even in those authors who do not explicitly declare it. (68–69)

---

42. Elsewhere Hermogenes concentrated squarely on invention. The extant *On Invention* attributed to Hermogenes may be spurious: see Wooten 1987:xi; Drury 1985:860. Kennedy 1983:102 dates it tentatively to the fourth century C.E. But the *On Staseis,* now well presented in Heath 1995, is certainly authentic, and stasis theory is a matter of invention.

43. He is not alone in this: I think particularly of the work of Chaim Perelman.

And so rhetoric and philosophy, those quarrelsome siblings, are once again inevitably brought face to face. They have had a long, scrappy history together, ever since Plato's Socrates expressed his complicated (and possibly ironic) attitudes toward rhetoric.[44] In the Greek-speaking world, the quarrel goes back further than Plato; the elder sophists, who (along with other Presocratic thinkers) helped to begin the systematization of philosophic discourse, were also (as we saw earlier) the first to systematize the teaching of rhetoric. As this phenomenon began to spread on the Greek mainland, it soon provoked questions about its use: What is the nature of language to reality? and What are the right and wrong uses of persuasive communication? Plato himself offers some provocative answers to both these questions; the dialogue is picked up by Isocrates, Aristotle, the Stoics, and later philosophers as well.[45]

Six Memos likewise requires that we face the metaphysical and ethical issues raised by the uses of literature: Calvino, aware of the perils of a liminal time such as our era, speaks (as we saw) of values "to be saved," and of the human faculty of "bringing visions into focus with our eyes shut . . . of *thinking* in terms of images" (92). Rhetors and audiences need such a faculty too; that is what underlies the use, in oratory, of *êthopoiïa*—the rhetor's projection to the audience of a character that is realistic, plausible, and trustworthy.[46] Thus the issue of focus, of imaginal thought, is of crucial importance for all art that is readily seen as mimetic—but also for occasions of oratory. Just what is mimesis? How shall we situate such a phenomenon in our "postmodern" world? Is it a second-order phenomenon, less real than reality, or ought the mimetic to be considered as real as the rest of the world around us?

Postmodernism is defined by Calvino as "the tendency to make ironic use of the stock images of the mass media, or to inject the taste for the marvelous inherited from literary tradition into narrative mechanisms

---

44. The reader who is interested in this fascinating treatment should at least read Plato's *Gorgias, Symposium,* and *Phaedrus.* But he has much else to say about rhetoric in the other dialogues as well.

45. Of ancient thinkers, it is Aristotle who provides the most thoroughgoing treatment of the issue, building (as I think) on the foundation laid by Plato for a philosophical rhetoric. His answers to these questions have certainly not satisfied everyone, which is partly why the quarrel continues to this day. On the quest for a philosophical rhetoric in antiquity, see, e.g., Kennedy 1999:53–97; more recent thinkers, such as Vico, Nietzsche, Ivor Richards, Kenneth Burke, Foucault, de Man, and Derrida, have revisited the same ground, sometimes asking the same questions in different ways, but not (in my opinion) providing more definitive answers.

46. Significantly, formal orations in ancient Greece were often ghostwritten by professional *logographoi* (speechwriters). Their work was in this respect closely parallel to what we might term the writing of fiction, since theirs was the charge of crafting êthos for another person to project when the oration was actually delivered. For more on this, see Kirby 1991a:200–203.

that accentuate its alienation" (95). We have left behind the more ingenuous epoch where such irony was not universal; in oratorical situations now we find ourselves ineluctably haunted by the discrepancy between seeming and being: what of an orator that embodies the Hermogenic principles of sincerity or modesty? Is she indeed sincere or modest, or is this empty mimesis, the merest figment and masquerade? If, as Calvino says, "all 'realities' and 'fantasies' can take on form only by means of writing" (99), then we need to consider the extent to which the orator, by virtue of speaking, inscribes a "reality"—or indeed a "fantasy"—onto the rhetorical situation. In our oral communication, as well as on our literary pages, these issues take on a far-reaching significance.

℮

As a kind of frontispiece to *Six Memos* is added the photograph of a sheet of paper with a handwritten list of the five lecture titles; the sixth is there too, ever so faintly—literally "under erasure"—and this is most fitting for the work of a child of the postmodern era, the age of the *opera aperta,* a man who knew intimately the boundaries of determinacy.[47]

It is a poignant coincidence, in fact, that this sixth, unwritten lecture was to have been on the topic of consistency. We live in a time that reminds us, more acutely than ever before, of the deep truth of Heraclitus, that all is in flux. In fact this becomes for us one of the hallmarks of life itself, to such an extent that the change *is* the consistency. While Calvino did not complete his memo on consistency, he did leave behind, in his fiction, some provocative observations on the topic:

> So here you are now, ready to attack the first lines of the first page. You prepare to recognize the unmistakable tone of the author. No. You don't recognize it at all. But now that you think about it, who ever said this author had an unmistakable tone? On the contrary, he is known as an author who changes greatly from one book to the next. And in these very changes you recognize him as himself.[48]

47. I am invoking, of course, the title of Umberto Eco's *Opera aperta;* the English edition (Eco 1989) is a partial translation of this but includes a good deal of other material as well. In Calvino's own work, see *If on a Winter's Night a Traveler* (Calvino 1981), whose very table of contents—not to mention its remarkable opening chapter—invites the reader to relate to the book in a variety of ways, as with Julio Cortázar's *Rayuela.* Each different act of reading virtually transmogrifies the work into a different novel. On the way in which the grammatical person of the narrator contributes to this openness in Calvino's novel, see Kirby 1992b.

48. Calvino 1981:9.

It may well seem that, in the strict sense, the only consistency in human life is to be found in death. In that sense Calvino left his sixth memo unwritten on the page, but composed it in his own passing in 1985. Here again we may turn to his fictional work:

> for Mr. Palomar being dead means resigning himself to remaining the same in a definitive state, which he can no longer hope to change. . . . This is the most difficult step in learning how to be dead: to become convinced that your own life is a closed whole, all in the past, to which you can add nothing and can alter none of the relationships among the various elements.[49]

Yet I wonder whether Calvino himself quite subscribed to this notion. Mr. Palomar is a notoriously tentative character; his most endearing quality is his penchant for musing, for contemplation, for rumination (or, put another way, his most maddening quirk is his tendency to vacillate, to equivocate, even to prevaricate). So it is not entirely surprising to read, in the same chapter, the following:

> The wave strikes the cliff and hollows out the rock, another wave arrives, another, and still another; whether he is or is not, everything goes on happening. The relief in being dead should be this: having eliminated that patch of uneasiness that is our presence, the only thing that matters is the extension and succession of things under the sun, in their impassive serenity. All is calm or tends toward calm, even hurricanes, earthquakes, the eruption of volcanoes. But was this not the earlier world, when he was in it? When every storm bore within itself the peace of afterward, prepared the moment when all the waves would have struck the shore, and the wind would have spent its force? Perhaps being dead is passing into the ocean of the waves that remain waves forever, so it is futile to wait for the sea to become calm.[50]

If this new perspective be seriously entertained, the whole traditional contrast between life and death may be turned inside out: the immemorial Western notions of life-as-change and death-as-fixity begin to slip, to blur, to metamorphose, both of them suffused with the luminosity characteristic of Calvino's writing.

49. Calvino 1985:124–125.
50. Calvino 1985:122.

The Revestiture of Myth

❧

Roberto Calasso's *The Marriage of Cadmus and Harmony*

Tutto si ripete, tutto ritorna, ma sempre
con qualche lieve torsione del significato.
—Roberto Calasso, *Le nozze di Cadmo e Armonia*

"[W]e enter the mythical when we enter the realm of risk, and myth is the enchantment we generate in ourselves at such moments. More than a belief, it is a magical bond that tightens around us. It is a spell the soul casts on itself. . . . In Greece, myth escapes from ritual like a genie from a bottle. Ritual is tied to gesture, and gestures are limited: what else can you do once you've burned your offerings, poured your libations, bowed, greased yourself, competed in races, eaten, copulated? But if the stories start to become independent, to develop names and relationships, then one day you realize that they have taken on a life of their own." [1]

I would give a great deal to have written those words myself. But they come in fact from Roberto Calasso's *The Marriage of Cadmus and Harmony*. By the time I put my hands on this book—originally published in 1988 in Italian as *Le nozze di Cadmo e Armonia*—it had already been translated into twelve languages. And not only this, but the publisher's

---

1. Calasso 1993:279. Hereafter, citations from this translation will typically be indicated by page number only, in the body of the text.

blurbs, taken from various book reviews, were comparing Calasso not
to scholars of mythology,[2] like Robert Graves or Joseph Campbell, but to
such ancient authors as Pindar, Euripides, and (especially) Ovid. Publisher's blurbs are, of course, notorious for their hyperbole—so much so
that one takes them with a grain of salt, if at all. Naturally, then, I was
initially suspicious at reading such extravagant accolades of Calasso. But
it was not long before Calasso's own stories began to take on, to use his
phrase, a life of their own for me. I surmise that most readers of *The
Marriage of Cadmus and Harmony* will have a similar experience.

In this chapter I want to assess a number of major aspects of this remarkable book, including the question of its genre, its treatment of the
concept of *the classical,* and its treatment of the concept of myth. Both
these latter ideas seem to have entranced Calasso in writing *The Marriage
of Cadmus and Harmony;* and I hope that in the course of my analysis,
some impression of the book's overall contours will emerge here. In addition, I want to discuss some of the explicitly semiotic observations that
Calasso includes in his text.

℃

Calasso is hardly bound by, or solely devoted to, the retelling of ancient
stories. He allows himself a remarkable degree of elbowroom for his
own philosophical speculation (and I use the term "philosophical" here
in a very loose sense: namely, to include every venue of intellectual
investigation), much more so than fiction writers have traditionally
been wont to do. And this fact raises the pressing issue of genre: how
are we to classify this work? No category immediately presents itself. It
is certainly not nonfiction in the normal sense of that word, since so
much of it retells the stories of the mythic and legendary past.[3] For the
same reason one would be hard put to classify it as an essay. But it is also
not fiction as the latter is typically conceived. It is not a work of philosophy in any traditional sense—not even, in fact, in such nontraditional
senses as those in which one might characterize as "philosophical" the
aphoristic collections of Nietzsche, or the historical/anthropological

2. As in my distinction between "semiosis" and "semiotics," I will endeavor in this chapter
to distinguish between "myth" and "mythology"—reserving the latter term to designate "the
study of myth." By "mythography" I mean the process of committing a myth to specific form,
typically written.

3. On the technical distinction (not always observed) between "myth" and "legend," see
above, chap. 1, n. 4.

investigations of Foucault. It is not verse, nor is it drama of any conventional kind.[4]

For all these reasons I am tempted to suggest a new category, one that I would like to call *critical fiction*. By "critical fiction" I do not quite intend what in current literary theory we call *metafiction,* in which the narrative consistently, purposefully, and for its own sake draws attention to the narrating process, although it might considered to be akin to that; in fact, we might properly consider some metafiction to be a species of the genus critical fiction.[5] Nor is critical fiction exactly the same type of reach toward the factual, the precarious situating of fictional characters in historical situations, that one finds in historical fiction. Critical fiction is a more purely self-reflexive and self-conscious kind of fiction, and also a kind of fiction in which the ordinary or hitherto time-honored rules of fiction seem not to apply. Traditional fictional narrative presents, in mimetic format,[6] a set (or several sets) of characters acting and speaking along the trajectory of a more or less unified course of events that we call a "plot." In such a traditional setup, the narration of these events is the primary focus and concern of the narrator, and narratorial observations are relegated to a minor role, if not completely eclipsed.[7] In critical fiction, by contrast, there is a disproportionately large space reserved for the kind of quasi-philosophical speculation that I have already mentioned; so much so, in fact, that at times—far from restricting such observations to a demure parenthesis—such speculation seems actually to assume the foreground. This phenomenon, the distinguishing hallmark of critical fiction, I designate the *critical aside.* Consider, for example, the following passages by Milan Kundera:

4. The unusual nature of Calasso's writing has provoked other, sometimes unfavorable, assessments. See, for example, André Aciman's review of Calasso 1994 (the original Italian of which was published five years before *Le nozze di Cadmo e Armonia,* although it was not published in English translation until a year after *The Marriage of Cadmus and Harmony*): "It is a difficult book, digressive, arcane, exhausting, seemingly senseless, perhaps totally senseless, spinning a vertiginously disjointed tale made up of scattered fragments stitched to numberless quotations and *faits divers,* ultimately leaving its reader as baffled and breathless as Schliemann must have felt on finally realizing that, without knowing it, he had dug a hole in King Priam's bathtub" (Aciman 1995:32). But some people find Ovid's poetry infuriating too.

5. On metafiction see especially Waugh 1984. For examples of metafiction in this sense, see, e.g., the creative works of Barth 1968, Pynchon 1973, Calvino 1981, and (not for the faint of heart) Ridley 1988.

6. I use the word "mimetic" in a consciously Aristotelian sense; on the topic see Kirby 1991b.

7. Kinds and degrees of narratorial invention in more conventional fiction are exhaustively investigated by Genette 1980.

I think, therefore I am is the statement of an intellectual who under-rates toothaches. *I feel, therefore I am* is a truth much more universally valid, and it applies to everything that's alive. My self does not differ substantially from yours in terms of its thought. Many people, few ideas: we all think more or less the same, and we exchange, borrow, steal thoughts from one another. However, when someone steps on my foot, only I feel the pain. The basis of the self is not thought but suffering, which is the most fundamental of all feelings. . . . . Suffering is the university of egocentrism.[8]

Unlike Parmenides, Beethoven apparently viewed weight as something positive. Since the German word *schwer* means both "difficult" and "heavy." Beethoven's "difficult resolution" may also be construed as a "heavy" or "weighty" resolution. The weighty resolution is at one with the voice of Fate (*"Es muss sein!"*); necessity, weight, and value are three concepts inextricably bound; only necessity is heavy, and only what is heavy has value.[9]

In both these and numerous other passages interspersed in his fiction, Kundera interrupts the flow of his main narrative to make observations of the sort I have been discussing. Such asides are different in kind from the typical textual matter that distinguishes ordinary metafiction, which is designed specifically to call attention to the narrative process itself—to the textuality of the text, one might say. A prime example of the latter would be the opening paragraphs of Calvino's *If on a Winter's Night a Traveler.*[10] The critical aside, by contrast, although it cannot help but draw some attention to its qualitative disparity from ordinary plot-advancing narrative, is included precisely because the author wants to discuss the material it presents, and to discuss it there. As such, of course, it cannot fail to highlight the presence of the narrator in the text (what Benveniste calls "discours" as opposed to "histoire").[11]

Calasso is a master of the critical aside. An example, chosen almost at random, is the following:

Behind what the Greeks called *eídôlon,* which is at once the idol, the statue, the simulacrum, the phantom, lies the mental image.

---

8. Kundera 1991:200.
9. Kundera 1984:33.
10. Those paragraphs, and the nature of their textuality, are discussed in Kirby 1992b: 10–12.
11. See Benveniste 1971: 205–215.

This fanciful and insubstantial creature imitates the world and at the same time subjects it to *a frenzy of different combinations, confounding its forms in inexhaustible proliferation*. It emanates a prodigious strength, our awe in the face of what we see in the invisible. It has all the features of the arbitrary, of what is born in the dark, from formlessness, the way our world was perhaps once born. But this time the chaos is the vast shadowy canvas that lies behind our eyes and on which phosphenic patterns constantly merge and fade. Such constant formation of images occurs in each one of us in every instant. But these are not the only peculiarities of the phenomenon. *When the phantom, the mental image, takes over our minds, when it begins to join with other similar or alien figures, then little by little it fills the whole space of the mind in an ever more detailed and ever richer concatenation.* What initially presented itself as the prodigy of appearance, cut off from everything, *is now linked, from one phantom to another, to everything.* (133, emphasis added) [12]

Traditional classical mythography offers nothing like this; nor does typical modern mythology. Part metaphysical postulation, part epistemological rumination, this paragraph taps into postmodern discourse (one thinks especially of Baudrillard) [13] with its discussion of the simulacrum (*simulacro*), on its way to what turns out to be a discussion of phenomenology and indeed of semiotics. Calasso's designation of the simulacrum as "arbitrary" is a direct legacy of Saussurean semiology, and readers who remember from chapters 1 and 2 my discussion of Peircean unlimited semiosis will notice the resonance with that in the portions I have italicized.

Other critical asides will offer philological and antiquarian data of the sort one would most expect to find in a literary commentary: "In [Euripides'] *Iphigenia in Aulis* we are hammered time after time with the verb *kteínein*, 'to kill,' while *thúein*, 'to sacrifice,' is used only rarely, the distance between the two being spanned by *spházein*, 'to slit a throat'" (107). Still others offer information of the historical or anthropological variety:

There is an object that represents one of the highest peaks of civilization, with respect to which all others we are familiar with are but watered down derivatives: the bronze caldron. In the China of the Shang dynasty it became the cult object around which

---

12. This passage is, among other things, a notable example of the unusually free hand given Calasso's translator, Tim Parks. The totality of Calasso's first sentence here is "All'origine del simulacro è l'immagine mentale."

13. See, e.g., Baudrillard 1983, Poster 1988. Baudrillard's notion of *hyperreality* in turn suggests Umberto Eco, which in turn brings us around to semiotics.

people's lives revolved. . . . It was then that the sacred vessel was
given a certain number of canonical forms (how many is still a
matter of debate). . . . In Doric Greece, the caldron was made in
just the one dominant form: the tripod. (150)

One has been trained to be wary of positing an identity between author and narrator, but because of the interruption of the narrative by the
critical aside—or, perhaps one should say, because of the way the narrative portions are interwoven with critical asides—the reader feels that the
author is very present in the text.[14] That is certainly the case in *The Marriage of Cadmus and Harmony*. Indeed one could almost believe at times
that Calasso's retelling of these myths was merely a vehicle for his philosophical musings. I would be tempted to say so, but it is the very raptur-
ous power and beauty of his narrative that convince me that he must have
taken great delight in retelling them for their own sake.

The Marriage of Cadmus and Harmony is by no means a conventional
work of classical scholarship. One of the particularly remarkable things
about Calasso is that he does not work as a professional classicist, but
rather as a publisher (indeed he has published the original Italian editions of his own books).[15] In view of this, the depth of his erudition
is sometimes breathtaking. Moreover, it is the rare professional scholar
who, at the end of the twentieth century, can traverse well-trodden literary ground and still find original, interesting, and important things to
say—and to say them in a fashion that might fairly be described as provocative or even gripping. But such is the case with Calasso. Take, for
example, his treatment of the Oedipus legend.[16] If I do not reproduce it
here, it is in the hope that my reader will be thereby enticed to search it
out for herself. I will, however, go so far as to say that one may dally with
Freud, parry with Lacan, speculate with Deleuze and Guattari, ruminate
with René Girard, and entertain the theories of scores of other scholars
and critics who presume to pronounce on the meaning of Oedipus, without finding scholarly work more original or memorable than these two
or three pages of Calasso.

When Calasso shifts into his analytic mode, he can be almost Aristotelian in the precision of his taxonomies. For example, when he is discussing the nature of the dealings between gods and mortals, he divides it

14. On the author as *scriptor*, see Kirby 1992b.
15. See Calasso 1983, 1988, 1996—the first three of "a projected series of five books . . .
which traces the birth of 'the Modern' out of the collapse of the classical world" (Banville
1999:16).
16. Calasso 1993:343–345 (= Calasso 1988:384–385).

into two categories: what he calls *hierogamy* and *sacrifice*. He takes the word "hierogamy" (Italian *ierogamia*) from the Greek term *hieros gamos*, the sacred marriage, which we usually find used to designate a ritual act where a human being is symbolically wedded to a god, typically in order to insure the fertility of the crops or the like. By the term "hierogamy" Calasso himself means the actual marriage between a god and a mortal, such as Zeus and Semele, or Aphrodite and Adonis. He categorizes hierogamy and sacrifice according to a calculus that reminds us of Freud's Eros and Thanatos: hierogamy, then, symbolizes, or epitomizes, passion, desire—everything that Eros is meant to entail, whereas sacrifice of course embodies Thanatos, the drive toward death. And Calasso subdivides sacrifice further still, under the headings of expulsion and assimilation. He says: "For all the variegated multiplicity of its forms, the practice of sacrifice can be reduced to just two gestures: expulsion . . . and assimilation" (291–292). *Expulsion* is itself further glossed as having to do with *purification*—people expel, that is, in order to purify—and *assimilation* is glossed as having to do with *communion:* in other words, we assimilate into our own bodies the body of the sacrificial victim. I imagine he also has in mind the notion that when assimilation is practiced by a group, it offers the opportunity for *communion* to the sacrificial *community* (seen most notably in our era in the Christian celebration of the Eucharist). Then he goes on to ask whether it might be a mistake—an "ancient misnomer," as he calls it (292)—to designate both these rituals—the ritual of expulsion and the ritual of assimilation—as *sacrifice*. "So it might seem," he says,

> at least until awareness of another phenomenon behind the two gestures brings them right back together again: hierogamy. Yet hierogamy does not involve any element of destruction, the one thing that kept the two extreme gestures of sacrifice together. How can we explain this? Hierogamy is the premise of sacrifice, but on the part of the gods. It is that first mixing of the two worlds, divine and human, to which sacrifice attempts to respond, but with a response that is merely human, the response of creatures living in the realm of the irreversible, creatures who cannot assimilate (or expel) without killing. To the erotic invasion of our bodies, we reply with the knife that slashes the throat, the hand that hurls the stone. (292)

At one point Calasso offers a most provocative definition: his answer to the age-old question "What is the classical?" This is not quite the same as asking, "What is a classic?," a question to which I shall return briefly at the end of this book. It is my sense that when we speak of the classical, in (for example) art or architecture, we are primarily offering an assessment of style. Here is what we are told in *The Marriage of Cadmus and Harmony:* "Looking at Athena, her breast fringed with snakes, her clear-cut mono-chrome face, we get a sense of what the classical is: a hybrid between the barbaric and the neoclassical" (243). It is very like Calasso to go for the theoretical jugular here, and not to shrink from addressing the big issues, but somehow this definition seems not quite satisfactory. It is clever, and what is more, it is thoughtful; but in the end, it seems to raise more questions than it answers. For to pit the classical against itself—or against its avatar, the neoclassical—is a classic case (if I may so express myself) of what the logicians used to call *petitio principii,* "begging the question." In its most literal sense, *petitio principii* means the quest, or request, for a beginning—that is, a search for a "square one" from which to begin a line of argument. Defined as an error of logic, however, begging the question means that one has assumed as a premise what needs to be made a conclusion—one has assumed as already proven the very thing one needs to prove. And as far as I can see, Calasso nowhere in *The Mar-riage of Cadmus and Harmony* offers any satisfactory definition of the neo-classical. So this definition of the classical, while promising, is not finally much help.

Perhaps we should step back for a moment and ask just what it is we mean by *definition.* A favorite pastime of Socrates, Plato, and Aristotle, the process of definition might be defined as telling the genus and prop-erties of a thing, or an attempt to ascertain its essential nature.[17] Other, more rough-and-ready varieties include the "ostensive definition," so named from the Latin *ostendo,* to "point at" or "show" (this is what Chief Justice Potter Stewart had in mind when he said that he could not define pornography, but knew it when he saw it), and the "stipulative defini-tion," where one more or less damns the torpedoes and says (stipulates) that a thing just *is* such-and-such. My sense is that, as in most delicate or difficult cases, these latter two types of definition are those more usually invoked in defining the classical. An ostensive definition of the classical would be, for example, to point at the Parthenon. A more stipulative

17. Naturally, in an era that is suspicious of essentialism of all stripes, such a tradition is not likely to be popular.

definition—but one that at least seeks to offer some pathway toward essential nature—has been very popular among art historians. The strategy in this case is to define the classical by polarity: that is to say, in distinction to something that is perceived to be nonclassical or even anticlassical. Most recently, the eighteenth-century classicism of Western Europe has been seen as somehow subverted by nineteenth-century romanticism. Hence the title of Sir Kenneth Clark's memorable book, *The Romantic Rebellion*.[18] By a process of exclusion, then, we may understand the classical by contrasting it with its opposite, the romantic. So far so good. But we are still not all that much closer to some knowledge of essence (if such can indeed be known)—because we also cannot conclusively say what would qualify as the romantic.

I propose to cut this Gordian knot by a combination of ostensive and stipulative definitions—since the terms "classical" and "romantic" finally gain meaning only from their subjective cultural applications. Ostending to the Parthenon, or the Palace of Versailles, or Monticello, I would stipulate that the classical in, say, architecture, depends from a sense of balance, even symmetry. The romantic, then, rebels (in every age) against this canon by insisting upon an aesthetically conscious *imbalance*. The style of art nouveau, with its studied carelessness and valorization of carefully proportioned asymmetry, would be the romantic style par excellence. I think these parameters may be extended to music as well: in such a schema, the balanced voicing of a Bach harpsichord fugue is classical in contrast with the romantic keyboard-mapping of a Rachmaninoff piano prelude, as are the harmonic textures of a Mozart sonata when compared to those of a Chopin nocturne.

But where does the postmodern fit into this schema? Is it on the side of the apes, or of the angels? To this pressing conundrum one can only answer, Yes. The postmodern refuses to be trammeled in the straitjacket of binarism, in the obligation to choose either X or non-X: it will have neither, or both. In fact, I would venture to say that the essence of the postmodern—if something so elusive and evanescent, so constitutionally opposed to essentialism, can even be said to have an essence—is *the rejection of binary categorization*. Thus postmodern architecture draws from, is even based upon, forms and canons inherited from the classical tradition, all the while playing with nonclassical and even anticlassical variations and fillips.

18. Clark 1973.

The implications here for language and thought, of course, are staggering. Out goes traditional logic, which is founded upon the Law of Noncontradiction, that most quintessentially binary of axioms.[19] Out go many of the procedures of life as we know it: our judicial system, for example, which is based on the binary "guilty/not guilty." But the gain, if gain it is, is the ability to see shades of mediation and modulation that were hitherto black and white: just the thing for an age of quarks, electron microscopy, and antimatter.

The idea itself is, however, nothing new. I could point to examples of it in the writings of the ancient Greek sophists, for example, or even in *Alice in Wonderland*. But the most salient point is, so could Calasso. If one looks again at his definition of the classical, one finds that he has not availed himself of binary distinctions like those upon which our own hobnailed definition was predicated: Calasso walks with a softer shoe. In fact, he poises the classical in between the barbaric and the neoclassical— that is, he jettisons the binary approach altogether. What he is doing here, I suggest, is offering a postmodern definition of the classical.

Nor is this casual or haphazard. I will go further and suggest that this strategy is emblematic of everything Calasso is about in *The Marriage of Cadmus and Harmony:* a postmodern redefinition of the classical. All the old tales are here, retold with loving familiarity. Shrewd connections are even drawn from story to story, in a manner reminiscent of Ovid's *Metamorphoses*. But the previous balance that protected all our familiar dyads—beginning and end, truth and falsehood, even good and evil—is irrevocably disturbed. Moreover, the classical scholar's neat distinction between primary (or ancient) and secondary (or scholarly) sources, once so serenely obvious, is here toyed with, called into question, and, finally, dissolved. The scholarly observations of Bachofen or Solmsen or Milman Parry are now, it seems, as worthy of citation (and in the same way) as the deathless verse of Pindar.

ẽ

Not content merely with this stratagem of deconstructing the classical, Calasso also cracks another age-old chestnut: the nature of myth. In an

19. Although it has antecedents in the extant writings of Parmenides and Plato, the Law of Noncontradiction was, to my knowledge, first enunciated by Aristotle himself (see *Metaphysics* Γ.3, 1005b). It states that "the same attribute cannot at the same time belong and not belong to the same subject in the same respect," and is designated by Aristotle as "the most certain of all principles." (I cite the translation in Barnes 1984:2.1588.)

era when classical scholars in some quarters are maintaining that the earliest Greeks themselves had no category that could be termed "myth," it takes some courage, even bravado, to grapple with this problem. And yet Calasso almost has no choice: this is a challenge he cannot ignore (or resist). As he himself says:

> For centuries people have spoken of the Greek myths as of something to be rediscovered, reawoken. The truth is it is the myths that are still out there waiting to wake us and be seen by us, like a tree waiting to greet our newly opened eyes. (280)

So we ourselves can hardly ignore the issue. But it is difficult to find an adequate definition of myth. One might be tempted to begin with that rather naughty one provided by Ambrose Bierce, in *The Devil's Dictionary:* "The body of a primitive people's beliefs concerning its origin, early history, heroes, deities and so forth, as distinguished from the true accounts which it invents later." [20] There seems something not quite right about that, but I leave it to my reader to decide what that is. My own definition of myth—which I offer hesitantly and provisionally—is as follows: "a set of narratives that embodies the symbolic values of an interpretive community." The *narratives* are stories told, although the telling may be in sculpture, painting, or music, instead of in words—that is, in any viable semiosic system. The *symbolic values* are those ideas, beliefs, hopes, and fears that strike so deeply to the heart of our being that we are compelled to speak of them again and again, sometimes encrypting them in highly enigmatic or figurative form; and an *interpretive community* is a group of people, however large or small, who share a common system of discourse, and the competence to decode it. [21]

Calasso has much to say about the topic of mythology. Now classicists have, of late, learned to be wary of this as a category; Marcel Detienne, the French anthropological classicist, maintains that the ancients themselves had no such category as "mythology" as long as the actual myths were alive for them. [22] If one accepts this premise, it probably follows

20. Bierce 1911 (s.v. "Mythology"). Bierce of course is not troubled to observe my distinction between myth and mythology. Max Müller (1891), less humorously, calls mythology "a disease of language."

21. I have borrowed the term "interpretive community" from Stanley Fish. There is no reason why an interpretive community might not number as small as two (perhaps even one, if one allows that mental monologue might be mythopoeic), or as large as the entire human race. In the case of myths, scholars tend to think of what I call interpretive communities in terms of discrete cultures, perhaps as distinguished by particular languages—again reinforcing the connection between language and myth.

22. Detienne 1986.

that as soon as one finds mythographers such as Apollodorus, writing in around 140 B.C.E., the category of "myth" is a dead one. In any case, it is surely right to say that the use that Homer or Pindar or Sophocles makes of these ancient stories about gods and heroes is of a very different order than the use that someone like Apollodorus is making of them, or even perhaps someone like Ovid in the *Heroides* and *Metamorphoses*. But of course Calasso is not an ancient author, and would not be afraid of engaging in mythology himself—which he does, right from the epigraph at the beginning of his book: "Queste cose non avvennero mai, ma sono sempre": "These things never happened, but are always." And this is a topic that I think it is fair to say Calasso is exploring all the way through the work.

In exploring the topic of myth and mythology in *The Marriage of Cadmus and Harmony,* one comes to another phrase that is often repeated throughout the book: "Ma com'era cominciato tutto?" "But how did it all begin?" He poses this question a number of times, proceeding to answer it himself with a variety of stories. And this quest for beginnings, for what the ancients called *aitiai*—"origins" or "causes"—is central to the nature of myth. The Greek word *aitia* is etymologically at the root of our *etiology,* a word unfortunately mostly reserved these days for the medical terminology of disease. This notion of *aitia* points to what we call the "myth of origin." Many myths are apparently told to answer the questions "Why" or "Whence"—Why is such-and-such a thing in our world the way it is? or Where did such-and-such a thing in our world come from? The story, for example, of Hades and Persephone, as it is told in the Homeric Hymn to Demeter, or by Euripides, or Ovid, or Claudian, may be offered as an etiological explanation—a myth of origin explaining why there is winter in our world. Another story one might invoke in this category is that of the Tower of Babel, in the biblical book of Genesis, which is offered as an explanation of how the different peoples of earth came to speak different languages instead of one common tongue.[23] This concept of the myth of origin, then, and the thirst for origins generally, is a notion that repeatedly draws Calasso's attention.[24]

23. In a lighter vein, one might invoke Kipling's *Just So Stories,* which have such inviting titles as "How the Leopard Got His Spots" and "How the Camel Got His Hump."

24. A similar motivation underlies Calasso's *Ka,* which focuses on Indic myth and legend (not without occasional reference to Greek analogues). On beginnings see, e.g., Calasso 1998:130, 191, 198. Other topics of key importance to *The Marriage of Cadmus and Harmony* are also treated in *Ka,* e.g., the nature and effects of language (Calasso 1998:24–25, 169, 172–174, 238–239, 315, 322, 366), the bovine species (168–169, 249–250), desire (66, 101–102, 105, 110, 192–193, 284, and passim), and ritual and sacrifice (50, 129–153, 199–204; literature and sacrifice are explicitly connected on 313). For Greek analogues, see, e.g., Eros ~ Kama (66), Orion ~ Prajâpali

I have said that myths are a set of narratives that embodies the symbolic values of an interpretive community. To put this another way, myths are a given culture's attempts to answer crucial questions about the world they live in. (Some of these are: What is the nature of the godhead? Where did we come from? What is love? Why must we work for a living? Why do we die?) The same might be said of Calasso's work: he tells stories that purport to answer a set of crucial questions vis-à-vis the symbolic values of our culture. This leads us to the conclusion that it would be possible to define Calasso's own writing, in this way, as mythic. But Calasso makes another, even more startling move: in constructing this narrative, he is attempting to answer questions about the ways in which myths themselves embody symbolic values. So I suppose in that sense it is *mythology,* or even what one might call *metamyth.* Some of these questions are, for example, Why do humans interact with the gods? and Why do we feel the need to tell stories about them? Calasso offers a wonderful answer to both of these questions:

> After that remote time when gods and men had been on familiar terms, to invite the gods to one's house became the most dangerous thing one could do, a source of wrongs and curses, a sign of the now irretrievable malaise in relations between heaven and earth. At the marriage of Cadmus and Harmony, Aphrodite gives the bride a necklace which, passing from hand to hand, will generate one disaster after another right up <to> the massacre of the Epigoni beneath the walls of Thebes, and beyond. At the marriage of Peleus and Thetis, failure to invite Eris leads to the Judgment of Paris in favor of Aphrodite and against Hera and Athena, and thus creates the premise for the Trojan War. Lycaon's banquet, where human and animal flesh are served together, brings about the Flood. . . .
>
> What conclusions can we draw? To invite the gods ruins our relationship with them but sets history in motion. A life in which the gods are not invited isn't worth living. It will be quieter, but there won't be any stories. And you could suppose that these dangerous invitations were in fact contrived by the gods themselves, because the gods get bored with men who have no stories. (387)

So the concept of the interaction between human and divine is inevitably tied up with the telling about it: with the creation of stories. Once again, myth is inevitably connected with language. When we feel the shadow

---

(56), Apollo ~ Indra (248), Agni ~ Hermes (253), Achilles ~ Krishna (339). The *Iliad* and *Mahâbhârata* are compared on 315.

of the Immortal, of Perfection, of sublime Beauty, fall across our path, we cannot avoid the frisson of ecstasy and of fear, that shiver of exhilaration that makes us feel doubly and triply alive. No more can we avoid telling about it, over and over again. Thus myth is born—and born through language.

When Calasso comes to address the topic of myth directly, he uses a recurrent metaphor of cloth or fabric. Now this cannot be coincidence, because in Italian as in Latin, the word for "text" comes from the verb for "to weave."[25] Indeed this is one of the great metaphors of Indo-European thought: the comparison of a text to something woven.[26] Both are the intricate artifacts of human ingenuity; both are produced, strand by strand, with painstaking care and infinite attention to detail; and both are in one way or another central to human culture. The ancients were as appreciative of a good weaver as of a good storyteller: Homer, in the *Odyssey,* for example, portrays Odysseus as a world-class spinner of tales, and Penelope as the craftiest (and most dilatory) of weavers; and their two narrative threads run parallel throughout their epic poem. In Ovid's *Metamorphoses,* the tale of Athena and Arachne shows not only the great admiration accorded to expert weaving, but the potential narrative power of the art of tapestry.[27] Here are some of the things Calasso has to say about myth, using this metaphor of cloth:

> No sooner have you grabbed hold of it than myth opens out into a fan of a thousand segments. Here the variant is the origin. Everything that happens, happens this way, or that way, or this other way. And in each of these diverging stories all the others are reflected, all brush by us *like folds of the same cloth* [*come lembi della stessa stoffa*]. (147–148, emphasis added)

Once again we see the interest in origins, in beginnings, and also in the way that the ancients spun out myriad different versions of their myths. Calasso goes on to talk about the way in which all these variant versions may be woven finally into a seamless whole, the very fabric as it were of our culture, a fabric that our forebears once wove and wore, and which—

---

25. Ital. *testo* (< *tessere*); Lat. *textus* (< *texere*). The Italian word for "cloth" or "fabric" is *tessuto.*

26. For the mythic connection with weaving, see Scheid and Svenbro 1996.

27. Ovid, *Metamorphoses* 6.3–145. Later in the same book Ovid tells the lurid story of King Tereus of Thrace, his wife Procne, and her sister Philomela (6.424–674). In a ghastly allomorph of the Jacob/Rachel/Leah motif, Tereus, wedded to one sister, not only desires the other but eventually rapes her, then cuts out her tongue. Philomela, now robbed of speech and held prisoner, weaves a tapestry that tells the story of her outrage, and sends it to her sister (571–586). Here the metaphor of *tessuto* as *testo* bleeds into the literal.

for our own sake, as much as for theirs, we cherish still, despite its great antiquity:

> We have lost the capacity, the optical capacity even, to place myths in the sky. Yet, despite being reduced to just their fragrant rind of stories [*ridotti alla loro scorza fragrante di storie*], we still feel the Greek myths are cohesive and interconnected, right down to the humblest variant, as if we knew why they were so. And we don't know. A trait of Hermes, or Artemis, or Aphrodite, or Athena forms a part of the figure, *as though the pattern of the original material were emerging in the random scatter of the surviving rags [come se la stessa stoffa si ritrovasse nella casualità dei brandelli superstiti]*. (280, emphasis added)

And, in one final instance of this profound and moving metaphor, Calasso not only makes his peace with the ravages of time, but also acknowledges that myth exerts an irresistible power—on himself and on us all:

> We shouldn't be too concerned about having lost many of the secrets of the myths, although we must learn to sense their absence, the vastness of what remains undeciphered. To be nostalgic would be like wanting to see, on raising our eyes to the sky, seven Sirens, each intoning a different note around each of the seven heavens. Not only do we not see the Sirens but we can't even make out the heavens anymore. And yet *we can still draw that tattered cloth around us,* still immerse ourselves in the mutilated stories of the gods. And in the world, as in our minds, *the same cloth is still being woven.* (280, emphasis added)[28]

Myths are, above all, signs, and in a book so full not only of mythic tales, but also of metamythical observation, it is perhaps unsurprising that we should find a certain amount of semiotic discussion as well. I have already mentioned Calasso's nod toward infinite semiosis. In a number of other places as well, he remarks on the nature of signs and their use. From among these I will discuss half a dozen passages that serve not only to tie together some of the book's pervasive themes, but to offer the beginnings (at least) of a semiotics of myth.

---

28. The Italian version of this passage ends thus: "Eppure *in quella stoffa tagliuzzata,* in quelle storie monche degli dèi possiamo ancora avvolgerci. E dentro il mondo, come dentro la nostra mente, *quella stoffa continua a tessersi*" (Calasso 1988 : 315; emphasis added).

> ◆ At one extreme of the mental image lies our amazement at
> form, at its self-sufficient and sovereign existence. At the other lies
> our amazement at the chain of connections that reproduce in the
> mind the necessity of the material world. It is hard to see those
> two opposite points in the phantom's spectrum. To see them si-
> multaneously would be unbearable. For the Greeks, Helen was
> the embodiment of that vision, beauty hatched from the egg of
> necessity. (133–134)

This paragraph actually follows directly upon the earlier passage that discusses the simulacrum. Its larger context is a lengthy discussion of the
figure and significance of Helen of Troy. Helen is personally a sign of
many things: of unattainable beauty, of desire strong enough to wreak
havoc and destruction, of the union of gods and mortals (her mother
was Leda, her father, Zeus). She is also the sign of the fickle woman: the
wife of Menelaus, king of Sparta, she was abducted by (or ran off with?)
Paris, son of the king of Troy. Helen herself, in the *Iliad* of Homer,
comments presciently on the semiosic significance that she and her peers
will have for those who come after them: "Upon whom Zeus placed a
wretched fate, so that hereafter / We might be the stuff of song for future
generations."[29]

In the classical period, Helen was worshiped as a demigod, and the
ancients had a story that it was not Helen herself who went to Troy, but
a simulacrum or likeness of the actual woman; this is the springboard for
Calasso's discussion of the simulacrum, which he takes in unexpected directions. In the ancient biographical tradition of the Greek lyric poets,
Stesichorus is said to have composed a poem that said Helen did go to
Troy, and to have been struck blind as a punishment; on composing a
"palinode" or retraction of this, he was said to have regained his sight.[30]
Thus already in antiquity we find anxiety over what Derrida has called
the "metaphysics of presence," and attention to the ways in which a sign
may, with its semiosic presence, stand for the absence of the object it
represents. We shall have more anon to say about presence and absence.

> ◆ The first enemy of the aesthetic was meaning. The symbol
> appears as an image that is also something else. The aesthetic ap-
> pears in a figure that is *like* many others. The god is a boy; he

---

29. *hoisin epi Zeus thêke kakon moron, hôs kai opissô / anthrôpoisi pelômeth' aoidimoi essomenoisi*
(*Iliad* 6.357–358, my translation).

30. For a reference to the Stesichorean simulacrum see Plato, *Republic* 586c. For the blinding,
palinode, and restoration of sight, Plato, *Phaedrus* 243a–b. On Helen generally, see Suzuki 1989,
Austin 1994.

appears on the scene like any Athenian boy, naked as they are, face
creased in a light smile. Often he has no attributes that might allow
us to recognize him. . . . Here meaning seems to melt away,
doesn't impose itself. What does impose itself is a presence, as if of
someone we don't know. And one doesn't think immediately of
any meaning, but of what appears to the eye. (241)

Here too we find attention to the nature of the sign. By positing *meaning*
as the enemy of the aesthetic, Calasso implies that the foundation of the
aesthetic experience is an experience of presence in the artifact: that, in
order to abstract (< Lat. *abstractus*, "dragged from") a meaning from a
thing, one must turn away from the presence of the thing itself. Thus
meaning becomes an "enemy of the aesthetic" because it necessitates, in
some sense, the absence of the artifact. This calculus of presence and absence will have still further impact on Calasso's text, as we shall see below.

> ◆ Among the most significant of epithets applied to Zeus is
> *Phanaîos,* "he who appears." . . . The supremacy of appearance
> [*apparenza*] begins with Zeus, and from it derive the tensions
> that galvanize Greek culture. The fact that Plato launched a de-
> vastat ing attack on appearance shows that appearance was still
> dominant and oppressive to him. The messenger of the realm of
> appearance is the statue. No other ancient language has such a rich
> vocabulary for referring to different kinds of images as Greek. . . .
> Breaking away in very early times from those philosopher-priests,
> the Magi, the Greeks generated a new race of philosophers, who
> were not priests and did not always dispense with images and find
> nothing at all to worship. But, before that could happen,
> appearance had to impose itself as a hitherto unknown force, a
> challenge. (246)

By invoking *appearance* Calasso is actually tapping into an ancient discussion of what the Greeks called *ta phainomena,* usually translated "the ap-
pearances," a term used to designate that which we apprehend via our
senses. The question, most simply put, is: Are *ta phainomena* themselves
real, or is there some nonphenomenal reality underlying them? [31] This is
precisely the battleground on which many bloody disputations have been
fought, beginning in ancient times. (1) *Hesiod,* in the archaic period, tells

---

31. The third logical possibility—that *ta phainomena* are not themselves real, *and* that there is
no nonphenomenal reality underlying them—was not widely entertained. It was apparently the
premise of the sophist Gorgias' (now lost) essay *On Not-Being,* and was (in later antiquity) a matter of some interest to Sextus Empiricus.

how the Muses told him, "We know how to tell many false things that are like real things, / And we know how, when we want, to speak true things,"[32] which shows already in the eighth century B.C.E. some awareness of the possibility of inconcinnity between the linguistic sign and its object.[33] Be that as it may, Hesiod does not seem to require a systematic explanation of *ta phainomena:* he is content to take the Muses' pronouncements as authoritative and sufficient *in ipsis.* (2) It is the Presocratics who seem to have been the first to be interested in explaining *ta phainomena* with an account that is not, like Hesiod's, simply an appeal to some external authority: their explanations are intended, in fact, to provide the authority for their beliefs.[34] This is why the Presocratic period of Greek philosophy is seen as such a milestone in the history of rational thought. (3) Plato's role in this unfolding drama of *ta phainomena* is an extraordinary and in some senses paradoxical one. On the one hand, he is (via Socrates) heir to the Presocratic high esteem of ratiocination and the application of logic to philosophical inquiry. On the other, he seems[35] (Calasso suggests) deeply suspicious of *ta phainomena,* viewing them as, at best, images or representations of the Forms, in which inhere all reality and truth. But his theory of the Forms is, in fact, an attempt to "save *ta phainomena*" by linking them, through the mechanism of participation, to something that is real.[36] Even had we not been made fully aware of the semiotic nature of the long-standing argument over *ta phainomena,* we could no longer ignore it after Plato. (4) *Aristotle* appeals to *ta phainomena* in an attempt to propound the logical underpinnings of scientific discovery. As G. E. L. Owen asserted in an essay now famous (and often responded to by other philosophers),[37] Aristotle takes *ta phainomena* as the beginning point of our knowledge of universals; thus (in a way different from Plato) it is important for Aristotle to "save *ta phainomena,*" for he maintains that they can actually tell us something significant about form.

32.   *idmen pseudea polla legein etumoisin homoia, / idmen d', eut' ethelômen, alêthea gêrusasthai* (*Theogony* 27–28, my translation).

33.   It is interesting that Calasso says that the supremacy of appearance "begins with Zeus," since the Muses in Hesiod are said always to begin and end their song with the praise of Zeus (*Theogony* 48). Most scholars in fact consider this line spurious, i.e., not to have been composed by Hesiod himself, but it does date from antiquity and is preserved in the ancient manuscript tradition.

34.   Curd 1998 argues that it is not until Parmenides that we find systematic arguments (as opposed to assertions) for basic positions.

35.   I say "seems" as a hedge against glib or careless interpretations of the Platonic texts, which are notoriously complex; on problems in interpreting Plato, see Kirby 1997b.

36.   This traditional view of Plato—now becoming less fashionable—might obscure the fact that Plato's suspicion of *ta phainomena* is in fact a legacy of the Presocratics, especially (again) Parmenides.

37.   Owen 1961.

Practically none of this is explicit in Calasso's text, of course, and yet it is so artfully and allusively constructed that he is able to suggest it all, and to show that he is aware of the philosophical implications at stake here. Moreover, by couching his critical aside in metamythic terms, he is able both to avoid the potentially ponderous intrusion of abstruse philosophical disquisition, and to weave this aside in subtly with his overall narrative. It is important to see that the concept of *phainomena* opens up the possibility for presence-in-absence via representation, that is, via semiosis.

> ◆ What happened in ancient Greece that had never happened
> before? A lightening of our load [*Un alleggerimento*]. The mind
> shrugged off the world with a brusque gesture that was to last a
> few centuries. When, in the geometric patterns of the vases, we
> begin to find rectangles inhabited by black figures, those figures
> already have an empty space behind them, a clearing, an area at
> last free from meaning [*il vuoto, un'area sgombra, finalmente senza
> significato*]. It was perhaps out of gratitude toward this insolent ges-
> ture that Greece celebrated in its tragedies the attempt, admittedly
> vain and doomed to be short-lived, to rid themselves of the con-
> sequence of gesture and action. (267–268)

Here the ostensible topic of discussion is the figure/ground distinction in visual art. The so-called Geometric period of Greek art spans from about 1000 to about 700 B.C.E., reaching its fullest expression in the ninth and eighth centuries. Vase paintings from this period are decorated, as the name suggests, with geometrical patterns such as zigzags and meanders, triangles, lozenges, and circles. Human and animal figures, when de-picted, tend to be highly stylized.[38]

In analyzing a visual representation, one might make the claim that the figure is the semiosic item, and that the ground against which it is figured is indeed a void, completely empty of signification (as Calasso explicitly says here). A good Peircean, of course, would maintain that the ground is as limitlessly semiosic as the figure. But the less revolutionary move is to consider the ground as a sort of visual silence — an empty space (*vuoto*) into which one puts the figure, and with it, signification.

What is less predictable, perhaps, is that Calasso draws the parallel between the static visual arts, such as painting and sculpture, and drama. Horace, in the first century B.C.E., famously compared literature to paint-ing (*Vt pictura poesis*); I take Calasso here, however, to be speaking not of the texts of Greek tragedies, but of the gestures and actions of the char-

---

38. For useful introductions to matters of Greek art, see, e.g., Striker 1959, Boardman 1973.

acters depicted (or at least of the actors onstage). This recognition that semiosis may be nonlinguistic is a move away from Saussure and in the direction of Peirce. It also speculates, although poetically and indeed somewhat obscurely, that the distinguishing of figure from ground suggested the possibility of *meaninglessness* in human action, and that Attic tragedy attempted to tap into this. Calasso calls that attempt "admittedly vain and doomed to be short-lived," because, in human affairs, meaning (that is, interpretation) creeps in willy-nilly: we seem to find the temptation to make sense of our lives, and of the world around us, irresistible.

Such an approach to the history of art is, of course, strictly speaking reductive—thousands of years before the beginning of the Geometric period, humans were painting figures on grounds—and such a monolithic reading of Greek tragedy is equally simplistic: it is easier to produce nihilistic interpretations of Euripides, for example, than of Aeschylus. But I am less inclined to attribute these lacunae to ignorance than to the fact that Calasso is moving swiftly, and (as I have said) poetically, through a great deal of material in this aside. The strength of such an aphoristic style is its pungent and frequently memorable effect; its inherent weakness is that it tends to the inchoate and the opaque. By stripping away every possible extraneity of thought, Calasso is able to advance, in a different direction, his meditation on presence and absence in semiosis: in the case of figure/ground representation, one might posit an instantiation of presence in the figure, and absence in the ground.

> ♦ With time, men and gods would develop a common language made up of hierogamy and sacrifice. The endless ways these two phenomena split apart, opposed each other, and mixed together corresponded to the expressions of that language. And, when it became a dead language, people started talking about mythology. (292)

This passage is of course from the section, discussed earlier, that deals with hierogamy and sacrifice. I maintained that these two phenomena correspond, respectively, to Freud's *eros* and *thanatos;* taken together, these two polar forces may stand for the totality of human existence. (Moreover, it is relatively easy to connect hierogamy with presence, via eros, and sacrifice with absence, via thanatos.) Once they are conceived of as signs of all that is most important to our race, it is no great reach to think of them in terms of a language, as Calasso does here. Their innumerable combinations suggest not only the now familiar phenomenon of unlimited semiosis, but—in a more specific metaphor—the interplay of vowels and consonants in human speech. Thus yet again is myth linked organically to language. And Calasso points up my distinction between myth and mythology by linking the latter with the hierogamy/sacrifice dyad as an eventually "dead language": when such a phenomenon per se is stepped back from, and turned into the object of intellectual scrutiny, one has moved to the metalevel.

Significantly, the entire book ends with a semiotic observation:

> ◆ Cadmus had brought Greece "gifts of the mind": vowels and consonants yoked together in tiny signs, "etched model of a silence that speaks"—the alphabet. With the alphabet, the Greeks would teach themselves to experience the gods in the silence of the mind, and no longer in the full and normal presence, as Cadmus himself had the day of his marriage. He thought of his routed kingdom. . . . Thebes was a heap of rubble. But no one could erase those small letters, those fly's feet that Cadmus the Phoenician had scattered across Greece, where the winds had brought him in his quest for Europa carried off by a bull that rose from the sea. (390–391)

There is much to remark upon in this final paragraph of the work. To take last things first: his final image—that of the bull from the sea carrying off Europa—links the very end of the book with its very beginning: "On a beach in Sidon a bull was aping a lover's coo. It was Zeus. He shuddered, the way he did when a gadfly got him. But this time it was a sweet shuddering. Eros was lifting a girl onto his back: Europa" (3).

Calasso's principal source for the tradition that Cadmus—or, more precisely, the Phoenicians (ancestors of today's Lebanese) who came to Greece with Cadmus—introduced the art of writing in Greece, is the historian Herodotus. Herodotus speaks of "Cadmean letters," [39] which he says is a writing system for the most part not very different from the Ionian letters with which he is more familiar. Much has been made of the fact that, unlike (a) hieroglyphs and other characters, which are pictographic, (b) syllabaries, which are not fully alphabetic, and (c) earlier Semitic writing systems (such as the Aramaic), which represent (with very few exceptions) consonants without vocalization, the Greek alphabet was the first writing system to be able to represent every vocalic and consonantal sound more or less equally, by one written sign each. [40] (It

---

39. *Kadmeïa grammata* (Herodotus 5.59).
40. Eric Havelock is the classical scholar who has most enthusiastically explored the implications of this historical fact—perhaps too enthusiastically in certain respects; see Kirby 1994:439– 440. For more on Greek writing and the development of the alphabet, see, e.g., Jeffery 1990; Immerwahr 1990; Powell 1989, 1991; Woodard 1997.

is also at the basis of our modern roman alphabet.) These "gifts of the mind" are undoubtedly the semiosic system that has the weightiest daily impact on the life of the scholar, as on that of the publisher (and we must not forget that Calasso is himself both of these). Unlike icons, which have a pictorial connection with their objects, letters are symbols that have a purely arbitrary association with the sounds for which they are signs. The less organic or representational the connection between sign and object, the less "present" the object may seem in the sign: and so we are back to absence and presence in language. In fact, Calasso appears in this passage to have fully digested the message of Derridean grammatology: namely, that language, and written language above all, carries implicit in itself the death of the metaphysics of presence.

Perhaps what we yearn for more achingly than anything else — though indeed we may not always couch it in these terms — is the ability to experience reality unmediated, to embrace That Which Is in all its plenitude, without any dissipation of richness or directness. One of the most entrancing aspects of the myths and legends of antiquity is that they portray memorable characters who seem to be having just such an experience. Often that experience is too much for them to bear: Semele, having importuned her lover Zeus to reveal himself to her in his full splendor, is instantly burned to cinders by the effulgence of his glory; Icarus, flying too close to the sun on his waxen wings, finds himself plunged into the sea below. Somewhere in our secret selves we acknowledge such human limitations as our own. So we content ourselves with experiencing the gods "in the silence of the mind," most often by reading, accepting deferral and absence in exchange for a presence so fervent and intense it might be the end of us. And yet that presence is in some sense present even in its absence; this paradox is what Calasso has in mind when he quotes Nonnus in reference to the "silence that speaks." Calasso's Cadmus seems to have some inkling (so to speak) of the weighty import of his legacy to Greece, those small letters that none could erase. The advent of such letters signals the end of the age of the gods, the end of myth (in one sense) and the beginning of mythology. It is also, lest we forget, what makes possible the advent of Calasso's book (as well as mine): that is, these letters of the alphabet are what enable him (and me) to be, in some sense, present even in our absence: to speak, it may be, even after our death. Poignant as it is, that may not be such a bad trade after all.

CODA

En ma fin gît mon commencement.
—*Mary Queen of Scots*

*O*ne ancient tradition, as I mentioned in chapter 1, whispers that the Sphinx learned her deadly riddle from the Muses themselves. This reminds us that a riddle and a secret have some important traits in common: they both embody the focused representation of ideas in words; their import is not universally known or understood; and for this reason they may require some explaining. In the case of the riddle of the Sphinx, not to know was fatal. While it may seem alarmist to take such an extreme stance vis-à-vis the secret of the Muses, we ought nonetheless to consider soberly what it would mean to Western culture to lose that secret entirely. As for Oedipus, so too for us: the answer to the riddle may well turn out to be our very selves, and we ignore it at our peril. And there are those who fear that we are indeed, even as we speak, losing it a bit more, day by day.

On the other hand, there are now (as in every generation) hopeful and encouraging signs that the secret indeed continues to be told. Hence the epigraph I have chosen for this coda: the motto of Mary Queen of Scots, "In my end is my beginning." On the one hand, it has a deeply mystical luster to it, like the Worm Ourobouros biting its tail, symbol of eternity; on the other, however, it expresses the great historical irony that, indeed, as far as concerned the throne of England, which she so desired, Mary's end was, politically, her beginning: upon the death of Elizabeth I, the crown of England did pass to the Stuarts, and specifically to Mary's son James; but because of the threat she posed to Elizabeth's sovereignty, this would and could never happen as long as Mary herself was still alive.

I draw this analogy to the death of classical antiquity and its rebirth in classicism. The latter, as we saw in Calasso's work, is typically nostalgic by nature: it idealizes the culture of an earlier era and civilization and harks back longingly to it.[1] Moreover, in the case of ancient Greece the

---

1. Again, one thinks, in certain respects, of Schiller's distinction between the naïve and the sentimental in poetry. See Schiller 1981.

127

classicizing process began quite early on: in both the Greek- and Latin-speaking worlds, the enshrinement of the so-called pure style known as Atticism was just such a gesture, signifying incontrovertibly that those who espoused it acknowledged classical Athenian Greek as the ne plus ultra of formal language. By the time of Erasmus, the practice of "Ciceronianism" carried this to such an extreme that there were those who insisted that a truly pure Latinity would draw only upon vocabulary that could be attested to in the extant writings of Cicero. All such positions are predicated on a Hesiodic notion of decline, looking back to a Golden Age when the exploits of mortals were greater than they could possibly be today.

When the imagery of the Golden Age was used by Vergil and his compeers, however, it was to celebrate (however aptly or otherwise) the reign of Caesar Augustus and his imposition of the *pax augusta*. For them, the notion was a cyclical one: *redeunt saturnia regna*. The Age of Gold is come again; let us rejoice and be glad. This attitude toward classicism is not so much nostalgic as empowering, and indeed that may account in part for the peculiar and enduring power of the poetry of Horace and Vergil. For them, the Golden Age was now. They heard the secret of the Muses retold firsthand; indeed, they told it themselves openly. Of course they had the undeniable (and perhaps unrepeatable) advantage of working in what was basically still a living tradition: Greek and Latin were still spoken and taught as living languages, belonging to living cultures (even if classical Hellenic culture was by then far past its greatest flower).

č

It is no surprise that each of the five writers considered in this book makes his own highly personal use of the classical materials he taps into. This will be a function not only of his personality, his individual predilection, and the message he wishes to convey, but also of the rhetorical exigencies of the literary genre in which he is working. As I have already indicated in my Prelude, I do not mean to suggest that Italian authors are the only ones to cherish their classical heritage. Similar studies could doubtless be carried out on groups of authors writing in French, Spanish, German, English, and so on. But there is no denying that we find a certain immediacy, a freshness, in the way the five writers I have discussed here deal with the classical material they handle.

Pasolini, like many creative geniuses of his ilk, was far ahead of his time, and the innovative nature of his work often sat ill with its first audiences. His cinematic projects routinely shocked their original audiences for their controversial subject matter. Even his semiotic speculations, as we saw in chapter 1, were not well received at first. Pasolini's use of the classical material appears to be a deeply personal one, the most overtly so of any of our five authors, because of his transparent self-revelation in interviews and commentaries on his film.

Edipo re points up a number of popular aspects of the classical tradition in modern life. First, of course, film is in some ways the preeminent artistic medium of our time; it reaches the masses in ways that books often do not—one need not even be literate to appreciate film—and (as Pasolini himself noted, and as we have discussed in chapter 1) film and real life are in some ways on equal footing semiosically. Moreover, film does for today what grand opera did for the eighteenth and nineteenth centuries: it unites visual spectacle, dramatic mimesis, music, and (sometimes) dance in a single overwhelming aesthetic experience. I imagine that no one would deny that the feature-length film, along with television productions and the music album (on CD or audiocassette), are the types of artistic production that currently see the widest commercial consumption in the West today. In this way, ironically, film might be said to parallel some of the social and aesthetic functions of Attic tragedy in its fifth-century heyday. Because of its remoteness from our own cultural milieu, we are liable to forget that Attic tragedy was presented to and for the whole citizenry of Athens.

A second way in which *Edipo re* reflects popular contemporary interaction with the classical tradition is its overtly Freudian appropriation of the Oedipus motif. The average nonclassicist is more likely to have heard of the Oedipus complex (and perhaps even to associate this with Freud) than to be familiar with the play of Sophocles; but of course it is to Sophocles that Freud is explicitly indebted, just as Pasolini is to Freud.

Eco, who is as close to the universal polymath as anyone now living, began his scholarly career as a mediaevalist, and that provided him with the historical and cultural information he needed to set his novel in the Middle Ages. His professional expertise in semiotics equipped him with the requisite knowledge to make *The Name of the Rose* a semiotic novel. But even these two competences, taken by themselves, would not have been able to provide the missing piece that his understanding of the Aristotelian *Poetics* supplied. The peculiar nature of that treatise—both in terms of what it lacks and of how the surviving torso has affected subsequent literary history—was a crucial aspect of the novel, and his interest in it was almost surely piqued by that of Borges.

It is difficult to imagine the oeuvre of Eco without its constant traffic to antiquity: Eco, trained as a mediaevalist, understands (and exploits) the intimate connection between the European Middle Ages and Greco-Roman antiquity. Indeed that connection is in some ways the premise of *The Name of the Rose*. We are asked to imagine a mediaeval monastic library housing precious manuscripts of ancient texts that have since disappeared, perhaps irrevocably, and for which classical scholars pine. That hunger for ancient books, embodied so literally in the novel by Jorge of Burgos, is difficult for nonbibliophiles to understand, but, by the same token, is something that everyone who has experienced it will poignantly recognize; the desire and fear that fuel it are at the basis of Ray Bradbury's *Fahrenheit 451*. In some ways, in fact, *The Name of the Rose* is a bibliophilic fantasy in which the reader may imagine a return, via mediaeval Europe, to the works of ancient Greece and Rome.

Tusiani's Latin poetry, as redolent of antiquity as any work discussed here, springs from an inspiration as personal as that of Pasolini, but because of its highly mannered formalist nature, one might well not suspect that his use of the Latin tongue sprang from a personal sense of alienation from both his natal and his adopted lands. Moreover, of the five authors, it is the work of Tusiani that constitutes the most extreme case of classicizing we have seen—at the formal level at least. On the other hand, as we noted in chapter 3, he is capable at times of using the classical language and metrical apparatus to couch subject matter of a completely contemporary (sometimes almost postmodern) nature. For Tusiani, the secret of the Muses means a return to the very fabric of the ancient text: the language and metric of ancient Rome. That he imports modern-day imagery and ideas (and a Christian *Weltanschauung*) into his work, does nothing to dilute the bloodlines of this genre: on the contrary, it points up the very continuity of the tradition, which lived on after antiquity into the Middle Ages and Renaissance and was never completely abandoned even after that. (Milton, for example, wrote a considerable body of classicizing verse in Greek and Latin, though it is now rarely read.) There are few practitioners of the craft of classical versification alive today who could pretend to rival Tusiani's inventiveness, fecundity, or sheer virtuosity, but the printing and reprinting of his books of Latin verse demonstrate that his readership is an abiding one.

Calvino's treatise on "literary values," which we have examined as a treatise on rhetorical style, is entirely contemporary in its own style and concerns. Apart from the occasional reference to an ancient author, no one unfamiliar with the classical rhetorical tradition would suspect any ancient antecedents to Calvino's work here, and certainly his fictional work is equally unlikely to make one look for such lines of filiation. Nonetheless, in both form and content it demonstrates its kinship with the classical *tekhnai* or rhetorical manuals, even to the level of specific detail. Indeed *Six Memos for the Next Millennium,* despite the contemporaneity we have noted, is as profoundly a part of the classical rhetorical tradition as the poetry of Tusiani is of the poetic. Without citing shop-worn exempla or tired pedagogical admonitions, Calvino nonetheless succeeds in reinscribing precisely the rhetorical and literary values that have been prized by litterateurs in the West since Plato at least. Moreover, he does so in ways that recall in minute detail the strategies of hand-books such as that of Hermogenes. That detail, combined with Calvino's well-known erudition and familiarity with Western literature from antiquity on, make it almost impossible to believe that *Six Memos* was not conceived as part of the rhetorical tradition in which at any rate it now stands.

Finally, Calasso's work is overtly postmodern in its bold appropriation of ancient tales in a very down-to-the-minute format—even, as we saw in chapter 5, an innovative and somewhat subversive format. He is at once endorsing the ancient tradition and pronouncing its funeral eulogy, taking away with one hand and giving back with the other. One reason that Calasso is repeatedly compared to Ovid is probably that *The Marriage of Cadmus and Harmony,* like the *Metamorphoses,* is itself constantly changing: topics are strung together in a seamless whole, but the author's mind seems constantly to flit and swerve from one tale or one idea to another, from legend to excursus and back again, almost without warning. This is the sort of book that inspires writers of book reviews to term it an "instant classic"—whatever that may mean.

The Marriage of Cadmus and Harmony is, of all the works we have examined, the most sweeping and comprehensive celebration of classical antiquity qua tradition. A principal theme of this book is the vast gulf that separates then from now, and the stern bargain that time forces us to strike in order to reclaim the past in any substantial way. Yet precisely by virtue of such an assertion, Calasso reveals his own tremendous intimacy with those stories and traditions of antiquity. The loss of unmediated presence has not, for Calasso himself, meant any loss of touch with the mythographic tradition, or with the power that those ancient symbols have carried for millennia. It is precisely this power that he purports to convey to his reader—to raise the hackles on our necks, if he can, by conjuring the spirits of the ancient past, to give us, if not the experience of the manifest presence of the gods, then some simulacrum of its effects. In his highly idiosyncratic way, this is what it means for Calasso to retell the secret of the Muses.

℃

I have already indicated my awareness that a celebration of the perpetuation of the Greco-Roman tradition is not going to meet with universal benevolence. In point of fact, the very notion of "classics" is going to be anathema to some in the Academy today. The more staunchly traditional among us may dismiss that anathema on the assumption that it merely indicates a shallow or callow valorization of the trendy and chic, or (what sometimes amounts to the same thing) an intellectual bandwagon to mount. But I have listened carefully to the protestations of academics who decry the uncritical embracing of the classical tradition, and I do not find them all to conform to this stereotype. On the contrary, they sometimes ask deeply searching questions, and demand unflinching self-reflection on the part of those who would embrace that tradition as history has constituted it. What about the ugly moral values it has sometimes perpetuated? What about the exclusivity of the hegemonic voices it has preserved, at the expense of marginalized groups? What about the very ossification of form and content a classical canon threatens to engender? These are not idle or negligible questions, and no classicist of conscience can afford to ignore them. I think they are worth keeping in mind, if we are to commit ourselves to cherishing works of art that we consider classics. Put most bluntly, Why *should* we continue to tell the secret of the Muses?

It is impossible to answer this question dispassionately—which fact itself should signal how high the stakes are here. Profound grievances may be detailed on both sides of the issue. On the one hand, to jettison the whole historical framework of Western aesthetics is to risk losing, with our past, a precious part of ourselves. On the other, it is undeniable that the classics have been an egregious tool of elitism, racism, sexism, and other forms of oppression. It is no coincidence, for example, that they formed the curricular cornerstones of the *humanistisches Gymnasium* in Germany and the public school/Oxbridge system in England—or that, as those nations began to move toward democracy, the class signifiers favored in these educational institutions also underwent radical change. So cogent arguments can be made both pro and contra. Perhaps it might refresh us to begin anew with some definitions.

What *is* a classic? I refused to address this question in chapter 5, but perhaps, in view of the Pandora's box I have opened here, it is time to do so now. Knowing that all such definitions are tendentious, limited, and limiting, I will nonetheless advance my own, if for no other purpose than to stimulate thought and dialogue on the matter.

1. *A classic is the best of its kind.* This aspect of the definition is already part of the ancient conception: *classis* may mean a "class" or "category," and in Aulus Gellius *classicus* means a writer of the highest rank (*Attic Nights* 19.8.15). So to speak of "classics" is to conceive, a priori, of standards of valuation in the arts, and to apply them hierarchically. What those standards may be, and how they are adjudicated, is I suppose external to this portion of the definition; but typical aesthetic standards in Western cultures have included beauty (again, whatever that is conceived to be) and artistic unity (although the postmodern project may in some ways be read precisely as a gesture toward dismantling, toward fragmentation). When we come to adjudicating standards, we must again attend carefully to the principle of charity and the danger of oppression. Who is being excluded when the list is drawn up, and why? What does the list look like when it is deemed complete? For, of course, canons are by definition limited; otherwise the notion of "best" becomes meaningless.

2. *A classic has withstood the test of time.* How much time? A year? A century? A millennium? This is not immediately obvious, and moreover may differ from genre to genre, or from culture to culture. But the notion of withstanding the test of time is precisely what has given rise to the oxymoron "instant classic." An important side-issue—and perhaps an impossible question to answer—is whether any given group of people can themselves authoritatively recognize a classic coming into being in their own midst, or whether at least one generation must pass first. Another question that must be frankly faced here is whether, at a certain point, a work of art ceases to withstand the test of time—and how this would be recognized. Is it at that moment no longer a classic? This leads into my next point.

3. *A classic taps into the mythic values of its culture.* This, of course, echoes our discussion of myth itself in chapter 5, and consciously so; for part of what gives us a sense that a work of art is a classic is that it seems to give access to what Joseph Campbell has felicitously termed the "Power of Myth": the ideas, or the tropes, or the very mode of execution of such a work, have a power to them that transcends mere innovation or cleverness or piquancy. Rather, they inspire, they instruct, they give hope. And that is, ultimately, the source of their enduring value. For as long as the

fabric of a given culture remains unrent, the same symbolic values will continue to hold their power for that culture.

I recognize that there is plenty of fodder under these three headings for incendiary political discourse, and (in particular) that they might be construed as part of the underpinnings for a retrograde, even reactionary, cultural movement: speaking of twentieth-century Italians, it was Mussolini who most strenuously made just such notions a part of his program of *Italianità*. And against such totalitarian programs we must ever remain vigilant.

As I suggested in my Prelude, there are rival metaphysics (as well as politics) at play in this discourse, and those rivalries will account in part for different stances toward the very notion of a classic, as well as toward the use one might make of it. Thus, for instance, the conflict that finds its epicenter in the National Association of Scholars.[2] Thus too, in the field of classics specifically, the firestorms over *Black Athena* and (more recent, and if possible, more acrimonious) *Who Killed Homer?*[3] Part of what these controversies make clear is that it is not just how we think and feel about the Greek and Roman classics that matters, but specifically how we *teach* them: like it or not, we cannot avoid problematizing the very future of Western humanistic education in terms of the classics. That topic, in its specifically professional and logistical aspects, is beyond the scope of this book. But this is why I offer my threefold response to the question "What is a classic?": how we answer that question, with the openest and most charitable of minds, will help us to discern where to go from here. I would like to think that, if we are willing to risk thinking expansively, inclusively, we may discover that the veneration of classics need not be an act of oppression, stifling, or cultural imperialism. Indeed, we are likely to find—to our delight—that every culture, every era, produces its own classics: that in every time and place the sublime waters of Hippocrene bubble up where the human spirit may slake its thirst for excellence, for beauty. The real question to begin from, at least, is: What is beautiful to me? Sappho, in her inimitable way, put it best:

> Some say that the loveliest thing on earth is a troop of horsemen;
> Others, a company of foot-soldiers;

2. For an assessment (both trenchant and tendentious) of the situation, see the entry in Nelson and Watt 1999: 182–192.

3. *Black Athena:* see, e.g., Bernal 1987, 1991; Lefkowitz 1996; Lefkowitz and Rogers 1996; and (a lucid, learned, and sober assessment of the whole affair) Levine 1998. *Who Killed Homer?* is, as of this writing, still brewing; see Hanson and Heath 1998, Beye 1998, Connolly 1998, Willett 1999, Martindale 1999, Green 1999, and Hanson and Heath 1999. The storm continues to rage in *Arion* (ser. 3) 7.2 (Fall 1999): 174–184.

Others still, a flotilla of ships.
But to me, the fairest thing on earth is whatever one loves.[4]

Whatever one loves. In context, Sappho uses this as a way of moving
fluidly into the world of epic legend, so as to invoke the intoxicating
beauty of Helen of Troy, and then to compare this to the beauty of her
own beloved.[5] But the words themselves evoke a strikingly intimate and
subjective mode of valuation: the fairest thing on earth will turn out to
be whatever one loves the best. Anyone who knows an artist—whether
they be writer, musician, dancer, actor, sculptor, painter—knows that it
is love that motivates these people to do what they do. Indeed it would
have to be so: in precious few cases could it possibly be for monetary
gain. But art is born of love, on the personal and individual level.

What happens next, sometimes, is that this love is communicated to,
and shared by, an audience: what seemed beautiful to the artist also comes
to seem beautiful to those who see or hear the work of art. When this happens in sufficient community, culture is born. And when those who share
commonality of culture agree that some work of art (1) is the best of its
kind, (2) *still* appears to be the best of its kind after some measurable lapse
of time, and (3) embodies, in some way, the mythic values they hold
dear—then such a work of art comes to have the value of a classic in that
culture.

If this is so—and I think it is—then there is no reason why we should
not recognize that each culture, as I have said, produces its own classics.
If these hark back to the classics of previous eras, that may be construed
as powerful evidence of cultural continuity between the two societies.
But that is the nature of goddesses: they are immortal. In my end is my
beginning. To hear the secret, we have only to listen—and to love. For
love (*philein*) is at the very root of philology, in its broadest sense. As a
new millennium sweeps over our horizon, the time is especially ripe for
us to take stock of what we do and why we do it.

I think it is also important to remark again, having said all this, upon
the dangers immanent/imminent in such a notion of cultural classics.
Astute readers of literature and criticism will be aware that this raises the
whole issue of a canon.[6] Already in the Alexandrian period, aficionados
of literature were fond of making canonical lists: the Ten Attic Orators;
the Five Epic Poets; the Nine Lyric Poets; the Ten Historians; and so on.[7]

4. Fragment 16 (Lobel-Page), 1–4 (my translation).
5. For more on how this priamel operates, see Kirby 1984–1985.
6. For more on the literary canon, and the place in it of the Greek and Roman classics, see
the introduction to Kirby 1998b, especially xxvii–xxxii (with extensive bibliography in the notes).
7. On these see O'Sullivan 1997.

This is all well and good; there will always be standards of excellence, and parameters by which one is judged to have hewed to those standards (or not). But the lesson of history is that, far too often, the rosters are composed of heterosexual white males; and, on a larger level, the lists that are held to matter are typically those of imperialist nations. I surmise the Muses are not so myopic as all that. Rather than reinscribe such an oppressive cultural past, I would like to conclude by asking my reader to think expansively and to imagine what a more inclusive canon might be like. In keeping with Sappho's intensely personal and subjective definition of the most beautiful, what books and authors might find their way into one's own personal canon? Which of these have meant the most among one's friends, in one's academic classes? Building a canon purposefully this way—from the individual to the community to the overall culture—may offer us a way to circumvent old patterns of hegemony and oppression. And who knows? Someday we may once again hear the sweet singing that, thousands of years ago, gave Hesiod to understand that he was in the presence of the numinous:

> Let us begin our song from the Heliconidae, the Muses,
> They who possess the great and holy mountain of Helicon;
> About the violet-dark spring they dance
> On their soft feet, and about the altar of mighty Zeus.
> And having bathed their soft skin in the waters of the Permessus,
> Or of Hippocrene, or of the holy Olmeius,
> On the height of Helicon they make their dances
> Fair and lovely, in rhythmic steps.
> Setting out from there, veiled in deep mist,
> Through the night they walk, singing in voices of surpassing
>   beauty . . .[8]

---

8. *Theogony* 1–10 (my translation).

Selected Latin Verse of Joseph Tusiani

 $\mathcal{B}$ ecause the reader may encounter some difficulty in obtaining copies of Tusiani's Latin verse, I append here the complete Latin text of each poem that I discuss in chapter 3. The texts of these poems are based, in each case, on the *editiones principes,* which have then been collated against the texts reproduced in Tusiani 1994 (which was edited by Emilio Bandiera). In any case these tend to differ principally in matters of capitalization and punctuation. I follow the practice of Tusiani 1994 in capitalizing the first word of each line. In *Funus in hortulo* 13 I have printed *terreor* instead of Bandiera's *terreo;* in *Lingua latina* I have indented the fifth line of each stanza (as in *Cantiuncula vespertina*) in order to mark the difference in meter. In *Photographema maritimum* (2, 4) I have restored the capital O of *Oceanus* and the *harena* of Tusiani's *editio princeps,* but have adopted Bandiera's *cuncta* (which is Tusiani's own revision of the *editio princeps*).

Funus in hortulo

Mortuus ante meos oculos (lacrimabile visu),
    Heu, tam vivus heri, parve sciure, iaces.
Quis furor eripuit vitam tibi nocte quieta
    Aut saxo stravit te redeunte die?
Heu, tam vivus heri, tu mobilis incola rami,   5
    Nunc immobilis es, nunc levitate cares.
Pes mihi longior, os quoque longius ecce videtur:
    Numina magnificant omnia quae rapiunt.
Ille sciurus ubi est, qui, percupidus nucis, ad me
    Gressibus ambiguis expediebat iter   10
Horrescensque manu mota remeabat in herbam
    Inde resumpturus cautum iter ad spolia?
Te terrebam egomet multum qui terreor a te
    Cuius finis ait finem hominis similem.

Laetus heri ardebam caudam palpare pilosam,   15
   Nolo hodie pavidus tangere corpus iners.
Parce mihi. Pala parvum tumulabo cadaver,
   Parve sciure, tuum. Me metus acer habet.

Hora litorea

Hymnos aequora cantitant,
   Aures qui insolito murmure leniunt.
Felix in sabulo sedens,
   Cantu caeruleo, cymba velut vaga,
Longinquam ad magicam insulam   5
   Nunc lente vehor a criminibus procul.
Procedens ita ad aureas
   Oras, ad regiones sine nomine,
Nil in mente habeo nisi
   Istam qua rapior musicam amabilem.   10
Quando—cogito—et unde ego
   Audivi similes harmonicos sonos?
Ventorumque aviumque vis
   Numquam tanta animo gaudia protulit
Nec possunt frutices novi   15
   Tam mire zephyris reddere gratias.
Haec est musica quae venit
   A tellure ubi pax regnat, ab insula
Longinqua et magica et mea
   Quae aeternum mihi erit deliciae et domus.   20

Lingua latina

Tu potens, metuenda, tu
Magna et imperiosa, me
Reddis ingenuum et pium,
O Latina loquela, tu
   Lex et ars mihi pura.   5

Non ducis tonitrum in foro,
Simplicem repetis mihi
Musicam; attonitum meum
Vincis ingenium novae
   Syllabis pietatis.   10

Me doces sonitu sacro
Arborum fremitus leves
Et maris melos intimum,
Siderum harmoniam vagam
    Noctis in patula umbra.   15

Audio omnia corda quae,
Ut cor istud, amant diem,
Corda quae, velut hoc meum,
Flent diem fugientem ab his
    Dulce olentibus oris.   20

Roma, amorem animae meae
Concinis. Celebratio
Gloriae optima amor mihi est.
Roma-Amor, mihi plus vales
    Servitudine mundi.   25

Naenia

Lalla me, lalla, longa et vexamina vitae,
Musica, multiplici sopi suadente susurro.
Lalla me leviter, loquere et de lumine et umbra
Una laetitia supra labentibus oclos.
Ut mater lenta lenta dulcedine nato   5
Cantat naeniolam somnum tenerumque precando,
Candida tu canta, mihi somnia dulcia donans.
Lalla me, lalla, donec languore revinctus
Ne plus desperem . . . sperem . . . dormire sit amen . . .   9
Lalla me . . . Cupio dormire . . . Mori . . . est . . . dormire . . .

Cantiuncula vespertina

Me pudet cecinisse, Amor,
Dona laetitiae tuae:
Terra adhuc lacrimas habet
Et minacior advenit
    Umbra noctis amara.   5

Umbra noctis amara iam
Labitur super ultima
Serta, et acre silentium

Muta reddit et irrita
   Vatis intima verba.   10

Vatis intima verba eunt
Quo tremor folii fugit,
Quo maris zephyrus meat,
Quo nitor perit aetheris
   Cum die pereunte.   15

Cum die pereunte, Amor,
Fac viri pereat scelus:
Culpa si manet horrida,
Nemo regna potest tua
   Voce vincere laeta.   20

Hypnosis Aprilis

Dulciter cane canticum,
Ver novum, foliis tuis,
Canticum sine termino
Dulciter cane canticum
Omnibus tremulis rosis   5
Et coloribus omnibus
Nunc per orbem ineuntibus,
Canticum cane dulciter
Rivulis refluentibus,
Dulciter cane dulciter   10
Ultimum mihi canticum,
Ver novum, mihi candidum
Canticum ultimum amabile
Dulciter cane quod meos
Impleat sonitu dies,   15
Ah, dies aliter sine
Musica, sine murmure
Ullius deitatis in
Me, cane ultimum et intimum
Canticum mihi dulciter,   20
Dulciter mihi canticum,
   Et beatus abibo.

In ascensu Domini

Ascendit Dominus: cur non ego, servus, ad astra?
Forti cum Domino sine servum ascendere victum,
Liber et ille erit in caelo, pars intima pacis.
Alae sunt Domino, sed servo est ardor eundi.
Solem a se genitum Dominus si attingit amando,   5
Nonne ab eodem sum fulgore animante creatus,
Nonne Creatoris vivebam in mente vidente
Ante triumphalem per culmina et aequora vitam?
Has inter nebulas natales non remanebo,
Non remanebo ubi mors et materies minuunt me.   10
Me quoque suscipiat dominatrix Ultima Causa
Ac me discordem renovet Concordia Prima.
Quid faciam in terra, Dominus si ascendit ad astra?
Et tu, mi Domine omnipotens, poteris sine servo
Excelsus Dominus cognosci? Ascendere noli,   15
Nunc sine me noli tua quaerere candida regna.
Annos extremos tibi notos hic remorare,
Ibimus et tandem coniunctim ad sidera digna.

Caeli interpres

Caeli interpres sum, caeli et mysteria canto:
    Audi me et tellus terribilis procul est.
Verbis humanis quae cessant esse loquela
    Et fieri incipiunt musica prima Dei,
Humanis verbis quae sicut sermo sonant sed   5
    Insolito splendent versicolore die,
Adloquor omnes qui cupiant cognoscere quae sint
    Gaudia Supremae magnifica Harmoniae.

Ver moribundum

Tu quoque, Ver, moreris, tu tam pretiosum et odorum?
Quam pulchrum et dulce est transire ab olente iuventa
Ad redolentius aestatis florum monumentum!
Tu quoque, Ver sanctum, moreris? Sit mors mea talis.
Ah, quid dico? Puer crevit novitque tremendum   5

Ingressum a tristi Septembri ad tristius omen
Octobris. Salve, moriturum Ver peramatum.
Vulneris antiqui nunc immemor, ecce serena
Morte tua vehor ad vitam immortalem ineuntem:
Flores post florem, post carmen carmina, lucem   10
Continuam super hanc plenam caligine terram.

Naenia garganica

Naenia nota dolens, ab odora valle remota
Ad me saepe venis, nostrum et modulamine lento
Cor lenis mentemque serenas ut plaga vento
Arsa refecta est. Nescio cur, sed musica moesta
Me renovat terraeque facit tolerabile pondus.   5
Quomodo dulce melos fieri fragrantia possit
Ignoro, sed amata ferunt tua murmura mundum
Omnis odoris: sic violae et spiramine menthae
Involvor, mollisque thymi croceaeque genistae.
Blandula naenia, me, bona naenia blandula, sopi,   10
Urbis ne piceas respirem auras miserandae.

Photographema maritimum

Unda tacet subito, subito tacet hora diurna:
    Sistunt ecce simul tempus et Oceanus.
Alta voce puer ridet ludens in harena
    Atque eius risus cuncta creata tenet.

Abrams, M. H. (1953). *The Mirror and the Lamp: Romantic Theory and the Critical Tradition*. New York.

Aciman, André (1995). "The Writer in His Labyrinth." Review of Calasso 1994. *New Republic* (26 June): 32–38.

Adams, Marilyn McCord (1987). *William Ockham*. 2 vols. Notre Dame.

Adams, J. N. (1982). *The Latin Sexual Vocabulary*. Baltimore.

Ahl, Frederick (1991). *Sophocles' Oedipus: Evidence and Self-Conviction*. Ithaca, NY.

Albeggiani, Ferdinando (1934). *Aristotele: La Poetica: Introduzione, traduzione, commento*. Florence.

Amengual, Barthélemy (1976). "Quand le mythe console l'histoire: Œdipe roi." *Études cinématographiques* nos. 109–111:74–103.

Ammendola, G., ed. (1953). *Edipo a Colono*. Torino.

Aristarco, Guido (1977). "Pasolini: Le cinéma comme 'langue'." *Études cinématographiques* nos. 112–114:109–126.

Austin, Norman (1994). *Helen of Troy and Her Shameless Phantom*. Ithaca, NY.

Austin, J. L. (1962). *How to Do Things with Words*. Oxford.

Bal, Mieke (1985). *Narratology: Introduction to the Theory of Narrative*. 2nd ed. Toronto. A translation of *De theorie van vertellen en verhalen*, Muiderberg 1980.

Balogh, Josef (1927). "Voces paginarum." *Philologus* 82:84–109, 202–240.

Banville, John (1999). "The Dawn of the Gods" *New York Review of Books* 56.1 (15 Jan. 1999): 16–18. A review of Calasso 1998.

Barnes, Jonathan, ed. (1984). *The Complete Works of Aristotle: The Revised Oxford Translation*. 2 vols. Princeton.

Barth, John (1968). *Lost in the Funhouse*. New York.

Barthes, Roland (1964). "Edipo." *Il menabò della letteratura* 7:5–6.

——— (1968). *Elements of Semiology*. New York. A translation of *Eléments de la sémiologie*, Paris 1964.

——— (1974). *S/Z*. New York. A translation of *S/Z*, Paris 1970.

Baudrillard, Jean (1983). *Simulations*. New York.

Belfiore, Elizabeth (1992). *Tragic Pleasures: Aristotle on Plot and Emotion*. Princeton.

Bennett, Helen T. (1988). "Sign and De-Sign: Medieval and Modern Semiotics in Umberto Eco's *The Name of the Rose.*" Pp. 119–129 in Inge 1988.

Benveniste, Emile (1971). *Problems in General Linguistics.* Coral Gables. A translation of *Problèmes de linguistique générale,* Paris 1966.

Bernal, Martin (1987). *Black Athena: The Afroasiatic Roots of Classical Civilization.* Vol. 1, *The Fabrication of Ancient Greece, 1785–1985.* New Brunswick.

—— (1991). *Black Athena: The Afroasiatic Roots of Classical Civilization.* Vol. 2, *The Archaeological and Documentary Evidence.* New Brunswick.

Beye, Charles Rowan (1998). [Review of Hanson 1998.] *Bryn Mawr Classical Review* 9:625–632.

Bierce, Ambrose (1911). *The Devil's Dictionary.* Vol. 7 of *The Collected Works of Ambrose Bierce.* New York.

Bloom, Harold, ed. (1988). *Sophocles' Oedipus Rex.* New York.

Blundell, Mary Whitlock (1990). *Sophocles' Oedipus at Colonus.* Newburyport.

—— (1998). *Sophocles' Antigone.* Newburyport.

Boardman, John (1973). *Greek Art.* 2nd ed. London. Originally published 1963.

Borges, Jorge Luís (1964). *Labyrinths: Selected Stories and Other Writings.* Ed. Donald A. Yates and James E. Irby. Enl. ed. New York. Originally published 1962.

—— (1978). *The Aleph and Other Stories, 1933–1969.* Ed. and trans. Norman Thomas di Giovanni. New York.

Bowra, C. M. (1944). *Sophoclean Tragedy.* Oxford.

Brevini, Franco, ed. (1981). *Per conoscere Pasolini.* Milan.

Brooks, Peter (1984). *Reading for the Plot: Design and Intention in Narrative.* New York.

Bruno, Giuliana (1994). "The Body of Pasolini's Semiotics: A Sequel Twenty Years Later." Pp. 88–105 in Rumble and Testa 1994.

Buchler, Justus, ed. (1955). *Philosophical Writings of Peirce.* New York.

Butler, Judith (1990). *Gender Trouble: Feminism and the Subversion of Identity.* New York.

Bywater, Ingram (1909). *Aristotle on the Art of Poetry.* Oxford.

Calasso, Roberto (1983). *La rovina di Kasch.* Milan.

—— (1988). *Le nozze di Cadmo e Armonia.* Milan.

—— (1993). *The Marriage of Cadmus and Harmony.* Trans. Tim Parks. New York. A translation of Calasso 1988.

—— (1994). *The Ruin of Kasch.* Cambridge, MA. A translation of Calasso 1983.

—— (1996). *Ka.* Milan.

—— (1998). *Ka: Stories of the Mind and Gods of India.* Trans. Tim Parks. New York. A translation of Calasso 1996.

Calvino, Italo (1981). *If on a Winter's Night a Traveler.* San Diego. A translation of *Se una notte d'inverno un viaggiatore,* Torino 1979.

—— (1985). *Mr. Palomar.* San Diego. A translation of *Palomar,* Torino 1983.

———— (1986). *The Uses of Literature.* San Diego. A partial translation of *Una pietra sopra: Discorsi di letteratura e società,* Torino 1980.
———— (1988). *Six Memos for the Next Millennium.* Cambridge, MA. A translation of *Lexioni americane: Sei proposte per il prossimo millennio,* Milan 1988.
———— (1999). *Why Read the Classics?* New York.
Campari, Roberto (1994). *Il fantasmo del bello: Iconologia del cinema italiano.* Venice.
Capozzi, Rocco, ed. (1997). *Reading Eco: An Anthology.* Bloomington.
Carruthers, Mary (1990). *The Book of Memory: A Study of Memory in Medieval Culture.* Cambridge.
Carson, Anne (1986). *Eros the Bittersweet: An Essay.* Princeton.
———— (1997). *Autobiography of Red: A Novel in Verse.* New York.
Clark, Kenneth (1973). *The Romantic Rebellion: Romantic versus Classical Art.* New York 1973.
Clarke, D. S., Jr., ed. (1990). *Sources of Semiotic: Readings with Commentary from Antiquity to the Present.* Carbondale.
Cohen, Michael (1988). "The Hounding of Baskerville: Allusion and Apocalypse in Eco's *The Name of the Rose.*" Pp. 65–76 in Inge 1988.
Cole, Thomas (1991a). *The Origins of Rhetoric in Ancient Greece.* Baltimore.
———— (1991b). "Who Was Corax?" *Illinois Classical Studies* 16:65–84.
Connolly, Joy (1998). [Review of Hanson 1998.] *Bryn Mawr Classical Review* 9: 632–639.
Cortázar, Julio (1966). *Hopscotch.* Trans. Gregory Rabassa. New York. Originally published as *Rayuela,* Buenos Aires 1963.
Costa, Antonio (1977). "The Semiological Heresy of Pier Paolo Pasolini." Pp. 32–42 in Willemen 1977. Originially published in *Teorie e metodi di analisi del linguaggio cinematografico,* Milan 1974.
Crane, R. S., ed. (1952). *Critics and Criticism: Ancient and Modern.* Chicago.
Curd, Patricia (1998). "Eleatic Arguments." Pp. 1–28 in Jyl Gentzler, ed., *Method in Ancient Philosophy.* Oxford.
Dahan, G. (1980). "Notes et textes sur la Poétique au moyen âge." *Archives d'histoire doctrinale et littéraire du Moyen Age* 47:171–239.
Dawe, Richard, ed. (1982). *Sophocles: Oedipus Rex.* Cambridge.
Deely, John (1990). *Basics of Semiotics.* Bloomington.
———— (1997). "Looking Back on *A Theory of Semiotics:* One Small Step for Philosophy, One Giant Leap for the Doctrine of Signs." Pp. 82–110 in Capozzi 1997.
Deleuze, Gilles, and Félix Guattari (1976). *Rhizome.* Paris.
———— (1983). *Anti-Oedipus: Capitalism and Schizophrenia.* Originally published as *L'Anti-Œdipe,* Paris 1972.
DelFattore, Joan (1988). "Eco's Conflation of Theology and Detection in *The Name of the Rose.*" Pp. 77–89 in Inge 1988.
Detienne, Marcel (1986). *The Creation of Mythology.* Chicago. A Translation of *L'invention de la mythologie,* Paris 1981.

Doob, Penelope Reed (1990). *The Idea of the Labyrinth from Classical Antiquity through the Middle Ages.* Ithaca, NY.

Douglas, Alan E. (1957). "A Ciceronian Contribution to Rhetorical Theory." *Eranos* 55:18–26.

Drury, Martin, ed. (1985). "Appendix of Authors and Works." Pp. 721–892 in Patricia E. Easterling and Bernard M. W. Knox, eds., *The Cambridge History of Classical Literature.* Vol. 1: Greek Literature. Cambridge.

Dupont-Roc, R., and J. Lallot (1980). *Aristote: La poétique.* Paris.

Durán, Manuel (1997). *La música de las esferas: De Pitágoras a Fray Luis (pasando por Platón).* Orange.

Eco, Umberto (1968). *La struttura assente.* Milan.

———— (1975). "Looking for a Logic of Culture." Pp. 9–17 in T. A. Sebeok, ed., *The Tell-Tale Sign: A Survey of Semiotics.* Lisse.

———— (1976). *A Theory of Semiotics.* Bloomington.

———— (1979). *The Role of the Reader.* Bloomington.

———— (1983a). *The Name of the Rose.* San Diego. A translation of *Il nome della rosa,* Milan 1980.

———— (1983b). "Horns, Hooves, Insteps: Some Hypotheses on Three Types of Abduction." Pp. 198–220 in Eco and Sebeok 1983.

———— (1984a). *Semiotics and the Philosophy of Language.* Bloomington.

———— (1984b). *Reflections on* The Name of the Rose. New York. A translation of *Postille a* Il nome della rosa, Milan 1983.

———— (1984c). "The Frames of Comic 'Freedom.'" Pp. 1–9 in Umberto Eco, V. V. Ivanov, and Monica Rector, *Carnival!* Berlin.

———— (1988a). "Prelude to a Palimpsest." Pp. xi–xv in Inge 1988.

———— (1988b) *The Aesthetics of Thomas Aquinas.* Cambridge, MA. A translation of *Il problema estetico in Tommaso d'Aquino,* Milan 1970, itself a revised version of *Il problema estetico in San Tommaso,* Torino 1956.

———— (1988c). "Intentio Lectoris: The State of the Art." *Differentia* 2:147–168, reprinted as pp. 44–63 of Eco 1990.

———— (1989). *The Open Work.* Cambridge, MA. A partial translation, with other material included as well, of *Opera aperta,* 3rd ed., Milan 1976. Originally published 1962.

———— (1990). *The Limits of Interpretation.* Bloomington.

———— (1993). *Misreadings.* San Diego. A translation of *Diario minimo,* Milan 1963.

———— (1994). *How to Travel with a Salmon and Other Essays.* San Diego. A translation of *Secondo diario minimo,* 1992.

———— (1995). *The Island of the Day Before.* New York. A translation of *L'isola del giorno prima,* Milan 1995.

———— (1997). "An Author and His Interpreters." Pp. 59–70 in Capozzi 1997.

Eco, Umberto, and Thomas A. Sebeok, eds. (1983). *The Sign of Three: Dupin, Holmes, Peirce.* Bloomington.

Edmunds, Lowell (1981). "The Cults and the Legend of Oedipus." *Harvard Studies in Classical Philology* 85:221–238.

———— (1985). *Oedipus: The Ancient Legend and Its Later Analogues*. Baltimore.

Edmunds, Lowell, and Alan Dundes, eds. (1983). *Oedipus: A Folklore Casebook*. New York. Reprinted Madison, WI, 1995.

Eliot, T. S. (1932). *Selected Essays: New Edition*. New York.

Else, Gerald F. (1957). *Aristotle's Poetics: The Argument*. Cambridge, MA.

———— (1965). *The Origin and Early Form of Greek Tragedy*. New York.

———— (1986). *Plato and Aristotle on Poetry*. Chapel Hill.

Evans, Dylan (1996). *An Introductory Dictionary of Lacanian Psychoanalysis*. New York.

Fagles, Robert, trans. (1982). *Sophocles: The Three Theban Plays: Antigone, Oedipus the King, Oedipus at Colonus*. New York.

Ferrero, Adelio (1977). *Il cinema di Pier Paolo Pasolini*. Venice.

Figueira, Thomas J., and Gregory Nagy, eds. (1985). *Theognis of Megara*. Baltimore.

Fisch, Max H., Christian J. W. Kloesel, et al., eds. (1981–). *Writings of Charles S. Peirce: A Chronological Edition*. 30 vols. projected. Bloomington.

Florescu, Vasile (1971). *La retorica nel suo sviluppo storico*. Bologna.

Ford, Andrew L. (1985). "The Seal of Theognis: The Politics of Authorship in Archaic Greece." Pp. 82–95 in Figueira and Nagy 1985.

Fortenbaugh, William W., ed. (1985). *Theophrastus of Eresus: On His Life and Work*. Rutgers University Studies in Classical Humanities 2. New Brunswick.

Freud, Sigmund (1953–1974). *The Interpretation of Dreams*. Vols. 4–5 of *The Standard Edition of the Complete Psychological Works of Sigmund Freud*, ed. J. Strachey et al., 24 vols., London. A translation of *Die Traumdeutung*, Leipzig 1900.

Fuhrmann, Horst (1988). "Umberto Eco und sein Roman *Der Name der Rose*: Eine kritische Einführung." Pp. 1–20 in Kerner 1988.

Fusillo, Massimo (1996). *La Grecia secondo Pasolini: Mito e cinema*. Florence.

Gantz, Timothy (1993). *Early Greek Myth: A Guide to Literary and Artistic Sources*. Baltimore.

Genette, Gérard (1980). *Narrative Discourse: An Essay in Method*. Ithaca, NY. A translation of "Discours du récit," itself a portion of *Figures III*, Paris 1972.

Gentili, Bruno, and A. Pretagostini, eds. (1986). *Edipo: Il teatro greco e la cultura Europea*. Roma.

Gerard, Fabien S. (1981). *Pasolini ou le mythe de la barbarie*. Bruxelles.

Gervais, Marc (1973). *Pier Paolo Pasolini*. Paris.

Giordano, Paolo (1994a). "Joseph Tusiani and the Saga of Immigration." Pp. 60–83 in Giordano 1994b.

————, ed. (1994b). *Joseph Tusiani: Poet, Translator, Humanist: An International Homage*. West Lafayette, IN.

Giovannoli, Renato, ed. (1985). *AA. VV. Saggi su* Il nome della Rosa. Milan.

Golden, Leon (1992). *Aristotle on Tragic and Comic Mimesis*. Atlanta.

Goldhill, Simon (1986). *Reading Greek Tragedy*. Cambridge.

Grafton, Anthony (1997). *Commerce with the Classics: Ancient Books and Renaissance Readers*. Ann Arbor.

Green, Peter (1999). "Mandarins and Iconoclasts." *Arion* (ser. 3) 6.3 (Winter 1999): 122–149.

Grube, George M. A. (1952a). "Theophrastus as a Literary Critic." *Transactions of the American Philological Association* 83 : 172–183.

——— (1952b). "Thrasymachus, Theophrastus, and Dionysius of Halicarnassus." *American Journal of Philology* 73 : 251–267.

——— (1961). *A Greek Critic: Demetrius on Style*. Toronto.

Halliwell, Stephen (1986a). *Aristotle's* Poetics. Chapel Hill.

——— (1986b). "The Place Where Three Roads Meet: A Neglected Detail in the *Oedipus Tyrannus*." *Journal of Hellenic Studies* 106: 187–190.

Hanson, Victor Davis, and John Heath (1998). *Who Killed Homer? The Demise of Classical Education and the Recovery of Greek Wisdom*. New York.

——— (1999). "The Good, the Bad, and the Ugly." *Arion* (ser. 3) 6.3 (Winter 1999): 150–195.

Hartshorne, Charles, and Paul Weiss, eds. (1931–1958). *Collected Papers of Charles Sanders Peirce*. 8 vols. Cambridge, MA.

Hendrickson, G. L. (1929). "Ancient Reading." *Classical Journal* 25 : 182–196.

Henrichs, Albert (1983). "The 'Sobriety' of Oedipus: Sophocles OC 100 Misunderstood." *Harvard Studies in Classical Philology* 87 : 87–100.

Herington, John (1985). *Poetry into Drama: Early Tragedy and the Greek Poetic Tradition*. Berkeley.

Heath, Malcolm (1995). *Hermogenes on Issues: Strategies of Argument in Later Greek Rhetoric*. Oxford.

Hester, D. A. (1977). "Oedipus and Jonah." *Proceedings of the Cambridge Philological Society* n.s. 23 : 32–61.

Hogan, Patrick Colm, and Lalita Pandit, eds. (1990). *Criticism and Lacan: Essays and Dialogue on Language, Structure, and the Unconscious*. Athens, GA.

Hopcke, Robert H. (1989). *Jung, Jungians, and Homosexuality*. Boston.

Housman, A. E. (1939). *The Collected Poems of A. E. Housman*. New York.

Hunt, R. W. (1980). *The History of Grammar in the Middle Ages: Collected Papers*. Ed. G. L. Bursill-Hall. Amsterdam.

Immerwahr, Henry R. (1990). *Attic Script*. Oxford.

Inge, M. Thomas, ed. (1988). *Naming the Rose: Essays on Eco's* The Name of the Rose. Jackson, MS.

Isay, Richard (1989). *Being Homosexual: Gay Men and Their Development*. New York.

James, J. (1993). *The Music of the Spheres: Music, Science, and the Natural Order of the Universe*. New York.

Janko, Richard (1984). *Aristotle on Comedy: Towards a Reconstruction of* Poetics *II*. Berkeley.

———— (1987). *Aristotle:* Poetics *I. With the* Tractatus Coislinianus, *Reconstruction of* Poetics *II, and the Fragments of the* On Poets. Indianapolis.

Jebb, Richard, ed. (1893). *Sophocles: The Plays and Fragments*. Part I, *The Oedipus Tyrannus*. 3rd ed. Cambridge. Originally published 1883.

————, ed. (1890). *Sophocles: The Plays and Fragments*. Part II, *The Oedipus Coloneus*. 3rd ed. Cambridge. Originally published 1889.

Jeffery, Lillian H. (1990). *The Local Scripts of Archaic Greece*. Rev. ed. Oxford. Originally published 1961.

Johnson, Allen W., and Douglass Price-Williams (1996). *Oedipus Ubiquitous: The Family Complex in World Folk Literature*. Stanford.

Johnston, Sarah Iles (1991). "Crossroads." *Zeitschrift für Papyrologie und Epigraphik* 88:217–224.

Kamerbeek, J. C., ed. (1967). *The Plays of Sophocles: Commentaries*. Part IV, *The Oedipus Tyrannus*. Leiden.

————, ed. (1984). *The Plays of Sophocles: Commentaries*. Part VII, *The Oedipus Coloneus*. Leiden.

Kassel, Rudolf, ed. (1965). *Aristotelis de arte poetica liber*. Oxford.

Kellner, Hans (1988). "'To Make Truth Laugh': Eco's *The Name of the Rose*." Pp. 3–30 in Inge 1988.

Kelly, H. A. (1979). "Aristotle-Averroes-Alemannus on Tragedy: The Influence of the 'Poetics' on the Latin Middle Ages." *Viator* 10:161–209.

Kennedy, George A. (1957). "Theophrastus and Stylistic Distinctions." *Harvard Studies in Classical Philology* 62:93–104.

———— (1963). *The Art of Persuasion in Greece*. Princeton.

———— (1972). *The Art of Rhetoric in the Roman World*. Princeton.

———— (1983). *Greek Rhetoric under Christian Emperors*. Princeton.

———— (1994). *A New History of Classical Rhetoric*. Princeton.

———— (1999). *Classical Rhetoric and Its Christian and Secular Tradition from Ancient to Modern Times*. 2nd ed. Chapel Hill. Originally published 1980.

Kerner, Max, ed. (1988). *". . . Eine finstere und fast unglaubliche Geschichte"? Mediävistische Notizen zu Umberto Ecos Mönchsroman "Der Name der Rose."* Darmstadt.

Kirby, John T. (1984–1985). "Toward a General Theory of the Priamel." *Classical Journal* 80:142–144.

———— (1991a). "Aristotle's *Poetics:* The Rhetorical Principle." *Arethusa* 24:197–217.

———— (1991b). "Mimesis and Diegesis: Foundations of Aesthetic Theory in Plato and Aristotle." *Helios* 18:113–128. Reprinted, in revised form, as Kirby 1996a.

———— (1992a). "Rhetoric and Poetics in Hesiod." *Ramus* 21:34–60.

———— (1992b). "Toward a Rhetoric of Poetics: Rhetor as Author and Narrator." *Journal of Narrative Technique* 22:1–22.

——— (1994). Review of Kathleen E. Welch, *The Contemporary Reception of Classical Rhetoric: Appropriations of Ancient Discourse* (Hillsdale, NJ, 1990). *Philosophy and Rhetoric* 27:434–440.

——— (1996a). "Classical Greek Origins of Western Aesthetic Theory." Chapter 1 of Beate Allert, ed., *Languages of Visuality: Crossings between Science, Art, Politics, and Literature*. Detroit.

——— (1996b). "Ancient Semiotics and Modern Scholarship: Giovanni Manetti's *Theories of the Sign in Classical Antiquity*." *Voices in Italian Americana* 7: 207–211. A review of Manetti 1993.

——— (1996c). "The Second Sophistic." Pp. 661–665 in Theresa Enos, ed., *Encyclopedia of Rhetoric and Composition: Communication from Ancient Times to the Information Age*. New York.

——— (1997a). "Aristotle on Metaphor." *American Journal of Philology* 118: 517–554.

——— (1997b). "A Classicist's Approach to Rhetoric in Plato." *Philosophy and Rhetoric* 30:190–202.

——— (1998a). Review of William W. Fortenbaugh and David C. Mirhady, eds., *Peripatetic Rhetoric after Aristotle* (New Brunswick, NJ, 1994). In *Philosophy and Rhetoric* 31 (1998): 160–164.

———, ed. (1998b). *The Comparative Reader: A Handlist of Basic Reading in Comparative Literature*. New Haven.

Kirby, John T., and Carol Poster (1998). "Klimax." Entry in *Historisches Wörterbuch der Rhetorik* vol. 4 (Hu–K). Darmstadt.

Knauer, Georg N. (1964). *Die Aeneis und Homer*. Göttingen.

Knox, Bernard M. W. (1954). "Why Is Oedipus Called *Turannos?*" *Classical Journal* 50:97–102.

——— (1957). *Oedipus at Thebes: Sophocles' Tragic Hero and His Time*. New Haven.

——— (1964). *The Heroic Temper: Studies in Sophoclean Tragedy*. Berkeley.

——— (1968). "Silent Reading in Antiquity." *Greek, Roman, and Byzantine Studies* 9:421–435.

Koster, W. J. W. (1936). *Traité de métrique grecque suivi d'un précis de métrique latine*. Leyden.

Kundera, Milan (1984). *The Unbearable Lightness of Being*. New York. A translation of *Nesnesitelná lehkost bytí*, 1984.

——— (1991). *Immortality*. New York. A translation of *Nesmrtelnost*, 1990.

Lacan, Jacques (1977). *Ecrits: A Selection*. New York. Selected and translated from *Ecrits*, Paris 1966.

Lattarulo, Leonardo (1982). *La ricerca narrativa tra logica e misticismo*. Roma.

——— (1985). "Tra misticismo e logica." Pp. 89–106 in Giovannoli 1985; reprinted from pp. 3–17, 36–42 of Lattarulo 1982.

Lauretis, Teresa de (1980–1981). "Re-reading Pasolini's Essays on Cinema." *Italian Quarterly* 82/83:159–166.

———— (1981). *Umberto Eco.* Florence.

———— (1984). *Alice Doesn't: Feminism, Semiotics, Cinema.* Bloomington.

Lawton, Ben (1980–1981). "The Evolving Rejection of Homosexuality, the Sub-Proletariat, and the Third World in the Films of Pier Paolo Pasolini." *Italian Quarterly* 82/83 : 167–173.

Lefkowitz, Mary R. (1996). *Not Out of Africa: How Afrocentrism Became an Excuse to Teach Myth as History.* New York.

Lefkowitz, Mary R., and Guy MacLean Rogers, eds. (1996). *Black Athena Revisited.* Chapel Hill.

Leitch, Vincent B. (1988). *American Literary Criticism from the Thirties to the Eighties.* New York.

Lemaire, Anika (1977). *Jacques Lacan.* London. Originally published Belgium 1970.

Levine, Molly Myerowitz (1998). "The Marginalization of Martin Bernal." *Classical Philology* 93 : 345–363.

Lewes, Kenneth (1988). *The Psychoanalytic Theory of Male Homosexuality.* New York.

Lloyd-Jones, H., and N. G. Wilson, eds. (1990). *Sophoclis fabulae.* Oxford.

Lobel, E. (1931). "The Medieval Latin Poetics." *Proceedings of the British Academy* 17 : 309–334.

Longo, O., ed. (1972). *Edipo re.* Florence.

Lucas, D. W. (1968). *Aristotle:* Poetics; *Introduction, Commentary, and Appendixes.* Oxford.

MacCannell, Juliet Flower (1986). *Figuring Lacan: Criticism and the Cultural Unconscious.* Lincoln.

McCartney, Eugene S. (1948). "Notes on Reading and Praying Audibly." *Classical Philology* 43 : 184–187.

Manetti, Giovanni (1993). *Theories of the Sign in Classical Antiquity.* Trans. Christine Richardson. Bloomington. A translation of *Le teorie del segno nell' antichità classica,* Milan 1987.

Mann, Jocelyn (1988). "Traversing the Labyrinth: The Structures of Discover in Eco's *The Name of the Rose.*" Pp. 130–145 in Inge 1988.

Martin, Wallace (1993). "Metaphor." Pp. 760–766 in Alex Preminger and T. V. F. Brogan, eds., *The New Princeton Encycolpedia of Poetry and Poetics.* Princeton.

Martindale, Charles (1999). "Did He Die, Or Was He Pushed?" *Arion* (ser. 3) 6.3 (Winter 1999): 103–121.

Mayer, August, ed. (1910). *Theophrasti* ΠΕΡΙ ΛΕΞΕΩΣ *libri fragmenta.* Leipzig.

Merrell, Floyd (1987). "An Uncertain Semiotic." Pp. 243–264 in Clayton Koelb and Virgil Lokke, eds., *The Current in Criticism: Essays on the Present and Future of Literary Theory.* West Lafayette.

———— (1992). *Sign, Textuality, World.* Bloomington.

———— (1995). *Peirce's Semiotics Now: A Primer.* Toronto.

Metz, Christian (1974). "Le cinéma: Langue ou langage?" Translated and anthologized in *Film Language: A Semiotics of the Cinema*, New York. Originally published 1964.

Miethke, Jürgen (1988). "Der Philosoph als Detektiv: William von Baskerville, Zeichendeuter und Spurensucher, und sein 'alter Freund' Wilhelm von Ockham in Umberto Ecos Roman 'Der Name der Rose.'" Pp. 115–127 in Kerner 1988.

Minio-Paluello, L. (1947). "Guglielmo di Moerbeke, traduttore della Poetica di Aristotele (1278)." *Rivista di filosofia neoscolastica* 39:1–17.

Motte, Warren F., Jr. (1986). *Oulipo: A Primer of Potential Literature.* Lincoln.

Müller, Friedrich Max (1891). *The Science of Language: Founded on Lectures Delivered at the Royal Institution in 1861 and 1863.* 2 vols. 3rd ed. New York. Originally published 1861.

Naldini, Nico (1994). "Pier Paolo, My Cousin . . . "Pp. 14–21 in Rumble and Testa 1994.

Nelson, Cary, and Stephen Watt (1999). *Academic Keywords: A Devil's Dictionary for Higher Education.* New York.

Newman, John Henry 1960. *The Idea of a University* (1852). New York.

Nussbaum, Martha C. (1986). *The Fragility of Goodness: Luck and Ethics in Greek Tragedy and Philosophy.* Cambridge.

O'Brien, Michael J., ed. (1968). *Twentieth-Century Interpretations of Oedipus Rex.* Englewood Cliffs, NJ.

O'Sullivan, Neil (1993). "Plato and Η ΚΑΛΟΥΜΕΝΗ ΡΗΤΟΡΙΚΗ." *Mnemosyne* (ser. 4) 46:87–89.

———. (1997). "Caecilius, the "Canons" of Writers, and the Origins of Atticism." Pp. 32–49 in William J. Dominik, ed., *Roman Eloquence: Rhetoric in Society and Literature.* London.

Ober, Josiah (1989). *Mass and Elite in Democratic Athens: Rhetoric, Ideology, and the Power of the People.* Princeton.

Owen, G. E. L. (1961). "*Tithenai ta phainomena.*" Pp. 83–103 in S. Mansion, ed., *Aristote et les problèmes de méthode.* (Papers of the the Second Symposium Aristotelicum). Louvain. Frequently reprinted, e.g., in G. E. L. Owen, *Logic, Science, and Dialectic: Collected Papers in Greek Philosophy,* Ithaca, NY, 1986.

Palmer, Martin, et al., trans. (1996). *Nan-hua Ching: The Book of Chuang Tzu.* London.

Parker, Andrew, and Eve Kosofsky Sedgwick, eds. (1995). *Performativity and Performance.* New York.

Parmentier, Richard (1987). "Peirce Divested for Non-intimates." *Recherches sémiotiques/Semiotic Inquiry* 7:19–39, now reprinted as pp. 3–22 of *Signs in Society: Studies in Semiotic Anthropology,* Bloomington 1994.

Pasolini, Pier Paolo (1967). *Edipo re.* Milan.

——— (1971a). "Why That of Oedipus Is a Story." Pp. 5–13 in Pasolini 1971b. A translation of "Perchè quella di Edipo è una storia," Milan 1967.

———— (1971b). *Oedipus Rex*. London. A translation of *Edipo re*, Milan 1967; the Italian edition includes the essay "Perchè quella di Edipo è una storia."

———— (1972). *Empirismo eretico*. Milan.

———— (1988). *Heretical Empiricism*. Bloomington. A translation of Pasolini 1972.

Pavese, Cesare (1965). *Dialogues with Leucò*. Ann Arbor. A translation of *Dialoghi con Leucò*, Torino 1947.

Peyronie, André (1988). "The Labyrinth." Pp. 685–719 in Pierre Brunel, ed., *Companion to Literary Myths, Heroes, and Archetypes*. London 1992. A translation of *Dictionnaire des mythes littéraires*, Paris 1988.

Pfeiffer, Rudolf (19681976). *History of Classical Scholarship*. 2 vols. Oxford.

Pickard-Cambridge, A. W. (1927). *Dithyramb Tragedy and Comedy*. Oxford.

Poster, Mark, ed. (1988). *Jean Baudrillard: Selected Writings*. Stanford.

Powell, Barry B. (1989). "Why Was the Greek Alphabet Invented? The Epigraphical Evidence." *Classical Antiquity* 8 : 321–350.

———— (1991). *Homer and the Origins of the Greek Alphabet*. Cambridge.

Prince, Gerald (1987). *A Dictionary of Narratology*. Lincoln, NE.

Puhvel, Martin (1989). *The Crossroads in Folklore and Myth*. New York.

Pynchon, Thomas (1973). *Gravity's Rainbow*. New York.

Rabe, Hugo, ed. (1913). *Hermogenis Opera*. Vol. 6 of *Rhetores Graeci*. Leipzig.

Ragland-Sullivan, Ellie (1986). *Jacques Lacan and the Philosophy of Psychoanalysis*. Urbana.

Ragland-Sullivan, Ellie, and Mark Bracher, eds. (1991). *Lacan and the Subject of Language*. New York.

Reinhardt, Karl (1979). *Sophocles*. Trans. Hazel Harvey and David Harvey. New York. A translation of *Sophokles*, 3rd ed. Frankfurt 1947; originally published 1933.

Rice, Michael (1998). *The Power of the Bull*. London.

Ridley, Philip (1988). *Crocodilia*. London.

Robert, Carl (1915). *Oidipus: Geschichte eines poetischen Stoffs im griechischen Altertum*. 2 vols. Berlin.

Robertson, D. W., Jr., trans. (1958). *Saint Augustine: On Christian Doctrine*. Indianapolis.

Roncoroni, Federico (1986). "Pasolini e il Corriere." Supplement to *Corriere della Sera*, 8 Oct. 1986.

Rorty, Amélie Oksenberg, ed. (1992). *Essays on Aristotle's Poetics*. Princeton.

Rosenmeyer, T. (1963), M. Ostwald, and J. Halporn. *The Meters of Greek and Latin Poetry*. Indianapolis.

Rosier, Irène (1983). *La grammaire spéculative des Modistes*. Lille.

Rostagni, Augusto (1945). *Aristotele: Poetica. Introduzione, testo, commento*. 2nd rev. ed. Torino.

Roudinesco, Elisabeth (1990). *Jacques Lacan and Co.: A History of Psychoanalysis in France, 1925–1985*. Chicago.

———— (1997). *Jacques Lacan*. New York.

Rumble, Patrick, and Bart Testa, eds. (1994). *Pier Paolo Pasolini: Contemporary Perpectives*. Toronto.

Russell, Donald A. (1964). *"Longinus" on the Sublime*. Oxford.

Rusten, Jeffrey (1996). "Oedipus and Triviality." *Classical Philology* 91 : 97–112.

Sacré, Dirk (1994). "Joseph Tusiani's Latin Poetry." Pp. 160–179 in Giordano 1994b.

Sandys, John Edwin (1903–1908). *A History of Classical Scholarship*. 3 vols. Cambridge.

Scheid, John, and Jesper Svenbro (1996). *The Craft of Zeus: Myths of Weaving and Fabric*. Trans. Carol Volk. Cambridge, MA. A translation of *Le métier de Zeus*.

Schiappa, Edward (1990). "Did Plato Coin *Rhêtorikê?*" *American Journal of Philology* 111 : 457–470.

——— (1999). *The Beginnings of Rhetorical Theory in Classical Greece*. New Haven.

Schmandt-Besserat, Denise (1999). *How Writing Came About*. Austin.

Schiller, Friedrich (1981). *On the Naive and Sentimental in Literature*. Trans. Helen Watanabe-O'Kelly. Manchester. A translation of *Über naive und sentimentalische Dichtung*, 1795.

Schmid, Wilhelm (1917–1918). "Die sogenannte Aristidesrhetorik." *Rheinisches Museum* 72 : 113–149, 238–257.

———, ed. (1926). *Aristidis qui feruntur libri rhetorici II*. Leipzig.

Schwartz, Barth David (1992). *Pasolini Requiem*. New York.

Segal, Charles (1993). *Oedipus Tyrannus: Tragic Heroism and the Limits of Knowledge*. New York.

——— (1995). *Sophocles' Tragic World: Divinity, Nature, Society*. Cambridge, MA.

Sebeok, Thomas A. (1997). Foreword to Capozzi 1997.

Shackleton Bailey, D. R., ed. (1985). *Q. Horati Flacci opera*. Stuttgart.

Shapiro, Michael (1983). *The Sense of Grammar: Language as Semeiotic*. Bloomington.

Snyder, Stephen (1980). *Pier Paolo Pasolini*. Boston.

Solmsen, Friedrich (1931). "Demetrius ΠΕΡΙ ΕΡΜΗΝΕΙΑΣ und sein peripatetisches Quellenmaterial." *Hermes* 66 : 241–267.

Stack, Oswald (1969). *Pasolini on Pasolini: Interviews with Oswald Stack*. London.

Stanley, Keith (1963). "Rome, ΕΡΩΣ, and the *Versus Romae*," *Greek, Roman, and Byzantine Studies* 4 (1963): 237–249.

Stephens, Walter E. (1983). "Ec[h]o in fabula." *Diacritics* 13 : 51–64.

Striker, Gisela (1959). *A Handbook of Greek Art: A Survey of the Visual Arts of Ancient Greece*. London.

Suzuki, Mihoko (1989). *Metamorphoses of Helen: Authority, Difference, and the Epic*. Ithaca.

Tamburri, Anthony Julian (1990). *Of Saltimbanchi and Incendiari: Aldo Palazzeschi and Avant-Gardism in Italy*. Cranbury, NJ.

Taplin, Oliver (1977). *The Stagecraft of Aeschylus: The Dramatic Use of Exits and Entrances in Greek Tragedy*. Oxford.

———— (1978). *Greek Tragedy in Action*. London.

Thomson, D. F. S., ed. (1978). *Catullus: A Critical Edition*. Chapel Hill.

Tusiani, Joseph (1955). *Melos cordis*. New York.

———— (1978). *Gente mia and Other Poems*. Stone Park, IL.

———— (1984). *Rosa rosarum*. Oxford, OH.

———— (1985). *In exilio rerum*. Avignon.

———— (1989). *Confinia lucis et umbrae*. Leuven.

———— (1992). *Il ritorno: Liriche italiane*. Fasano di Brindisi.

———— (1994). *Josephi Tusiani Neo-Eboracensis carmina latina: Raccolta, introduzione e traduzione di Emilio Bandiera*. Fasano di Brindisi.

———— (1998). *Josephi Tusiani Neo-Eboracensis carmina latina II: Raccolta, introduzione et traduzione di Emilio Bandiera*. Lecce.

Veeser, H. Aram (1988). "Holmes Goes to Carnival: Embarrassing the Signifier in Eco's Anti-Detective Novel." Pp. 101–115 in Inge 1988.

Vellacott, Philip (1971). *Sophocles and Oedipus: A Study of the Oedipus Tyrannos*. London.

Viano, Maurizio (1993). *A Certain Realism: Making Use of Pasolini's Film Theory and Practice*. Berkeley.

Waterfield, Robin, trans. (1993). *Plato: Republic*. Oxford: Clarendon Press.

Watson, Burton, trans. (1968). *Nan-hua Ching: The Complete Works of Chuang Tzu*. New York.

Waugh, Patricia (1984). *Metafiction: The Theory and Practice of Self-Conscious Fiction*. London.

Webster, T. B. L. (1969). *An Introduction to Sophocles*. 2nd ed. Originally published Oxford 1936.

West, David (1995). *Horace Odes I: Carpe Diem*. Oxford.

West, M. L. (1982). *Greek Metre*. Oxford.

Whitman, Cedric (1951). *Sophocles: A Study of Heroic Humanism*. Cambridge, MA.

Wilamowitz-Moellendorff, Ulrich von (1921). *Geschichte der Philologie*. Leipzig. Translated by Hugh Lloyd-Jones as *History of Classical Scholarship*, Baltimore 1982.

Wiles, David (1997). *Tragedy in Athens: Performance Space and Theatrical Meaning*. Cambridge.

Wilkinson, L M. P. (1963). *Golden Latin Artistry*. Cambridge.

Willemen, Paul, ed. (1977). *Pier Paolo Pasolini*. London.

Willett, Steven J. (1999). "Can Classicists 'Think Like Greeks'?" *Arion* (ser. 3) 6.3 (Winter 1999): 84–102.

Wilson, Nigel (1992). *From Byzantium to Italy: Greek Studies in the Italian Renaissance*. Baltimore.

Winkler, John J. (1989). "The Ephebes' Song: *Tragôidia* and *Polis*." Pp. 20–62 in Winkler and Zeitlin 1989.

Winkler, John J., and Froma I. Zeitlin (1989). *Nothing to Do with Dionysos? Athenian Drama in Its Social Context*. Princeton.

Winnington-Ingram, R. P. (1980). *Sophocles: An Interpretation*. Cambridge.

Woodard, Roger D. (1997). *Greek Writing from Knossos to Homer: A Linguistic Interpretation of the Origin of the Greek Alphabet and the Continuity of Ancient Greek Literacy*. New York.

Wooten, Cecil W. (1983). *Cicero's* Philippics *and Their Demosthenic Model*. Chapel Hill.

——— (1987). *Hermogenes'* On Types of Style. Chapel Hill.

Zecchini, Giuseppe (1985). "Il medioevo di Umberto Eco." Pp. 322–369 in Giovannoli 1985.

Zeitlin, Froma I. (1989). "Playing the Other: Theater, Theatricality, and the Feminine in Greek Drama." Pp. 63–96 in Winkler and Zeitlin 1989.

Žižek, Slavoj (1992). *Enjoy Your Symptom! Jacques Lacan in Hollywood and Out*. New York.

VINCIT QVI PATITVR.

Pynchon, Thomas, 106 n. 5
Pythagoras, 93

quantitative verse (see meter)
Queneau, Raymond, 50 n. 61
quickness, as literary value, 92, 94–96
Quintilian (Marcus Fabius Quintilianus),
65 n. 24, 82 n. 4, 84, 94, 94 n. 30,
97 n. 38, 99 n. 41

Rachmaninoff, Sergei, 112
rapidity (gorgotês), in rhetorical style, 90
rappresentare, 19 n. 43
ratiocination, 121
reading in antiquity, 90, 90 n. 23
reality, 17, 101, 125 (see also Forms,
hyperreality)
referent (semiological), 20, 33 n. 11
refutation (elegkhos), in rhetoric, 89
Renaissance, xiii, xvi, 59 n. 10, 130
repetition (epanalêpsis), in rhetoric, 89
at beginning of phrase (epanaphora), 90
at end of phrase (antistrophê), 90
as rhetorical strategy, 95
representamen, 33, 34
representation, 10, 17, 32, 39, 52–53, 125
(see also mimesis)
resurrection, 68 n. 31, 69
rhetor, 97, 100
rhetoric, 82–86, 82 n. 3, 97, 101, 101 n. 44
Rhetoric to Alexander, 84
Rhetorica ad Herennium, 65 n. 24, 84
rhizome, 48–50, 49 n. 59
rhythm, in speech, 88, 89, 90
Riccoboni, Antonio, 53
Richards, Ivor A., 101 n. 45
riddle (ainigma), in rhetoric, 87
Ridley, Philip, 106 n. 5
romanticism, 112
Rome (ROMA), anagram of AMOR, 64,
64 n. 20
Rostagni, Augusto, 38
Rotimi, Ola, 2

sacrifice, 110, 123
saphês, saphêneia (see clarity)
Sappho, 38, 134–135, 136
Saussure, Ferdinand de, 11, 108

Schickele, Peter (P. D. Q. Bach), 2
Schiller, Johann Christoph Friedrich
von, xv
concept of the "naïve" and "sentimental," xvi, 127 n. 1
Schliemann, Heinrich, 106 n. 4
Schober, Franz, 62
Schubert, Franz, 62
scriptor, 109 n. 14
self-correction (epidiorthôsis), as rhetorical
figure, 91
self-interruption (aposiôpêsis), as rhetorical
figure, 91
sêmeion (sêma, sêmainein), 11 n. 18, 33, 34
semeiotic, 32 n. 5
vs. semiology, 18–20, 32, 32 n. 5
vs. semiosis, 11, 11 n. 17, 32 n. 5, 105 n. 2
Semele, 110, 125
semiology, 11, 15
semiosis, 11, 14, 19, 31–33, 39, 53
unlimited, 15, 33 n. 11, 46, 49, 49 n. 59,
108, 118, 122, 123
semiotics, 11–12, 32, 105, 118, 129
in antiquity, 32 n. 9
of imagination, 96, 108
of myth, 118–125
Semitic writing systems, 124
semnos, semnotês (see solemnity)
servus, 68 n. 31
Sextus Empiricus, 37, 120 n. 31
Shakespeare, William, 63 n. 18, 76 n. 47
Shaw, George Bernard, 25
Shelley, Percy Bysshe, xi
sidus, 69 n. 34
sign, 11–14, 16, 18, 21, 33–37, 33 n. 11,
118, 120, 124, 125 (see also
representamen)
signification, 53, 122 (see also
representation)
signifier and signified (semiological),
33 n. 11
Simonides, 84
simplicity (apheleia), in rhetorical style, 88,
90, 91
simulacrum, 108, 119
sincerity (alêtheia), in rhetorical style, 91,
102
Sirens, 118